A signal contribution to the international h
precision and confidence they explain the inti
nisms for securing relief from religious persecution and make them available
to human rights advocates everywhere. May we hope that this essential guidebook will be translated into many languages.

—Holly J. Burkhalter, *Vice President of Government Relations,*
International Justice Mission

This guidebook outlines practical and clear strategies for advocates of religious
freedom. As Pope Benedict XVI reminded us on his visit to the United States,
"The task of upholding religious freedom is never completed." This book will
help advocates to uphold religious freedom and by so doing promote justice
and peace in the world.

—Cardinal McCarrick, *Archbishop of Washington*

INSTITUTE *for* GLOBAL ENGAGEMENT

The Institute for Global Engagement (IGE) promotes sustainable environments for religious freedom worldwide. As a faith-based organization, IGE
believes firmly in universal human dignity and is committed to the protection
of all faiths through the rule of law. IGE encourages governments to respect
their citizens' right to religious freedom and educates people of faith to exercise
that right responsibly. Operating at the nexus of faith, culture, security, development, and the rule of law, IGE's relational diplomacy—currently focused
on East and Central Asia—enables respectful dialogue and practical agreements that help transition countries toward sustainable religious freedom.

International Religious Freedom Advocacy

A Guide to Organizations, Law, and NGOs

H. Knox Thames
Chris Seiple
Amy Rowe

BAYLOR UNIVERSITY PRESS

Book Design by Jenny Hunt
Cover Design by Andrew Brozyna, ajbdesign
Cover image © 2009 Digital Vision/PunchStock

The views expressed by Knox Thames are his own and are not necessarily those
of the U.S. Government, U.S. Department of State, or the U.S. Commission on
International Religious Freedom.

Library of Congress Cataloging-in-Publication Data
Thames, H. Knox, 1974-
  International religious freedom advocacy : a guide to organizations, law, and
NGOs / H. Knox Thames, Chris Seiple, Amy Rowe.
     p. cm.
  Includes index.
  ISBN 978-1-60258-179-1 (pbk. : alk. paper)
  1. Freedom of religion--Handbooks, manuals, etc. 2. Freedom of religion
(International law)--Handbooks, manuals, etc. 3. Religious tolerance--
Handbooks, manuals, etc. 4. Human rights--Handbooks, manuals, etc. 5.
International agencies--Handbooks, manuals, etc. I. Seiple, Chris. II. Rowe,
Amy, 1980- III. Title.

  BV741.T43 2009
  323.44'2--dc22

                                        2009003704

Printed in the United States of America on acid-free paper.

CONTENTS

Appendices

Acknowledgments

International Religious Freedom Advocacy is first and foremost dedicated to those brave souls being persecuted for their faith and to their tireless advocates bravely confronting oppression and violence. They are not alone, and I hope that this book will in some way help alleviate their suffering. I also want to thank Chris Seiple and the Institute for Global Engagement for their assistance in helping make the book a reality. The chapters written by Chris Seiple and Amy Rowe on Vietnam and NGO activity, as well as their collaboration on the conclusion, provide important insights and round out the book. Thanks are also due to Dennis Hoover at IGE, who was extremely helpful in guiding this work through the publishing process. In addition, I would like to thank the following individuals for their willingness to review early drafts and provide comments: Joanna Chellapermal with Christian Solidarity Worldwide, Jeremy Gunn with the American Civil Liberties Union, Jocelyn Penner with World Vision International, and Angela Wu with the Becket Fund for Religious Liberty. Lastly, I would like to thank my wife Shelley for her support and helpful feedback.

—*Knox Thames*

I am most grateful to our partners worldwide—in the U.S., but especially overseas—who have taught me the strategies for promoting religious freedom in a manner that honors the local culture and the rule of law. God has richly and practically blessed our work at the Institute for Global Engagement through these global citizens.

—*Chris Seiple*

Many thanks to Knox Thames for his experience, vision, and hard work on this project. Thanks to Chris Seiple, whose belief in me allowed me the privilege of working for religious freedom around the world. Thanks to the entire staff, past and present, of the Institute for Global Engagement, whose friendship, insights, and support have enriched me in our work together: Judd Birdsall, Rachael Boeve, Meagan Carner, Jared Daugherty, Lucy Dunderdale, Rebecca Haines, Dennis Hoover, Christin Klaasen, Amy McDowell, Matthew Scott, Margaret Ann Seiple, Amb. Robert Seiple, Hien Vu, Joshua White, and countless talented research associates. Special thanks to the victims of religious freedom abuses in Sudan, Pakistan, and Vietnam, from whom I learned so much. Most of all, thanks to Trent for taking the midnight-to-three shift with our daughter so I could work on this book.

—*Amy Rowe*

1

OVERVIEW OF INTERNATIONAL RELIGIOUS FREEDOM ADVOCACY

Around the world, persons of faith continue to face serious obstacles to the full and free enjoyment of religious freedom, whether from Christian, Muslim, or other religious communities. Religious freedom is perhaps the most personal of human rights, as it goes to the very core of a human being. Yet limitations, abuse, and persecution are a daily occurrence, with some estimating that more than half of the world's population cannot fully enjoy this cherished fundamental freedom.

At the same time, religious freedom protections are well established at the international level. International law recognizes religious freedom as a universal human right. Treaties and international agreements guarantee and reinforce the right of individual and communal religious freedom. Placing limitations on individual belief is never permitted, and communities of believers must be allowed to congregate for worship and study. Because of these wide protections, religious freedom is considered a part of "customary international law," and thereby every country in the world must protect this human right, even if they have not signed any treaties or joined international organizations. Of course, despite states pledging to uphold and defend these norms, implementation is inconsistent, even among European countries. Considering the ongoing abuses and robust international protections, many advocates want to take action on behalf of those suffering elsewhere, but they may not know how. This guidebook is written for them.

Bob Seiple, the first U.S. Ambassador-at-Large for International Religious Freedom and founder of the Institute of Global Engagement, has spoken about how persons of good will observe repression from their homes but are prevented from taking action by the unfamiliar maze of governmental and international offices and mechanisms, as they do not know where to go and who to approach. Without firsthand experience working with international institutions, many find it difficult, if not impossible, to engage effectively.

The purpose of the book is to show religious freedom advocates the path from their homes to the international stage. The following pages are intended to be used as a guidebook for engagement, providing helpful insights into the tangled web of international organizations and international law, and the nongovernmental organizations (NGOs) with which they interface.

International Religious Freedom Advocacy will focus on the practical and is neither an exhaustive encyclopedia nor an academic treatise debating the "theology" of religious freedom. Numerous works that explore the various shades of religious liberty already exist. The purpose of this book is not to retrace that well-worn path, but rather to be a user-friendly, straightforward tool for empowering would-be advocates to effectively promote religious freedom.

Therefore, each chapter will contain a brief overview of an international organization and will then highlight relevant mechanisms and offices that can address religious freedom concerns. The information should serve as an initial starting place for strategies, with the reader applying the information to individual situations or concerns. No specific countries are discussed, except for the United States in Chapter 8. The chapter does not discuss domestic U.S. issues but rather highlights the unique array of American governmental institutions that exist to promote religious freedom internationally. The guidebook also contains two case studies, which will contextualize how advocates have used international mechanisms to successfully promote and defend this fundamental right. The final chapter describes the role of NGOs and the various ways they can work to advance religious freedom.

Advocacy Avenues

In examining the various international institutions, one of three different types of resource will be identified: policymakers, monitoring bodies, and complaint recourse mechanisms.

Policymakers

Policymakers include governmental authorities, international officials, and elected leaders. These individuals oversee or influence policies that touch on religious freedom concerns, either through direct involvement with human rights issues or by following specific countries. Consulting policymakers should be the first step for activists, because they can mobilize untapped political capital on behalf of a cause.

To be effective, advocates must build relationships and consistently provide current and accurate information, highlighting succinctly the facts about problematic situations. When reaching out to policymakers, advocates should

- build compelling but accurate presentations to convince policymakers of the urgency of a situation
- demonstrate how a response fits into their broader policies
- build support for governments/organizations to act.

Whenever policymakers are profiled, the section will highlight

- the role and responsibilities of the individual or office
- how the policymaker can help promote religious freedom
- advocacy suggestions
- contact information.

Monitoring Bodies

Monitoring bodies are those offices tasked with tracking the respect for various human rights, including religious freedom, and issuing reports. Monitoring bodies can be special oversight agencies or commissions, as well as individual rapporteurs and ombudsmen. They can work systematically to examine a range of issues or countries, track governmental compliance and write reports, or respond directly when problems arise and raise concerns directly with an offending government.

Advocates should strive to keep monitoring bodies apprised of specific infringements on religious freedom. These organizations can conduct their own investigations, traveling to countries and questioning government officials about problematic laws and policies. Also, advocates should work to have specific religious freedom situations referenced in reports issued by monitoring bodies, which is an effective way of raising the issue at the international level.

Whenever a monitoring body is profiled, the section will highlight

- the function and focus of the individual or office
- the processes followed by the monitoring body
- how the monitoring body can advance religious freedom
- advocacy suggestions
- contact information.

Complaint Recourse Mechanisms

Complaint recourse mechanisms offer advocates a judicial procedure to pursue justice for the victims they represent. Coming in the form of international courts or quasi-judicial review systems, these bodies can provide victims with a ruling that directs a state to undertake particular action or award monetary damages. However, these procedures are not a panacea. The decisions are not always binding, and compliance can be uneven. The mechanisms have complicated rules on admissibility, and while useful in raising the profile of a situation or moving a government to end problematic activities or provide redress, they take time and a long-term commitment to see a case through to a verdict.

If religious freedom advocates wish to use a complaint recourse mechanism regarding a specific government, they must determine

- what treaties the country has ratified (and not just signed)
- what reservations (if any) were made
- whether the country has accepted international supervision.

Whenever a complaint recourse mechanism is discussed, the section will highlight

- the type and structure of the procedure
- the admissibility requirements for a petition alleging religious freedom violations
- the procedures followed when considering a complaint
- the type of remedies provided (binding vs. nonbinding)
- advocacy suggestions
- contact information.

ADVOCACY 101

By moving governments and international institutions to act, religious freedom advocacy can save lives, free prisoners, and increase religious liberties. Within the international system, there are many ways for religious freedom advocates to engage effectively and push for change—they can conduct direct advocacy, meet with governmental and international policymakers, publicize, report on compliance to monitoring bodies, and use international complaint mechanisms. To be effective, advocates generally undertake these activities by joining or working with NGOs committed to religious freedom.

While it is difficult for individuals and NGOs to convince governments to change policies, international organizations can be a force multiplier. A government will care little about the views of private citizens or foreign advocates, but it will become much more focused on problematic policies when an organ of the United Nations or another international body raises concerns. Advocates should therefore concentrate on engaging international institutions and mobilizing their political leverage towards a government that is violating religious freedom. NGOs often act as the vital catalyst and go-between.

When developing a plan of action, religious freedom advocates should consider the following.

- First, before rushing to international organizations, advocates should initially work to resolve the matter domestically. States are primarily responsible for their own compliance with international religious freedom standards. Relationships with local policymakers can often be more effective in resolving a situation than all the international attention in the world. NGOs with strong, positive relationships with governments can play an important role in this process. However, if the situation is life threatening, or if domestic remedies have been exhausted or will not result in a proper response, then advocates should look abroad.

- Second, determine whether the country is a member of any regional multilateral organizations. Many countries are part of regional organizations that have established their own human rights standards, with some maintaining complaint mechanisms that allow individuals to bring petitions about religious freedom violations. Advocates should also research what monitoring bodies receive human rights complaints and take their concerns there, typically under the auspices of a recognized and reputable NGO. If regional systems fail or the country in question does not participate, then look higher.

- Lastly, at the global level is the United Nations. There are a variety of UN tools available that provide some type of redress mechanism or investigative procedure. Advocates should work to activate one of these UN monitoring bodies or complaint mechanisms on behalf of the victims they represent. Advocates can also look for support from U.S. institutions and agencies or other sympathetic governments.

SPEAKING OUT IN TRUTH

Anyone wishing to advocate for the oppressed and persecuted must act wisely and with great discernment. For every good story about international advocacy freeing a religious prisoner or reforming laws, there is another about an overly aggressive or troublingly ill-informed activist causing more harm than good.

The Hippocratic Oath for advocates is "do no harm." This rule is an absolute. Advocates must coordinate their efforts with the victims or the victims' families, as they will bear the brunt of any response to international advocacy. Victims and their families must be fully aware of the possible ramifications and consent to action—their lives may literally be at stake.

It is also important for religious freedom advocacy groups to speak out against all forms of religious persecution and repression, even if their coreligionists are not affected or persons of no faith are targeted. There is strength in numbers, and often a positive conclusion in one case will be useful to others in similar situations. Governments will try to "buy" the silence of groups by providing benefits or freedoms exclusive to their communities. Advocates should avoid this temptation: if not everyone can enjoy religious freedom, then there is not complete religious freedom for anyone.

Advocates must also be very careful about the facts. If they are found to exaggerate or misrepresent, or to be ill informed, then they will have a difficult time persuading persons of power and influence. One key issue is the use of vocabulary. Sometimes, in an attempt to induce a faster international response, advocates are tempted to exaggerate and make a situation sound more compelling. For instance, the word *persecution* is often carelessly thrown around without any thought as to its true meaning. This overuse only cheapens the term and lessens the impact when describing an actual situation of persecution, hindering an advocate's effectiveness. It is an issue of trust. Once policymakers and monitoring bodies become aware of the loose usage of terminology, they will be much more difficult to persuade and motivate to action.

INTERNATIONAL LAW AND RELIGIOUS FREEDOM

At its core, the freedom of religion guarantees an individual's right to *forum internum*, the protection of an individual's personal beliefs and commitments. This would include theistic, nontheistic, and atheistic beliefs. Religious freedom also protects the *forum externum*, manifestations of religious belief undertaken by individuals or groups of individuals, but with some narrow limitations.

When approaching policymakers, monitoring bodies, or complaint recourse mechanisms, advocates should frame their arguments within the international standards guaranteeing religious freedom. Provisions protecting religious freedom are part of the larger subset of international law on human rights. To properly understand these international standards, it is important to be familiar with how human rights and religious freedom protections fit into the international legal system.

Originally, international law was about relations between states focused on issues beyond a country's borders. States were the only legitimate actors, and their sovereignty was viewed as unassailable. State rights trumped individual rights, and so within its borders a state could act as it wished and was immune from outside pressures. However, as the international system matured and developed from the 1700s to the 1900s, individual rights were gradually recognized.

The major transition from the state-centric focus to a more individualistic approach came after the atrocities of World War II and the Nuremberg trials. Establishment of the UN provided the architecture for a human rights system protecting an array of individual rights, which include religious freedom. Nations now generally agree that all persons have inherent, inalienable rights, neither bestowable nor removable by governments. Consequently, the power of state sovereignty has receded and individual rights have grown.

The French jurist Karel Vasak identified three general categories of rights, which are widely accepted today as a useful framework for understanding the different types of rights:

- **First Generation Rights**: *Civil and Political*—negative obligation—government should not prohibit or limit (most widely recognized)
- **Second Generation Rights**: *Economic, Social, and Cultural*—positive obligation—government should provide
- **Third Generation Rights**: *Peace, Development, and Environment*—positive obligation (just now emerging and least accepted).

As religious freedom is a personal liberty, it falls under First Generation Rights. Consequently, the right is protected through a variety of different international agreements and human rights treaties, which recognize personal freedoms and limit the actions of governments. These protections come in a variety of forms, with the most common being a treaty. A treaty is a formal, legally binding agreement between states, in which governments agree to uphold certain standards and ensure their laws and policies comply. Human rights treaties usually create individual rights and state obligations, and are sometimes called "covenants," "conventions," or "charters." A treaty can be amended through a "protocol," which often adds additional rights or introduces new mechanisms to enforce the treaty. Importantly, states party to a treaty are not obligated to ratify a protocol. When treaties and protocols "enter into force" after a certain number of countries have ratified or adopted the agreement, they are activated and have legal force and effect.

States can sometimes make "reservations" to treaties, explaining how they will not fully implement certain provisions. Reservations are acceptable as long as they do not eviscerate the purpose of the treaty. For instance, the United States regularly makes reservations to provisions in human rights agreements prohibiting "hate speech," noting that it cannot implement these provisions due to First Amendment speech protections. Lastly, under certain circumstances, states are permitted to "derogate" from their treaty obligations. Derogation enables governments legally to limit certain rights in times of national emergencies or war, although religious freedom is usually protected from any derogation.

Religious freedom is well entrenched in numerous UN human rights treaties, covenants, and conventions. Many jurists therefore agree that religious freedom has risen to the level of customary international law, which means it is a universal right that governments must respect, even if they have not signed any human rights treaties. For instance, Article 18 of the UN Universal Declaration of Human Rights speaks directly to religious freedom. It recognizes that "Everyone has the right to freedom of thought, conscience, and religion. This right includes freedom to change his religion or belief, and freedom, either alone or in community with others and in public or private, to manifest his religion or belief in teaching, practice, worship, and observance." Similar language on religious freedom is found in other UN agreements.

In addition to the United Nations, groups of countries have developed regional organizations, similar in structure to the United Nations but limited in geographical scope. These are recognized under Chapter VIII of the UN Charter and bind states together into regional arrangements and agreements. Three regions of the world—Europe, the Americas, and Africa—have created specific agreements establishing additional human rights and religious freedom protections that overlap with the Universal Declaration. (Asia lacks any regional human rights bodies. In late 2007, the Association of Southeast

Nations [ASEAN] did agree to establish a human rights body, but nothing concrete has been established as of this writing.)

Regional systems are usually only as strong as the region's cohesiveness. European structures are consequently the most developed, providing robust human rights and religious freedom protections. For instance, the European Court of Human Rights, the strongest of the international judicial bodies, has repeatedly ruled that religious freedom is one of the foundations of a democratic society and must be respected.

Notably, international documents do not define what constitutes a religion. Drafters have rightly not attempted to define the concept of religion, as it would be an impossible task. What one may consider sacred, another may consider sinful. Readers will find in subsequent chapters, however, that international agreements from the UN and regional systems offer a variety of expressions describing religious freedom:

- freedom of religion
- freedom of religion or belief
- freedom of conscience and of religion
- freedom of thought, conscience, and religion
- freedom of thought, conscience, religion, or belief.

The more specific a description, the better it protects religious freedom. So "freedom of thought, conscience, religion, or belief" includes elements of religious freedom additional to those found in the other renderings. However, the simplest wording—freedom of religion—is also understood to include those broader concepts, as the phrase is construed broadly. Also noteworthy is religious speech, either through word or dress, as it can also be protected under separate provisions concerning freedom of expression.

Religious freedom is unique from other human rights in that, for its full enjoyment, a variety of other rights must also be protected. The multifaceted and interdependent nature of this right can be seen in several ways: to meet collectively for worship or religious education, the freedom of association must be respected; to allow the sharing of religious views, which is often a part of a belief system, speech freedoms must be enjoyed; to provide for some type of community legal status, laws must not discriminate on religious grounds; to maintain or own a place of worship, property rights must be respected; to obtain sacred books and disseminate religious publications, media freedoms must be protected.

In touching these other rights, religious freedom can be either easier or harder to advocate for. It may be easier, as activists can attack limitations from a variety of angles and build broader coalitions with organizations not solely focused on religious freedom. It may be harder, however, if religious freedom limitations are an unintended casualty of a broader governmental policy focused on other domestic political concerns.

RELIGION AND THE STATE

The ways in which religion and the state are related by law around the world varies from country to country and region to region. These relationships are often part of a larger historical narrative involving the role of religion in a country's development and evolution. As nations emerged, some established a particular religion as a way to cultivate national identity. Examples range from the Church of England in the United Kingdom to the Islamic faith in Saudi Arabia.

Today some nations have divested religion, removing it from governmental power and, in extreme cases, completely from the public square: France's strict secularism of *laïcité* compares with officially atheistic communist countries. Many nations from all regions of the world have no established faith, such as Albania, Brazil, the Netherlands, South Africa, Thailand, and the United States. Some have recently disestablished the state church, as Norway did in 2008 and Sweden in 2000. Neither of the world's two most populous countries—China and India—have a state religion.

So while state practice toward establishing an official religion varies, virtually all governments provide some mechanism for granting legal status to religions. These laws help facilitate the work of a religious community by allowing it to obtain juridical personhood for administrative purposes. This status is important, as it can make it easier for a religious community to rent or purchase property, import materials, enter into contracts, and avoid personal liability for ministers, as well as obtain benefits such as state subsidies, access to coreligionists in jail or the military, access to schools, and ability to conduct marriage/funeral services. As will be discussed below, legal status provisions become problematic when governments condition the enjoyment of religious freedom by requiring registration with the state.

TYPICAL LIMITATIONS ON RELIGIOUS FREEDOM

Violations of religious freedom come in a variety of pernicious forms and are not limited to any one region. The most egregious actions are usually found under nondemocratic regimes, yet even in Western countries, lesser forms of religious freedom violations can arise from governmental and private harassment, limitations, and discrimination. As the UN Special Rapporteur on Freedom of Religion or Belief stated in a 2006 report,[1] "Acts of religious intolerance or other acts that may violate the right to freedom of religion or belief can be committed by States but also by non-State entities or actors. States have an obligation to address acts that are perpetrated by non-State actors and which result in violations of the right to freedom of religion of others. This is part of the positive obligation under article 18 [of the Universal Declaration]."

The International Religious Freedom Act, passed by the U.S. Congress in 1998, provides a useful explanation of what can constitute a violation of religious freedom:

(A) arbitrary prohibitions on, restrictions of, or punishment for

i. assembling for peaceful religious activities such as worship, preaching, and prayer, including arbitrary registration requirements;

ii. speaking freely about one's religious beliefs;

iii. changing one's religious beliefs and affiliation;

iv. possession and distribution of religious literature, including Bibles; or

v. raising one's children in the religious teachings and practices of one's choice.[2]

It also lists other actions that would qualify, if they were "committed on account of an individual's religious belief or practice." These actions include detention, interrogation, forced labor, imprisonment, forced religious conversion, beating, torture, rape, enslavement, murder, and execution.

There is a continuum advocates should be aware of when describing a situation:

Persecution—Repression—Harassment—Limitations—Discrimination

Persecution is ground zero for religious freedom violations. *Webster's Dictionary* defines the act of persecution as "to harass or punish in a manner designed to injure, grieve, or afflict; specifically to cause to suffer because of belief." Religious persecution is the most violent, egregious, and extreme repression of religious freedom and can include torture, beatings, imprisonment, loss of property, rape, slavery, murder, and forced conversion. If the circumstances are especially grave, persecution can come in the form of prohibition of religious activities, like corporate worship, education, and proselytizing. Persecution can occur at the hands of government agents or non-state actors. It can be interreligious, intrareligious or a combination of both. For acts to constitute religious persecution, they should be systemic, ongoing, and on account of religious or nonreligious beliefs. In these circumstances, religious groups are often forced underground and must meet secretly, fearing for their well-being and their lives.

The key distinction between persecution and repression is how governments enforce these limitations. *Repression* would describe situations in which believers are prohibited from meeting publicly, religious practice is made illegal, and proselytizing is banned. Repressive governments would use temporary detention, fines, court cases not resulting in prison sentences, and police raids to intimidate believers into submission. These actions violate international norms, but they would not evidence a systematic policy using violent force to bring compliance.

Harassment, limitations, and discrimination, while not rising to the level of persecution, can come in a variety of forms that inappropriately limit religious freedom. Examples of harassment would include overapplication of neutral laws to limit religious activity, as well as police unexpectedly attending religious services or taking pictures of participants as they leave. Threatening actions taken by non-state actors, such as vandalism with little or no response from law enforcement, would also qualify. These incidents would not be part of a wider policy and would occur sporadically. Limitations would include problems with obtaining permits to meet publicly or to use buildings for worship, or restrictions limiting religious speech. Discrimination could come in the form of laws benefiting certain religious communities over others, or through societal actions against particular religious communities.

Recurring examples of harassment, limitations, or discrimination include the following:

Religion Laws—Facilitation vs. Control

Religious freedom is usually guaranteed in a constitution, and in many countries additional religion laws are created to implement those provisions. Ideally, these laws do not overregulate but facilitate religious freedom, aiding the activities of religious groups through the provision of simple mechanisms granting legal personality, nonprofit status, or ways to accept charitable donations. Unfortunately, in many cases the opposite has developed, with specially designed religion laws creating convoluted requirements to place communities in a perpetual catch-22 situation and prevent their religious activity, if not make it outright "illegal."

Registration Schemes—Too Much Information

Registration schemes that fall outside of international standards seek to control rather than facilitate the enjoyment of religious freedom for all. In many countries, registration with the government is required for a group to practice "legally" or to enjoy a corporate status. Often, these systems require special governmental bodies to review doctrines. This is problematic; it places the state in the inappropriate position of determining what constitutes a religion, and it can lead to discrimination against new or minority religious communities. Other times, registration can be denied if the name of a religious group is considered too similar to another, or is deemed to use symbols attributed to another religious community. If officials are looking for reasons to deny a registration application, these vague provisions provide ample justification.

Tiers—Some Are More Equal Than Others

Problematic religion laws often establish de facto, if not de jure, tiers for religious communities. In these systems, tiers can take the form of different levels of religious community status. They can also come in the form of recognizing one or a few religious groups as "traditional," thereby discriminating against all other groups and placing them in a permanent second class status. In either situation, historic faith communities are often automatically assigned to the top level, while minority groups must go through a burdensome registration process for a lesser status. Usually these conferrals of status come with benefits: state funding, avoidance of registration, and tax breaks.

Thresholds—The Numbers Game

Thresholds often accompany tiered systems and utilize numerical criteria for placing groups on different levels. In these situations, religion laws require congregations to have a certain number of adult members. If this number is below one hundred, the requirement is generally viewed as benign. However, if it reaches into the thousands, then the threshold is discriminatory. Laws can also establish temporal restrictions, requiring religious groups to operate in the country for a certain period of time before qualifying for registration or a higher level of recognition. These schemes prevent minority religious communities from enjoying the same status as traditional groups and from having access to certain legal protections and benefits discussed earlier.

Free Speech Limitations—The Gag Rule

An increasing number of countries have placed limitations on free speech, to regulate public sharing of religious belief that intends to persuade the listener to another point of view. Sometimes this is disguised under the premise of respecting family integrity or protecting social harmony. There is growing use of the concept of "proper" and "improper" proselytism. Proselytism is improper if individuals are pressured to convert or monetary or material gain is offered to induce conversion. Increasingly, a number of countries have placed restrictions on religious speech, with some providing criminal penalties for insults against religious officials or for "defaming" a religion. In one example, a pastor in Western Europe was prosecuted for committing "hate speech" because of the content of his sermon. In another country, a student was sentenced to death for "defaming" Islam by circulating information questioning the official interpretation of Islam. Religious speech limitations also include prohibitions on religious expression through dress, be it clerical vestments or the Muslim headscarf.

National Security—False Justification

Many times, governments will cite national security as a reason to limit religious freedom. The justification is a permissible limitation under international standards for certain human rights, like freedom of expression. However, international agreements protecting religious freedom do not recognize national security as a permissible justification to limit religious manifestations, but only "public safety, order, health, [and] morals or the fundamental rights and freedoms of others."[3] Jurists have also firmly established that this is a narrow list of limitations, for employment only in rare occasions.

TIME TO ENGAGE

Religious freedom advocacy is not for the faint of heart. The reasons for religious oppression can vary, but oppressors will not surrender easily or admit freely to violating fundamental human rights. When confronted with such violations, it will take time, dedication, honesty, persistence, and conviction to see an end of the abuses.

Yet advocates can make a difference—sometimes lifesaving—by leveraging international political will against persecution and repression. Advocates can move organizations and governments to act, by reaching out to policymakers and simply making them aware of abuses. Advocates can help encourage positive change by publicizing and documenting abuses for monitoring bodies. Religious freedom advocates can see wrongs righted by utilizing international complaint mechanisms and advocating for justice.

The pages that follow will equip advocates for action, if they are ready and willing to take up the cause.

2

UNITED NATIONS

Created out of the ashes of World War II and the Holocaust, the United Nations (UN) is the world's preeminent international organization. While often criticized for its bureaucracy and slow response, there are many positive aspects to the UN. Designed to help nations work together, the purpose of the organization is to maintain international peace and security and solve international problems, be they economic, social, cultural, or humanitarian in nature. The founding UN Charter declares one of its primary goals to be the promotion of respect for human rights and fundamental freedoms. This simple but momentous reference for the first time recognized world consensus that human rights were of global concern. Building on this, subsequent UN conventions and covenants have enumerated these rights and concretely established religious freedom as a fundamental freedom.

The UN is headquartered in New York, with major offices in Geneva, Vienna, and Nairobi. It is a complex organization, with six principal organs overseeing fifteen agencies and other specialized departments. From an advocacy perspective, however, the UN system is best viewed in two categories: treaty-based bodies and charter-based bodies.

Treaty-based bodies are autonomous and consist of independent experts who monitor the implementation of certain treaties. They operate under limited mandates based on the scope of specific international treaties and covenants, and have jurisdiction only over those countries ratifying the agreement. The relevant example from a religious freedom perspective is the Human Rights Committee from the International Covenant on Civil and Political Rights.

Charter-based bodies are those specifically set forth in the UN Charter with broad mandates. Relevant bodies include the Security Council, the General Assembly, and the Economic and Social Council, as well as the Human Rights Council (and its predecessor the Commission on Human Rights).

Charter-based bodies are political in nature, and their membership is composed of state representatives.

Nongovernmental Involvement

The UN provides "consultative status" for advocacy groups and nongovernmental organizations, which permits them to participate in UN meetings. NGOs must apply for this status, and of all the various international organizations, the UN accreditation process is the most complex. Therefore, it will be discussed at length at the end of the chapter.

RELIGIOUS FREEDOM COMMITMENTS

UN religious freedom commitments are found in the so-called "International Bill of Rights," comprised of three documents—the Universal Declaration of Human Rights, the International Covenant on Civil and Political Rights, and the International Covenant on Economic, Social and Cultural Rights. These documents add specific rights to the general references to human rights and fundamental freedoms found in the UN Charter. However, at the time of UN Charter approval, it was unclear just what form the International Bill of Rights would take.

Universal Declaration of Human Rights

Passage of the Universal Declaration of Human Rights (UDHR) came first and is the foundational document of the international human rights system. Drafted under the supervision of Eleanor Roosevelt as Chair of the Commission on Human Rights, it was the first attempt by the world community to codify human rights standards after the atrocities of World War II. The UN General Assembly (discussed below) approved the Universal Declaration without any objections in 1948.

While General Assembly resolutions are nonbinding, the Universal Declaration is viewed as a "common standard of achievement" against which to measure government actions. Several provisions of the Universal Declaration are not recognized as universal rights by many countries, such as the right to work or to leisure. However, Article 18 on religious freedom is widely supported. It clearly states that all individuals have the right to change their religion, as well as to manifest their beliefs, either alone or corporately, through worship or other practices.

Article 18
Everyone has the right to freedom of thought, conscience and religion; this right includes freedom to change his religion or belief, and freedom, either alone or in community with others and in public or private, to manifest his religion or belief in teaching, practice, worship and observance.

Universal Declaration of Human Rights

Other parts of the Universal Declaration speak to religious freedom. Article 2(1) of the Universal Declaration condemns religiously based discrimination that would limit the enjoyment of these rights. Article 19 protects all forms of speech, including religious expression.

International Covenants

After the approval of the UDHR, two more documents followed. The Commission on Human Rights unsuccessfully attempted to create one legally binding covenant in the 1950s and 1960s that would make actionable the UDHR's aspirational rights, but these efforts failed due to the political climate of the Cold War. Consequently, two separate treaties were created, the International Covenant on Civil and Political Rights (ICCPR) and its sister document, the International Covenant on Economic, Social and Cultural Rights (ICESCR).

Focusing on political rights, the ICCPR speaks specifically to religious freedom, unlike the ICESCR. In addition, the ICCPR provides a more elaborate enunciation of the right to religious freedom than the UDHR. Since it is a treaty, its provisions are also legally binding, unlike the declaratory UDHR. Article 18 of the ICCPR deals directly with religious freedom. Building upon the religious freedom guarantees found in the UDHR, ICCPR Article 18 goes further in positive and negative ways. On the negative side, the UDHR language about "freedom to change his religion or belief" was altered in ICCPR Article 18(1) to "freedom to have or to adopt a religion or belief of his choice," which came at the insistence of Saudi Arabia. However, the intent of the drafters is still clear—governments must protect the *forum internum* and recognize the right of individuals to freely follow the religion of their choice. This outlook is bolstered by Article 18(2), which declares that no one may be coerced into joining a religion.

The Article 18(3) limitation clause focuses only on external displays of religion and not internal, personal beliefs. It holds that religious freedom is not absolute, but the reasons for limiting it are very narrowly construed. So while it is possible to limit legitimate religious practices, it is only in exceptional circumstances.

Article 4 has important implications for Article 18 rights. Article 4 protects religious freedom by specifically stating that governments cannot limit these rights during a public emergency. Only six other rights are given this protection along with religious freedom.

Article 18

1. Everyone shall have the right to freedom of thought, conscience and religion. This right shall include freedom to have or to adopt a religion or belief of his choice, and freedom, either individually or in community with others and in public or private, to manifest his religion or belief in worship, observance, practice and teaching.

2. No one shall be subject to coercion which would impair his freedom to have or to adopt a religion or belief of his choice.

3. Freedom to manifest one's religion or beliefs may be subject only to such limitations as are prescribed by law and are necessary to protect public safety, order, health, or morals or the fundamental rights and freedoms of others.

4. The States Parties to the present Covenant undertake to have respect for the liberty of parents and, when applicable, legal guardians to ensure the religious and moral education of their children in conformity with their own convictions.

International Covenant on Civil and Political Rights

Similar to the Article 2 antidiscrimination clause of the UDHR, Article 2 of the ICCPR commits contracting states to ensure that all individuals in their territory enjoy the rights described in the Covenant and to respect those rights, without regard to religion. Article 19 protects freedom of expression, which would include religiously motivated speech and proselytism. Later, Article 26 promises that all persons are equal before the law, regardless of religion or belief.

The last component of the International Bill of Rights, the International Covenant on Economic, Social and Cultural Rights, has a different focus and only touches upon religious freedom. Like the UDHR and the ICCPR, Article 2 provides expansive guarantees that rights declared in the ICESCR may not be limited based on religion. Article 13(3) provides for the right of religious education, in a similar fashion to ICCPR Article 18(4).

Treaty-Based Bodies—the Human Rights Committee and the First Optional Protocol to the ICCPR

Monitoring Body and Complaint Recourse Mechanism

The Human Rights Committee, established by ICCPR Article 28, is the primary treaty-based body of concern to religious freedom advocates. Its role is to monitor the implementation of the ICCPR. The Committee has eighteen independent members, selected from State Parties to the Covenant, who are experts of "high moral character and recognized competence in the field of human rights." The members are elected for a four-year term with the possibility of one reelection. The Committee meets in three sessions each year in New York and Geneva.

Monitoring Process

Under ICCPR Article 40, State Parties are committed to submitting reports every five years on "the factors and difficulties, if any, affecting the implementation" of the Covenant. Consequently, the original role of the Committee was to review these submissions and provide "concluding observations," highlighting positive examples of implementation, but also areas of concern. In executing this function, the Committee reviews both government submissions and government answers to oral and written questions, as well as reports from advocacy groups, NGOs, and other UN agencies.

The Committee also issues "general comments"—its interpretation of how to implement the provisions of the Covenant. For instance, it stated in 1998 that the "fundamental character" of religious freedom is "reflected in the fact that this provision cannot be derogated from, even in time of public emergency."[1]

Complaint Admissibility

The Committee was given a complaint recourse mechanism through the approval of the First Optional Protocol to the Covenant in 1976. Expanding the Committee's role significantly, the Protocol empowered the Committee to receive communications from individuals from those countries ratifying the Protocol who assert a violation of their ICCPR rights. Countries may also file complaints against other state parties. One hundred and five countries have now ratified the First Optional Protocol.

Nations ratifying the First Optional Protocol
Algeria, Andorra, Angola, Argentina, Armenia, Australia, Austria, Azerbaijan, Barbados, Belarus, Belgium, Benin, Bolivia, Bosnia and Herzegovina, Bulgaria, Burkina Faso, Cameroon, Canada, Cape Verde, Central African Republic, Chad, Chile, Colombia, Costa Rica, Côte d'Ivoire, Croatia, Cyprus, Czech Republic, Democratic Republic of the Congo, Denmark, Djibouti, Dominican Republic, Ecuador, El Salvador, Equatorial Guinea, Estonia, Finland, France, Gambia, Georgia, Germany, Ghana, Greece, Guatemala, Guinea, Guyana, Hungary, Iceland, Ireland, Italy, Kyrgyzstan, Latvia, Lesotho, Libya, Liechtenstein, Lithuania, Luxembourg, Macedonia, Madagascar, Malawi, Mali, Malta, Mauritius, Mexico, Mongolia, Namibia, Nepal, Netherlands, New Zealand, Nicaragua, Niger, Norway, Panama, Paraguay, Peru, Philippines, Poland, Portugal, Republic of the Congo, Republic of Korea, Romania, Russian Federation, Saint Vincent and the Grenadines, San Marino, Senegal, Serbia, Seychelles, Sierra Leone, Slovakia, Slovenia, Somalia, South Africa, Spain, Sri Lanka, Suriname, Sweden, Tajikistan, Togo, Turkmenistan, Uganda, Ukraine, Uruguay, Uzbekistan, Venezuela, Zambia

For allegations of abuse to be heard by the Committee's complaint redress procedure, claimants must have exhausted all available domestic remedies, if such remedies are available, or the government must have unreasonably prolonged the granting of a remedy. Anonymous submissions will not be accepted, and the issue must not be pending before another "procedure of international investigation or settlement." Third parties can bring complaints, preferably with the written consent of the victim.

Article 1 – Complaint Admissibility
A State Party to the Covenant that becomes a Party to the present Protocol recognizes the competence of the Committee to receive and consider communications from individuals subject to its jurisdiction who claim to be victims of a violation by that State Party of any of the rights set forth in the Covenant. No communication shall be received by the Committee if it concerns a State Party to the Covenant which is not a Party to the present Protocol.

Article 5
1. The Committee shall consider communications received under the present Protocol in the light of all written information made available to it by the individual and by the State Party concerned.
2. The Committee shall not consider any communication from an individual unless it has ascertained that:
    (a) The same matter is not being examined under another procedure of international investigation or settlement;

(b) The individual has exhausted all available domestic remedies. This shall not be the rule where the application of the remedies is unreasonably prolonged.

3. The Committee shall hold closed meetings when examining communications under the present Protocol.

4. The Committee shall forward its views to the State Party concerned and to the individual.

Optional Protocol to the International Covenant on Civil and Political Rights

Complaint Procedure

A submission will first be reviewed for admissibility by the Office of the High Commissioner for Human Rights, acting as Committee secretariat. If deemed admissible, the Committee will first share the submission with the offending country. Within six months, the offending country must provide the Committee with an explanation clarifying the matter and explaining any remedies provided. The Committee does not have fact-finding capabilities, and so is reliant on submissions provided by the individual complainant and the respondent government.

Remedies

If deemed admissible, the Committee will consider the submitted information and adopt "views" on the merits of the case. These decisions find either a violation, a nonviolation, or a combination of the two (if there are many elements in a complaint). The findings are forwarded to both parties and then made public after the end of the Committee session. If a violation of the Covenant is found, the Committee will issue views that recommend remedial action. States are obligated under the ICCPR to provide for an effective remedy, and the Committee's Special Rapporteur on Follow-up on Views will work to ensure compliance with the recommendations.

Advocacy Actions

The Human Rights Committee provides a useful avenue to pursue religious freedom abuses committed by, or permitted by, a country that has joined the First Optional Protocol. Importantly, its decisions are nonbinding, but it nonetheless provides a high-profile, public venue to raise concerns. Any Committee ruling against a State Party would place increased international pressure on a government to reform its policies and practices. Advocates can also provide information in the form of documentation about abuses of religious freedom for Committee reports.

Contact Information

Human Rights Committee
http://www.unhchr.ch/html/menu2/6/hrc.htm
Petitions Team
Office of the High Commissioner for Human Rights
United Nations Office at Geneva
1211 Geneva 10, Switzerland
Fax: + 41 22 917 9022
tb-petitions@ohchr.org

Charter-Based Bodies

As mentioned previously, charter-based bodies were not established through specific UN treaties or covenants but were specifically set forth in the UN Charter. They include the Security Council, the General Assembly, and the Economic and Social Council, as well as the Human Rights Council (its predecessor was the Commission on Human Rights).

Security Council and the Secretary General

Policymakers

The UN Security Council is perhaps the best-known organ of the UN. The UN Charter gives the Council responsibility for maintaining international peace and security. The Council is comprised of five permanent members—China, France, the Russian Federation, the United Kingdom, and the United States—and ten nonpermanent members elected by the General Assembly every two years. Each Council member has one vote. Approval of a substantive matter requires nine affirmative votes, including the five permanent members. The well-known veto power comes from this, as all five must vote affirmatively for a matter to be approved.

The Secretary General of the UN is the highest profile UN official, representing the organization and serving as spokesperson. The UN Charter describes the Secretary General as the "chief administrative officer," but also empowers him to "bring to the attention of the Security Council any matter which in his opinion may threaten the maintenance of international peace and security." Consequently, the Secretary General has great latitude to act on a variety of issues, including human rights. The Secretary General has also appointed Special Representatives to serve as his personal envoys, and they focus on a range of country and issue portfolios. The General Assembly appoints the Secretary General at the recommendation of the Security Council, therefore giving the permanent members a potential veto. Ban Ki-moon of the Republic of Korea took office in January 2007 as the eighth UN Secretary General and will serve a renewable five-year term.

Advocacy Actions

The Security Council is the highest and most powerful UN body. Questions of religious freedom are rarely dealt with here, and when they are, the stakes are usually very high, making this venue difficult to access for religious freedom advocates. However, advocates can forward information to the Secretary General and his personal envoys about religious freedom abuses and request intervention.

CONTACT INFORMATION

UN Secretary General Ban Ki-moon
http://www.un.org/sg/
760 United Nations Plaza
New York, NY 10017

Personal Representatives of the Secretary General
http://www.un.org/Depts/dpko/SRSG/

GENERAL ASSEMBLY

Policymakers

The General Assembly is the world's congress, where every member state has one representative with one vote. Serving as the main deliberative body of the UN, the General Assembly discusses issues of international peace and security, as well as human rights and fundamental freedoms. Any decisions, declarations, or resolutions on these issues require a two-thirds-majority vote, and the General Assembly regularly speaks to human rights issues around the world. However, these statements are nonbinding on member states. At the same time, General Assembly declarations can impact religious freedom.

The most well-known General Assembly declaration is the previously discussed Universal Declaration, which speaks to religious freedom among other things. However, the best example of a declaration focused directly on religious freedom is the 1981 Declaration on the Elimination of All Forms of Intolerance and of Discrimination Based on Religion or Belief. Alarmed by "manifestations of intolerance and by the existence of discrimination in matters of religion or belief," the General Assembly resolved to "adopt all necessary measures for the speedy elimination of such intolerance in all its forms and manifestations and to prevent and combat discrimination on the ground of religion or belief" (Introduction to the Declaration).

The nonbinding Declaration, drafted over several decades, covered a number of issues relating to religious freedom. Article 1 of the Declaration basically reiterates the ICCPR Article 18(1–3) verbatim, but with one notable modification. Stating that the right of religious freedom shall include "freedom to have a religion or whatever belief of his choice," the drafters omitted the right to "adopt" a religion of one's choice found in ICCPR Article 18(1). This seemingly harmless wordsmithing represented another attempt by certain governments to further winnow the right of individuals to change their religion.

In more positive areas, Article 2 of the Declaration does state that persons shall not be discriminated against on account of their religion or belief. Article 3 declares that "discrimination between human being on the grounds of religion or belief constitutes an affront to human dignity and a disavowal of the principles of the Charter of the United Nations," the Universal Declaration of Human Rights, and the international covenants on human rights. Article 4 follows with a pledge for all states to "take effective measures to prevent and eliminate discrimination on the grounds of religion or belief" in the enjoyment of all human rights.

Article 6 is perhaps the most valuable clause of the Declaration, as it spells out the specific freedoms incorporated into the enjoyment of religious freedom. These include the rights to gather for worship and maintain facilities for worship and education; the right to acquire materials for worship or religious practice; the right to write and issue religious publications; the right to receive donations; the right to freely select religious leadership; and the right to maintain international contacts.

Article 6
In accordance with article I of the present Declaration, and subject to the provisions of article 1, paragraph 3, the right to freedom of thought, conscience, religion or belief shall include, inter alia, the following freedoms:

(a) To worship or assemble in connection with a religion or belief, and to establish and maintain places for these purposes;

(b) To establish and maintain appropriate charitable or humanitarian institutions;

(c) To make, acquire and use to an adequate extent the necessary articles and materials related to the rites or customs of a religion or belief;

(d) To write, issue and disseminate relevant publications in these areas;

(e) To teach a religion or belief in places suitable for these purposes;

(f) To solicit and receive voluntary financial and other contributions from individuals and institutions;

(g) To train, appoint, elect or designate by succession appropriate leaders called for by the requirements and standards of any religion or belief;

(h) To observe days of rest and to celebrate holidays and ceremonies in accordance with the precepts of one's religion or belief;

(i) To establish and maintain communications with individuals and communities in matters of religion and belief at the national and international levels.

Declaration on the Elimination of All Forms of Intolerance and of Discrimination Based on Religion or Belief

Advocacy Actions

With every UN member state represented, the General Assembly provides a unique opportunity for religious freedom advocates to raise issues of concern with a broad array of governments. The General Assembly meets year round, but its high-level session that convenes each September at the UN headquarters in New York City provides advocates with an opportunity to meet with representatives from countries with problematic records, as well as with those from countries willing to support religious freedom. The Third Committee on Social, Cultural, and Humanitarian issues is where human rights issues are discussed. A religious freedom resolution is introduced in this committee each year, and this committee is where the UN Special Rapporteur on Freedom of Religion or Belief presents his or her annual report. While advocates can only observe the Third Committee, they can lobby delegations before and after the morning and afternoon sessions. Advocates can aid sympathetic delegations by providing language with religious freedom references for possible incorporation into resolutions and decisions, as well as supporting the work of the Special Rapporteur. Advocates need to apply for consultative status to attend UN General Assembly sessions.

CONTACT INFORMATION

General Assembly
http://www.un.org/ga/
760 United Nations Plaza
New York, NY 10017

Non-Governmental Organizations Section
http://www.un.org/dpi/ngosection/index.asp
Department of Public Information
Room S-1070 J, K, L
New York, NY 10017
Tel: (212) 963-6842
Fax: (212) 963-6914
dpingo@un.org

UN HUMAN RIGHTS COUNCIL

Monitoring Body

The main charter-based body dealing with human rights is the UN Human Rights Council. The Human Rights Council and its predecessor, the Commission on Human Rights, are not mentioned in the UN Charter, but both were created by bodies designated as "principal organs" of the UN in the UN Charter. The UN Charter-based Economic and Social Council (ECOSOC) created the Commission on Human Rights in 1946, under its power to "set up commissions in economic and social fields for the promotion of human rights." (ECOSOC is of interest to advocates, as it also handles NGO accreditation, which will be discussed later.) Likewise, the UN Charter-based General Assembly established the new Human Rights Council in 2006. The UN Charter allows the General Assembly to establish "subsidiary organs as it deems necessary for the performance of its functions" (UN Charter, Art. 22). Therefore, while only indirectly linked to the UN Charter, both the Commission and now the Council are considered charter-based bodies.

The Human Rights Council is relatively new, as the UN General Assembly voted overwhelmingly to replace the increasingly dysfunctional Commission on Human Rights with the new Human Rights Council in March 2006. The creation of the Council was part of a larger effort to reform the UN and improve its ability to speak to human rights issues. The problematic Commission on Human Rights was not all bad, as it did issue a variety of resolutions on human rights situations around the world. For example, the Commission criticized Turkmenistan in 2003 and 2004 for its poor record on human rights and mentioned problems concerning religious freedom. However, the Commission was rightfully criticized for the narrowness of its focus and for allowing abusive human rights violators to participate in the fifty-three-seat body. For instance, Libya held the Commission chairmanship in 2003.

Process

The Human Rights Council is now the lead intergovernmental organization within the UN system for monitoring human rights violations. It has been tasked with promoting universal respect for human rights and fundamental freedoms by assessing compliance with human rights principles, reviewing these standards, and providing technical assistance to requesting governments. The Council meets three times a year, with the possibility of additional special sessions, and reports to the General Assembly. In taking the place of the Commission, the Council has assumed responsibility for "special procedures," which allows the Council to name special rapporteurs, representatives, and working groups to investigate specific human rights issues. These representatives and groups can review specific cases under a country or thematic mandate set by the Council.

The forty-seven country representatives participating on the Council are selected by a majority vote in the General Assembly. Members must "uphold the highest standards in the promotion and protection of human rights," as well as undergo periodic reviews of their domestic compliance. Notwithstanding these standards, current members include countries with problematic human rights records, such as China, Cuba, Pakistan, Russia, and Saudi Arabia.

The Council has established the Universal Periodic Review mechanism (discussed below), as well as an Advisory Committee to support its work. The Advisory Committee replaced the former Sub-Commission on the Promotion and Protection of Human Rights and is composed of eighteen experts serving in their personal capacity for a renewable three-year term. The Advisory Committee researches issues of concern to the Council, undertaking various human rights studies and making recommendations to the Council. Members meet for two ten-day sessions each year, with the possibility of additional meetings if deemed necessary by the Council. Notably, the Council has "urged" the Advisory Committee to work with NGOs, and its annual sessions are open to NGOs with consultative status with ECOSOC.

Despite the restructuring, not all are convinced by the Council. Some governments (such as the United States) were skeptical about whether reforms had introduced enough safeguards to prevent the same type of problems from resurfacing in the new body. Initial Council activities have been worrisome. The only country-specific decision approved at the first meeting in 2006 was against Israel; it did not speak to human rights situations elsewhere. In 2007 and 2008, the Council passed resolutions endorsing laws to combat "defamation of religions." Sponsored by Pakistan on behalf of the Organization of the Islamic Conference, the vote was far from unanimous, but both resolutions were approved. While sounding positive, the problematic resolutions justify limitations on religious freedoms and free speech. The defamation concept could be used against dissident members of the majority faith, persons of no faith, or minority faith communities to stifle the sharing of their personal beliefs with others outside their community.

Advocacy Actions

Considering that the Human Rights Council is the premier human rights body, religious freedom advocates should engage the Council and attend its annual sessions. NGOs may speak during most Council sessions and raise issues of concern about specific countries. NGOs also play an important role in lobbying Council members about pending resolutions, to encourage either certain votes or the inclusion of better language. Council meetings therefore provide an opportunity to make delegations aware of specific religious freedom violations, with the possibility of the issue being discussed before the main UN human rights body. Advocates will also need to obtain consultative status to attend Council sessions.

CONTACT INFORMATION

Human Rights Council
http://www.ohchr.org/english/bodies/hrcouncil/
Human Rights Council NGO Liaison Office
Office of the Director-General
Room 153
Palais des Nations
1211 Geneva 10
Switzerland
Tel: + 41 22 917 21 27
Fax: +41 22 917 05 83
ungeneva.ngoliaison@unog.ch

UNIVERSAL PERIODIC REVIEW
Monitoring Body

The Human Rights Council has established a new procedure called Universal Periodic Review (UPR). The first session began in 2008, and over a four-year period, every UN member state will have its human rights record reviewed to determine its compliance with UN standards. A working group of countries conducting the reviews will consider information from nongovernmental organizations and special procedures, as well as state submissions. NGOs may attend these sessions, and they are also webcast on the internet.

Process

The General Assembly resolution that established the Human Rights Council stated that the Council shall "undertake a universal periodic review, based on objective and reliable information, of the fulfillment by each State of its human rights obligations and commitments in a manner which ensures universality of coverage and equal treatment with respect to all States; the review shall be a cooperative mechanism, based on an interactive dialogue, with the full involvement of the country concerned and with consideration given to its capacity-building needs."[2] The goal of these reviews is, among other things, to improve the "human rights situation on the ground" and help fulfill a state's "human rights obligations and commitments."

The reviews, led by a troika of countries randomly selected, will occur three times a year during a two-week session in Geneva. Each review will be based on documents provided by the government under review, a compilation of UN reports prepared by the Office of the High Commissioner for Human Rights, and "additional, credible and reliable information provided by other relevant stakeholders." "Stakeholders" include NGOs, and countries under review are encouraged to consult domestic stakeholders when preparing their reports.

Advocates wishing to provide information must meet the deadlines for each tranche of reviews, as established by the Office of the High Commissioner for Human Rights. In addition, these submissions cannot exceed five pages (but may include a longer report); must cover only the past four years; must be written in English, Spanish, or French; and must follow the preparation guidelines.

Advocacy Actions

Advocates should engage the Universal Periodic Review process, both domestically and in Geneva, by providing the government under review information as well as by providing submissions to the UN. NGOs need not have consultative status to provide information or to attend the UPR sessions. Advocates may ask the country under review questions from the floor, but they will be competing with other NGOs and countries for a very limited amount of time. As Council members may also ask questions, advocates should work with sympathetic delegations to encourage specific questions on issues or situations of concern.

CONTACT INFORMATION

Universal Periodic Review
http://www.ohchr.org/EN/HRBodies/UPR/Pages/UPRmain.aspx
OHCHR Civil Society Unit
Palais des Nations
1211 Geneva 10
Switzerland
Tel: +41 22 917 9656
Fax: +41 22 917 9004
UPRsubmissions@ohchr.org
civilsocietyunit@ohchr.org (NGOs)

Human Rights Council Complaint Procedure

Complaint Recourse Mechanism

In 1970, the Economic and Social Council (ECOSOC) adopted Resolution 1503, "Procedure for Dealing with Communications Relating to Violations of Human Rights and Fundamental Freedoms," which provided an avenue for the then Human Rights Commission to receive complaints. The "1503 Procedure" represents the oldest human rights complaint recourse mechanism in the UN system, and the Human Rights Council has since assumed responsibility for this mechanism. In 2007, the Council reviewed the 1503 Procedure and altered its modalities to "be more victims-oriented" and to streamline the process. The new Human Rights Council Complaint Procedure is important for religious freedom advocates, as it allows the Council to address "consistent patterns of gross and reliably attested violations of all human rights and all fundamental freedoms occurring in any part of the world and under any circumstances." Consequently, the Complaint Procedure can be invoked for even non-UN-member countries, making it the only universal complaint mechanism available to date.

It is too soon to determine whether the changes will improve the mechanism, as the former 1503 Procedure had its drawbacks. Some argued it presented only a mirage of an effective recourse to justice, due to the incredible secrecy of the process. The 1503 Procedure was highly confidential, as decisions were not made public and applicants were not informed of decisions. The Council would only announce which countries were under examination, so it was difficult to raise international awareness. In addition, while a complaint could refer to individual contraventions of human rights, the 1503 Procedure only reviewed situations involving gross and systematic violations. If a complaint survived the rigorous review process, the findings were nonbinding, there were no damages awarded, and individual remedies were not prescribed. The new Human Rights Council Complaint Procedure will maintain this nonbinding, confidential nature, so many of these shortcomings will likely remain.

Complaint Admissibility

The Human Rights Council Complaint Procedure is available for victimized individuals or groups who allege "gross and reliably attested violations"[3] of human rights and fundamental freedoms. Thousands of requests are received each year, so submissions must be well tailored and succinctly specify the relevant facts of the alleged violations. The submission must also relate the violations to the Universal Declaration of Human Rights or other human rights conventions and demonstrate that the violations are widespread, affecting more than just one person or a few individuals. Persons or organizations with "direct and reliable" knowledge of violations, but who are not the victims themselves, may also file complaints. Importantly, these third-party groups are not required to have consultative status with the UN. The victims do not have to be citizens of the offending state, but submissions may not be anonymous (names can be kept confidential). As with a Human Rights Committee inquiry, domestic remedies must be exhausted, shown to be ineffective, or unreasonably delayed.

Complaint Procedure

Communications received under the Complaint Procedure are first vetted by the Chairman of the Working Group on Communications. Anonymous complaints or those obviously outside the Complaint Procedure's parameters are immediately rejected. Surviving petitions are passed to the full Working Group on Communications for the next stage of review. Offending governments are notified of that action and asked to submit information. The petitioner will receive notice that the communication is being forwarded, but no other information about the process will be conveyed, regardless of the final outcome.

The five members of the Working Group on Communications are selected from the Human Rights Council Advisory Committee to serve a renewable three-year term. The Working Group meets twice a year to review communications and make initial admissibility decisions. Communications that are "manifestly ill-founded communications"[4] or fall outside of rights recognized in the Universal Declaration will be screened out. Importantly, the Working Group can combine communications that together expose a pattern of gross violations. The number of cases advanced each year by the Working Group is small. However, NGOs can informally contact individual Advisory Committee members to advocate on cases of concern. Complaints meeting these requirements are forwarded to the Working Group on Situations for the next screening stage.

The Working Group on Situations is composed of five representatives from the Human Rights Council, so it is more political in nature. Members are appointed for a renewable one-year term and meet twice a year to review communications recommended by the Working Group on Communications and state responses. The Working Group on Situations issues a report to the Human Rights Council about situations of gross human rights violation and presents recommendations for Council action.

Once before the Human Rights Council, the communication goes through a two-step, closed-door review process. First, the offending country is invited to provide its side of the story, and Council members may raise questions with government representatives. Notably, the applicant is not provided the same opportunity. During the adjournment, the Council will review the submitted materials and government responses. The Council will announce its final decision or resolution at the second closed meeting, where concerned governments may also be present, but not applicants.

Remedies

A Council decision can take one of four forms: (1) reject the application and discontinue consideration; (2) postpone and keep the situation under review until additional information becomes available; (3) initiate a study of the situation and appoint an independent expert; and (4) discontinue the private Complaint Procedure and discuss the issue publicly.

The decision and findings are nonbinding and will remain confidential, unless the offending government agrees otherwise (which rarely happens). However, the Council Chair will announce publicly which governments have been examined under the Complaint Procedure.

Advocacy Actions

Despite reforms, the Human Rights Council Complaint Procedure is painstakingly slow, complicated, and nontransparent. However, religious freedom advocates should remember that the Complaint Procedure is taken very seriously by the Human Rights Council. Despite not knowing the final disposition of a complaint, the process can be worthwhile for advocates, as it potentially forces governments to explain actions limiting religious freedom before the UN's preeminent human rights council, a body composed of fellow countries.

CONTACT INFORMATION

Human Rights Council Complaint Procedure
http://www2.ohchr.org/english/bodies/chr/complaints.htm
Human Rights Council and Treaties Division
Complaint Procedure
OHCHR-UNOG
1211 Geneva 10, Switzerland
Fax: + 41 22 917 9011
CP@ohchr.org

SPECIAL RAPPORTEURS

Monitoring Body

The Human Rights Council, like its predecessor the Commission on Human Rights, may use its "special procedures" power to create and appoint Special Rapporteurs. Special Rapporteurs are independent experts selected to continuously examine discreet topics in light of relevant UN documents. A number of different Special Rapporteurs exist, with foci ranging from arbitrary executions to violence against women, and these experts report to the Human Rights Council and the General Assembly. The Special Rapporteur on Freedom of Religion or Belief is the main interlocutor for religious freedom advocacy groups. However, the Special Rapporteur on the Promotion and Protection of the Right to Freedom of Opinion and Expression could address situations where religiously based speech has been limited. In addition, the Special Rapporteur on Contemporary Forms of Racism, Racial Discrimination, Xenophobia and Related Intolerance has been tasked with examining anti-Semitism, Christianophobia, and Islamophobia.

However, the Special Rapporteur on Freedom of Religion or Belief is the most relevant Special Rapporteur for advocates and was created in 1986 by the Commission on Human Rights. The 1981 Declaration on the Elimination of All Forms of Intolerance and of Discrimination Based on Religion or Belief provides the terms of reference for the Special Rapporteur's work in examining incidents and government actions that were in violation of those enunciated standards. In 2004, Asma Jahangir of Pakistan was appointed the Special Rapporteur. She has been active—from July 2006 to June 2007, she sent fifty-three communications raising concerns about allegations of religious freedom abuses to twenty-nine different governments.

Process

In accomplishing the assigned task, the Special Rapporteur on Freedom of Religion or Belief looks to receive information from NGOs, religious communities, and advocates regarding potential or actual violations of religious freedom. Advocates can submit communications about religious freedom abuses on behalf of victims, and UN consultative status is not required. In examining the compliance of State parties, the Special Rapporteur will review

1. whether constitutional and legislative systems are adequately protecting religious freedom;

2. whether religious facilities and shrines, as well as religious expressions, are protected;

3. whether registration requirements hinder the ability of individuals or communities to manifest their religious beliefs;

4. whether individuals may gather freely for worship and maintain worship facilities, as well as whether the dissemination of religious publications is allowed;

5. whether individuals may establish religious institutions, as well as charitable and humanitarian organizations;

6. whether persons are abused or tortured because of their religious beliefs; and

7. whether government officials—either civil servants, law enforcement officials, or military personnel—discriminate on religious grounds.

In response to credible allegations of abuse and urgent appeals, the Special Rapporteur can take direct action. She is empowered to communicate these concerns directly with the offending government and to request clarification and information as well as the taking of preventative steps. These communications come in two forms—urgent appeals and letters of allegation. Urgent appeals place governments on notice about actual or imminent violations of religious freedom and request immediate intervention. Letters of allegation are employed after the perpetration of an abuse, to request a clarification and to signal international concern about the situation.

The Special Rapporteur may also conduct country visits to better assess the situation and hold consultations with governmental, nongovernmental, and religious groups. For instance, between 2005 and 2008, she visited a diverse array of countries—Nigeria, Sri Lanka, France, Azerbaijan, the Maldives, Tajikistan, the United Kingdom, Angola, India, and Turkmenistan. An invitation must be extended from the government before any trip can proceed, but the Special Rapporteur can write and request an invitation. After a visit, the Special Rapporteur will issue recommendations regarding corrective measures to effectively promote religious freedom. The Special Rapporteur annually submits public reports to the Human Rights Council and the General Assembly regarding her work, findings, and a list of states not providing requested invitations for country visits.

The office welcomes information from advocates regarding actual, but also potential, violations of religious freedom, allowing advocates to engage the Special Rapporteur before a situation deteriorates. To facilitate the submission and review of information, the Special Rapporteur's office has developed a model questionnaire for individual complaints (see appendix II). Details are important, but specific names can be held confidentially, if requested, to protect victims from further repercussions.

Advocacy Actions

Advocates for religious freedom are encouraged to contact the Special Rapporteur on Freedom of Religion or Belief about issues of concern, as it is the only UN mechanism devoted entirely to religious freedom concerns. The Special Rapporteur has proven to be a powerful voice for religious freedom across the globe, so religious freedom advocates should use the questionnaire to make the Special Rapporteur aware of problematic situations. Advocates should also consider contacting the Special Rapporteur who focuses on speech freedoms when religious expression is limited, as well as the Special Rapporteur on Racism.

CONTACT INFORMATION

Special Rapporteur on Freedom of Religion or Belief
http://www2.ohchr.org/english/issues/religion/index.htm
c/o Office of the High Commissioner for Human Rights
United Nations at Geneva
8-14 Avenue de la Paix
1211 Geneva 10
Switzerland
Fax: +41 22 917 90 06
freedomofreligion@ohchr.org
urgent-action@ohchr.org

Special Rapporteur on the Promotion and Protection of the Right to Freedom of Opinion and Expression
http://www2.ohchr.org/english/issues/opinion/index.htm
c/o Office of the High Commissioner for Human Rights
United Nations Office at Geneva
1211 Geneva 10
Switzerland
Fax: +41 22 917 9006
urgent-action@ohchr.org

Special Rapporteur of the Commission on Human Rights on Contemporary Forms of Racism, Racial Discrimination, Xenophobia and Related Intolerance
http://www2.ohchr.org/english/issues/racism/rapporteur/index.htm
c/o Office of the High Commissioner for Human Rights
United Nations Office at Geneva
1211 Geneva 10
Switzerland
Fax: +41 22 917 9006
urgent-action@ohchr.org

OFFICE OF THE UNITED NATIONS HIGH COMMISSIONER FOR HUMAN RIGHTS

Monitoring Body

Outside of the treaty-based and charter-based system are the Office of the UN High Commissioner for Human Rights (OHCHR) and the High Commissioner for Human Rights. They were established in 1993 in response to increasing work by the UN on issues involving human rights, and thus also religious freedom. The High Commissioner leads the work of the OHCHR and has a broad mandate to promote the full realization of human rights through interactions with governmental and nongovernmental organizations, as well as by coordinating UN programs. The High Commissioner travels widely and will regularly speak publicly about specific issues of concern. The current High Commissioner is Navi Pillay, who was appointed in July 2008 by the Secretary General and approved by the General Assembly. Her term is for four years, with the possibility of one renewal.

Process

The OHCHR is headquartered in Geneva and has primary responsibility for promoting the respect of UN human rights norms by all countries and working to ensure proper translation of international commitments into local laws, policies, and practices. The OHCHR also serves as the secretariat to the previously discussed treaty-based Human Rights Committee and the charter-based Human Rights Council, providing logistical support. Two OHCHR Divisions, the Human Rights Procedures Division and the Operations, Programs and Research Division, carry out the Office's work.

In addition, the OHCHR has established field presences and regional offices in a number of countries, to monitor the human rights situation or to investigate specific abuses. While the role differs from country to country, these presences generally work to ensure the full implementation of a country's human rights commitments into law

OHCHR field presences

OHCHR Country Offices
Angola, Togo, Uganda, Palestine (territory), Cambodia, Nepal, Serbia (including Kosovo), Colombia, Guatemala, Mexico, Bolivia

OHCHR Human Rights Components of Peace Missions
Burundi, Central African Republic, Chad, Côte d'Ivoire, Democratic Republic of the Congo, Ethiopia/Eritrea, Guinea Bissau, Liberia, Sierra Leone, Somalia, Sudan, Iraq, Afghanistan, Timor-Leste, Georgia/Abkhazia, Haiti

OHCHR Human Rights Advisors
Great Lakes region of Africa, Guinea, Niger, Rwanda, Indonesia, Papua New Guinea, Sri Lanka, Kyrgyzstan, Republic of Moldova, Russian Federation, Serbia, South Caucasus, the former Yugoslav, Republic of Macedonia, Ecuador, Guyana, Nicaragua

Regional OHCHR Offices (operating or planned)
Africa: Southern Africa (Pretoria); East Africa (Addis Ababa); Central Africa (Yaoundé); West Africa (planned)
Arab region: Middle East and the Gulf (Beirut); North Africa (planned); General Region (planned in Qatar)
Asia and the Pacific region: South-East Asia (Bangkok); Pacific (Suva)
Europe, North America, and Central Asia: Central Asia (Almaty); North America (New York)
Latin America and the Caribbean: Latin America (Santiago); Central America (planned)

and practice at both the national level and the local level, as well as to lend assistance and protection to victimized groups or individuals.

The OHCHR can also conduct rapid responses to quickly deteriorating human rights situations in an attempt to provide protection. Possible actions range from the High Commissioner speaking publicly or through a press release, to initiating fact-finding or monitoring missions, to reinforcing OHCHR field presences.

The OHCHR relies heavily on civil society and nongovernmental organizations, including religious communities and their advocates. In 2004, the OHCHR appointed a special liaison officer to strengthen the OHCHR's engagement, in recognition of how NGOs can serve as an early warning system, providing the UN with the latest information about abuses.

Advocacy Actions

The High Commissioner for Human Rights is the premier human rights advocate in the international system. Consequently, religious freedom advocates would be wise to keep the High Commissioner, the supporting OHCHR, and the various OHCHR field presences apprised of situations of abuse against religious freedom. Advocates can request that the High Commissioner incorporate these concerns into her statements and visits, as well as instruct other offices to inquire about problematic situations.

CONTACT INFORMATION

Office of the UN High Commissioner for Human Rights (OHCHR)
http://www.ohchr.org/
UNOG-OHCHR
Palais des Nations
1211 Geneva 10
Switzerland
Tel: +41 22 917 9000

Human Rights Complaints:
Petitions Team
Office of the UN High Commissioner for Human Rights
UNOG-OHCHR
Palais des Nations 8–14
Avenue de la Paix
1211 Geneva 10
Switzerland
Fax: +41 22 917 9022
tb-petitions@ohchr.org

CONSULTATIVE STATUS

Article 71 of the UN Charter established a role for nongovernmental organizations, allowing them to consult UN organs about matters of concern.
Referred to as "consultative status," it is required for NGOs wishing to engage
the General Assembly, the Human Rights Council, or the Sub-Commission
on the Promotion and Protection of Human Rights. Registration to attend
and speak at UN meetings, such as the annual Human Rights Council session, is also contingent on holding consultative status. Applications for this
accreditation are reviewed by the ECOSOC Committee on Non-Governmental Organizations, which is composed of nineteen member states.

Eligibility

The eligibility requirements are as follows:

- concern with matters under the competency of ECOSOC or a subsidiary body
- aims and purposes in harmony with principles of the UN Charter
- two years of existence (proven by nonprofit status or other government
  registration)
- established headquarters
- democratically adopted constitution
- authority to speak for its members
- representative structure
- appropriate mechanisms of accountability to members
- funds from nongovernmental sources
- democratic and transparent decision-making processes.

Three levels of consultative status exist: General, Special, and Roster.

- General consultative status is granted to large NGOs with worldwide
  activities and interests, "concerned with most of the activities of the
  Council and its subsidiary bodies."[5]
- Special consultative status is reserved for NGOs with specialized
  interests over a narrower agenda, engaging "only a few of the fields of
  activity covered by the Council and its subsidiary bodies."[6]
- Roster status is for NGOs who only "make occasional and useful contributions to the work of the Council or its subsidiary bodies" and do
  not hold general or special consultative status.[7]

Process

Interested NGOs must first write a letter of intent to the NGO Section of the Department of Economic and Social Affairs, asking for recognition in one of the three categories. Once received, the Department will mail an application package and questionnaire. It is incumbent upon the NGO to finish completely the application and return it to the Department so that it can be forwarded to the Committee on Non-Governmental Organizations for consideration. Incomplete applications will not be forwarded.

The Committee on Non-Governmental Organizations meets only twice a year to consider applications. NGOs scheduled for review will be notified, and two representatives have the option of attending the session in New York City. If they do not attend and their application is deferred, they may then wish to participate at the next session and answer any questions. Once completed, the Committee may recommend a consultative status, defer an application to allow for clarification of its questions, or recommend a different status than what was requested. Final recommendations are communicated to the NGO and reported to ECOSOC for approval.

ECOSOC can either approve or reject Committee recommendations. The Department of Economic and Social Affairs sends notification of final decisions to NGOs. Those obtaining general or special consultative status are required to submit every four years a report of their activities and contributions to the work of the UN.

CONTACT INFORMATION

NGO Section of the Department of Economic and Social Affairs
http://www.un.org/esa/coordination/ngo/
ECOSOC
One United Nations Plaza, Room DC1-1480
New York, NY 10017
Tel: (212) 963-8652
Fax: (212) 963-9248
desangosection@un.org

3

EUROPEAN UNION

The European Union is probably the best-known regional organization. Casual observers are familiar with the EU's currency (the Euro) and its internal visa-free travel (the Schengen Agreement). However, the EU is much more than currency and customs agreements—the European Union is a supranational and intergovernmental organization bringing together twenty-seven member countries from across Europe. With over five hundred million citizens living across roughly 1.6 million square miles and speaking twenty-three languages, the European Union is becoming more and more of an international force.

Headquartered in Brussels, Belgium, the EU is built around the principles of human rights, democracy, and rule of law, and it is often referred to as the United States of Europe. While similarities exist with the U.S. system, it is a unique actor on the international stage, sharing some characteristics of a federation of states and some of an international organization comprised of sovereign countries. EU member states have freely agreed to relinquish their sovereignty in certain areas, such as international trade, while agreeing only to cooperate in others, like security and defense.

European Union members
Austria, Belgium, Bulgaria, Cyprus, Czech Republic, Denmark, Estonia, Finland, France, Germany, Greece, Hungary, Ireland, Italy, Latvia, Lithuania, Luxembourg, Malta, Netherlands, Poland, Portugal, Romania, Slovakia, Slovenia, Spain, Sweden, United Kingdom

As is generally true with many facets of the international system, the origins of the EU stem from post-World War II politics. With European economies in shambles and struggling to recover, Belgium, France, West Germany, Italy, Luxembourg, and the Netherlands agreed to establish the European Coal and Steel Community in 1951 to streamline and promote the sharing of raw materials. It was a resounding success, and two more international bodies were established a few years later—the European Atomic Energy

Community Treaty and the European Economic Community Treaty. Over time, these three agreements and their participating countries become known as the European Communities.

From this, the European Union emerged and was formally established in 1993 by the Maastricht Treaty. The treaty established EU policies on monetary issues and foreign policy matters, dividing them between three "pillars" of focus, within which the main EU bodies operate. The first pillar concerns economic, social, and environmental policies, but religious freedom matters can fall under the second and third pillars—either the Common Foreign and Security Policy or Freedom, Security and Justice.

- The first pillar reflects the areas of the three foundational agreements that established the European Communities—economic, social, and environmental policies. As a result, member states have relinquished their sovereignty and the EU has complete "competency" to govern issues falling into these categories.

- The second pillar established the Common Foreign and Security Policy (CFSP) and empowered the EU to take joint action in foreign and security matters. Unlike with the first pillar, the EU is not delegated full authority and CFSP is an area of intergovernmental cooperation. Many countries believed foreign policy and military matters to be too sensitive to surrender completely to the EU. Reforms in 1999 now enable the member states to act on behalf of the EU if two-thirds agree to take action. Promoting respect for human rights (which includes religious freedom) is considered to be a general CFSP objective.

- The third pillar focuses on freedom, security and justice, which individual countries also deemed too important to be controlled completely by the EU. The focus is intra-EU, and issues falling under this pillar include asylum, immigration, criminal matters, police cooperation, drug trafficking, trafficking in persons, the fight against terrorism, and human rights (and therefore also religious freedom in EU countries).

Nongovernmental Involvement

The European Union has a policy of working with NGOs and welcomes the involvement of nongovernmental organizations in deliberations and consultations. Neither the Council of the European Union nor the European Commission maintains an accreditation process, and anyone can meet with EU officials willing to speak with them. Advocacy groups wishing regularly to approach the European Parliament should obtain a lobby-ist parliamentary pass. Valid for a maximum of one year, the pass gains advocates entry into Parliament buildings and the ability to attend most committee meetings. Applicants will need to demonstrate that they will regularly attend Parliament sessions and that they have residency in an EU country, and they must provide a copy of their identification and an attes-tation of good conduct from the police or other local authority. A refer-ence from a Member of the European Parliament might also be requested. Advocates not needing regular access to the Parliament can still request meetings with individual parliamentarians, who can sign them in for indi-vidual meetings.

Advocates should also consider joining one of the human rights-focused NGO coalitions that operate in Brussels, such as the Human Rights and Democracy Network (HRDN) or the European Platform on Religious Intolerance and Discrimination (EPRID). They are known entities to EU officials and parliamentarians and so can help facilitate meetings to raise issues of concern.

Contact Information

Human Rights and Democracy Network (HRDN)
http://www.act4europe.org/code/en/about.asp?Page=41

Religious Freedom Commitments

The Charter of Fundamental Rights outlines the political rights of all EU citizens. While speaking to a variety of issues not all universally recognized as human rights, its language on religious freedom is consistent with interna-tional norms. Article 10 parallels what is found in the Universal Declaration and the International Covenant, while also expressly providing for the right to change one's religion. It guarantees individual and communal religious free-dom, as well as the right to manifest those beliefs. Article 10 does not provide a limitations clause, but one is contained in Article 52 concerning all the rights enumerated in the Charter. Other relevant articles would be Article 11 on freedom of expression, which would protect religious expression, and Article 12, which prohibits religiously based discrimination. Unique to the Charter is Article 22, which requires that the EU respect religious diversity.

> **Article 10—Freedom of thought, conscience and religion**
> 1. Everyone has the right to freedom of thought, conscience and religion. This right includes freedom to change religion or belief and freedom, either alone or in community with others and in public or in private, to manifest religion or belief, in worship, teaching, practice and observance.
> 2. The right to conscientious objection is recognised, in accordance with the national laws governing the exercise of this right.
>
> **Article 22—Cultural, religious and linguistic diversity**
> The Union shall respect cultural, religious and linguistic diversity.
>
> **Charter of Fundamental Rights of the European Union**

The Charter's status is unique, as it is not considered a treaty or legally binding document, but rather a proclamation of human rights that all EU member states should uphold. It has not been directly approved by EU countries, but rather by the leaders of the three main EU organs—the Presidents of the European Parliament, the Council of the European Union, and the European Commission—obligating these entities (described below) to uphold these standards.

Member states will only become legally obligated to the Charter upon ratification of the European Constitution. Formally known as the European Constitutional Treaty, the text was approved in 2004 by all EU heads of state, but it will not enter into force until each member state ratifies. While 18 nations have done so already, both France and the Netherlands voted against ratification in 2005. After the "no" votes, a less ambitious and scaled-back version, the Lisbon Treaty, was put forward for unanimous approval, but Ireland voted it down in 2008. Consequently, the future of ratification efforts is unclear. If ratification ever occurs, Article I-9 of the draft European Constitution declares that the "rights, freedoms and principles" set forth shall be recognized by the entire Union. During the 2007 EU summit, the member states agreed to discuss creating a watered-down version of the Constitution, in hopes of passing some type of agreement. However, until all twenty-seven states agree on the form of the Constitution, the Charter will remain an important nonbinding agreement on states that reflects European standards on human rights and religious freedom.

In addition to the Charter, the EU has developed Guidelines on specific human rights issues to provide direction for EU activities. The Guidelines currently cover the death penalty, torture and other forms of ill-treatment, human rights dialogues with third countries, children affected by armed conflicts, human rights defenders, and international humanitarian law. Notably, religious freedom has not been selected.

ORGANS OF THE EUROPEAN UNION

The three main bodies of the European Union that are of interest to religious freedom advocates are the European Parliament, the European Commission, and the Council of the European Union. Representing different branches of the EU, a variety of checks and balances have been instituted between the three bodies. The EU does maintain a court, the Court of Justice of the European Communities (usually referred to as the European Court of Justice), but as of now it does not have jurisdiction over human rights violations. A fourth independent agency, the European Union Agency for Fundamental Rights (FRA), monitors EU members regarding their fulfillment of human rights obligations.

EUROPEAN PARLIAMENT

Policymakers

The European Union maintains a parliamentary body, with representatives elected every five years from their home countries in nationwide referenda. Of the international parliamentary systems, the European Parliament acts the most like a national congress. Its members are tasked with representing their constituents' interests at the EU level. As the EU has expanded, so has the body. It currently comprises 785 Members of the European Parliament (MEPs). Elected from all twenty-seven countries, members do not sit in national blocs, but rather in EU-wide political groups representing every part of the political spectrum. The Parliament is led by a president elected for a term of two and a half years.

The Parliament also has two seats—the official seat in Strasbourg, France, and another in Brussels, Belgium, with the rest of the EU institutions. With offices and committees based in Brussels, much of the work of the Parliament is conducted there, and that is where most human rights lobbyists concentrate their activities. However, all 785 MEPs will travel to Strasbourg, France, every month for a week-long plenary session. EU officials and MEPs have repeatedly discussed making Brussels the official seat, but it is unclear whether these discussions will progress any further (and unlikely that France would agree).

In addition to MEPs, permanent staff support the committee structure, as well as being assigned to a regional or country desk. The political groups will often have staffers focusing on human rights as well. The European People's Party has gone further, assigning individuals to focus specifically on religion and politics.

Process

While similar to a national congress, the European Parliament does not maintain the same level of power. It cannot initiate legislation and must share its legislative role with the Council of the European Union. The Parliament can recommend through a report that the European Commission present a specific legislative proposal to the Council. It can only jointly approve legislation, directives, and regulations relating to the first pillar, where the EU enjoys full competency. The Parliament also shares a role with the Council in the budgetary process, deciding revenues and approving expenditures.

The Parliament can, however, approve nonbinding resolutions on any topic. These can be quite lengthy and speak to a whole range of issues. Those speaking to human rights situations are referred to as urgency resolutions. To pass, no direct vote is taken, but political groups reach an agreement beforehand at a working group meeting. Approved texts become a part of the permanent record. More importantly, approved resolutions represent the opinion of a majority of parliamentarians on the issue in question, which can send a powerful signal and increase the value of the nonbinding statement.

The Parliament regularly investigates and reports on issues of concern, often focusing on human rights. An MEP will be appointed to lead the investigation as a rapporteur and draft the report. Advocates can seek to meet with the MEP and provide background information and recommendations. Advocates can also request that other MEPs introduce amendments to the report at a later stage. In addition to discreet reports, the Parliament prepares an annual report on human rights, and a different rapporteur is nominated every year.

Like national congresses, the Parliament does play an important oversight role with EU institutions, especially the European Commission. The Parliament is responsible for approving each new slate of twenty-seven Commissioners for the European Commission. Its supervisory role is also made manifest through its power to submit parliamentary questions to the Commission and the Council, which they are obligated to answer.

The parliamentarians, much like members of the U.S. Congress, will often take up specific issues of individual interest and work within the parliamentary structures to highlight supported causes. MEPs can meet independently with ambassadors and government representatives, as well as send letters to heads of state raising their concerns about religious freedom violations. They can also use parliamentary mechanisms, such as resolutions or declarations, to effectively raise an issue.

MEP activism can also be conducted through the twenty standing committees and thirty-five informal caucuses. Of the various committees, three are of most interest to religious freedom advocates. While the European Parliament cannot create law or policies directing the foreign affairs of the member states, the Committee on Foreign Affairs does play a consultative role in the formation of the Common Foreign and Security Policy. Part of its jurisdiction specifically concerns human rights issues outside of the EU. Its jurisdiction consequently overlaps with the Committee on Human Rights, which is the main forum for addressing violations of fundamental freedoms and religious freedom outside the EU. For matters within the EU space, the Committee on Civil Liberties, Justice and Home Affairs is responsible for ensuring the human rights of EU citizens under the Charter of Fundamental Rights. All can convene hearings to investigate and examine reports of human rights abuses.

Lastly, parliamentarians also maintain more informal caucuses called "delegations" that focus on individual countries or groups of countries. Any of the thirty-five delegations can convene roundtables to discuss issues of interest and undertake country visits.

Delegations
EU-Croatia; EU-Former Yugoslav Republic of Macedonia; EU-Turkey; EU-Mexico; EU-Chile; Switzerland; Iceland and Norway and European Economic Area (EEA); Russia; South-East Europe; Ukraine; Moldova; Kazakhstan, Kyrgyzstan, Uzbekistan, Tajikistan, Turkmenistan and Mongolia; Armenia, Azerbaijan and Georgia; Belarus; Israel; Palestinian Legislative Council; Maghreb; Mashreq; Gulf States, Yemen; Iran; United States; Canada; Central America; Andean Community; Mercosur; Japan; People's Republic of China; Southeast Asia, ASEAN; Korean Peninsula; Australia and New Zealand; South Africa; NATO; South Asia; India; Afghanistan

---

Advocacy Actions

Lobbying MEPs on issues regarding religious freedom can prove fruitful when attempting to influence policy, either on specific religious freedom cases or more systematic abuses. MEPs can ask written questions and introduce urgency resolutions, as well as raise concerns in their committee meetings and when questioning representatives from the European Commission or Council of the European Union. They can also meet with embassy officials from governments with problematic religious freedom records and write heads of state about their concerns. Advocates can send information about issues of concern to relevant committee and delegation MEPs and staff. In addition, advocates can ask relevant committees and delegations to arrange hearings on situations.

CONTACT INFORMATION

European Parliament
http://www.europarl.europa.eu/
Rue Wiertz
1047 Brussels
Belgium
Tel: +32 2 284 21 11
Fax: +32 2 284 69 74

EUROPEAN COMMISSION

Policymakers

The European Commission constitutes something akin to an executive branch of a national government. It acts independently and represents the entity of the European Union and the common interests of all member states, and maintains a significant focus on human rights. Only the Commission can propose new legislation at the EU level, which the European Parliament and Council of the European Union can reject or adopt. It is often referred to as the "guardian of the treaties," as it ensures the proper application by member states of the various EU agreements and institutional decisions. The Commission is fully involved in the formulation of the Common Foreign and Security Policy with the Council of the EU. The Commission can also focus on issues of particular interest—for instance, in 2006 it held a meeting with Christian, Jewish, Muslim, and Buddhist leaders to discuss ways to promote inter-religious tolerance.

Process

The Commission is led by a President, usually a former head of state, who is nominated by the Council of the European Union and elected by the Parliament for a five-year term. The current President is José Manuel Barroso of

Portugal. The Commission is accountable to the Parliament, so Commissioners meet regularly with the Parliament to explain and justify its policies, as well as to respond to written and oral questions from MEPs.

There are twenty-seven Commissioners, one from each EU member, with each having a distinct issue portfolio. Appointed for a five-year term, the present Commission will work through October 2009. Commissioners do not represent their countries but are responsible for different thematic areas of policy, ensuring proper treaty application or representing the EU abroad. Before a slate of Commissioners is put before the European Parliament and the Council of the European Union for approval, the portfolios responsible for the more high-profile topics are the subject of intense negotiations between EU states and with the Commission President.

Commissioner portfolios of interest to advocates would be:

- Freedom, Security and Justice—most recently held by former Italian Foreign Minister Franco Frattini, and the position oversees the monitoring of the fundamental rights of EU citizens

- External Relations and European Neighbourhood Policy—currently held by former Austrian Foreign Minister Benita Ferrero-Waldner, who engages with non-EU countries

- Enlargement—currently held by former Finnish MEP Olli Rehn, who supervises the possible expansion of the EU into the Western Balkans and Turkey

Commissioners oversee Directorate-Generals (DGs), which are the departments responsible for different policy portfolios. Acting like government agencies, DGs are the main bureaucracy of the European Union. Commissioners can be responsible for more than one DG, and DGs can cross more than one Commissioner's area of responsibility. For instance, the Directorate-General for the External Relations (DG RELEX) covers external relations and enlargement, while the Directorate-General for Justice, Freedom and Security is solely under that one Commissioner's purview. Within DG RELEX there is a Human Rights and Democracy Unit, with one official specifically assigned to follow religious freedom matters. The Commission has also established the European Instrument for Democracy and Human Rights (EIDHR), which funds a range of projects with nongovernmental organizations to promote human rights.

The formation of the current Commission was not a smooth process. Italy originally designated Dr. Rocco Buttiglione for the Freedom, Security and Justice portfolio. However, his candidacy came under intense scrutiny by

CONTACT INFORMATION

European Union
http://europa.eu
http://europa.eu/pol/rights
http://europa.eu/geninfo/mailbox/
inst_en.htm

European Commission
http://ec.europa.eu/
http://ec.europa.eu/staffdir/index.
htm (staff directory)
Tel: + 32 2 299 11 11
oib-info@ec.europa.eu

**José Manuel Barroso, President of
the European Commission**
http://ec.europa.eu/
commission_barroso/president
European Commission
1049 Brussels
Belgium
Tel: + 32 2 298 81 50
sg-web-president@ec.europa.eu

**Commissioner for Freedom,
Security and Justice**
http://ec.europa.eu/
commission_barroso
European Commission
B-1049 Brussels
Belgium
Tel: +32 2 299 11 11
Fax: +32 2 292 13 49

**Directorate-General for Justice,
Freedom and Security**
http://ec.europa.eu/justice_home
European Commission
B-1049 Brussels
Belgium
Tel: +32 2 299 11 11

**Benita Ferrero-Waldner, Commis-
sioner for External Relations and**

European Neighbourhood Policy
http://ec.europa.eu/
commission_barroso/ferrero-
waldner
Tel: +32 2 299 49 00

**Directorate-General for External
Relations
(DG RELEX)**
http://ec.europa.eu/
external_relations
European Commission
Rue de la Loi 170 (CHAR 13/03)
B-1049 Brussels
Belgium
Tel: +32 2 299 90 44
Fax: +32 2 299 92 88

**Olli Rehn, Commissioner for
Enlargement**
http://ec.europa.eu/
commission_barroso/rehn
olli.rehn@ec.europa.eu
Tel: +32 2 295 79 57
Fax: +32 2 295 85 61

**Directorate-General for
Enlargement**
http://ec.europa.eu/dgs/enlargement
European Commission
Rue de la Loi 200 (CHAR 04/145)
B-1049 Brussels
Belgium
elarg-02@ec.europa.eu

**European Instrument for Democ-
racy and Human Rights (EIDHR)**
http://ec.europa.eu/europeaid/
where/worldwide/eidhr/
index_en.htm
EuropeAid-EIDHR-Mailing-List@
ec.europa.eu
EuropeAid-EIDHR@ec.europa.eu

the European Parliament after he referred to homosexuality as a "sin." The Parliament cannot reject individual candidates, but only the entire slate of proposed Commissioners, and it threatened to do just that. To resolve the conflict, the Commission President withdrew Buttiglione's name, despite the devout Catholic's pledge that his personal moral views would not impede his efforts to ensure the rights of all EU citizens.

Advocacy Actions

The European Commission is the institutional center of the European Union and therefore can influence EU policies on religious freedom, both inside and outside the EU. Advocates should try to contact Commissioners with relevant portfolios and ask for assistance with specific situations. Requested actions could include having the EU raise concerns bilaterally or begin monitoring a situation through one of their missions. Advocates should also meet with staff in DG RELEX or DG Justice, Freedom and Security concerning problematic countries inside and outside the EU space and provide information. The Commission does not maintain any general registration or accreditation requirements for activists.

COUNCIL OF THE EUROPEAN UNION

Policymakers

The Council represents the twenty-seven member states and is considered the main decision-making body of the EU. Ministers from each EU country sit on the various committees of the Council that relate to their expertise (e.g., the Minister of Agriculture sits on the Agriculture and Fisheries Committee), which is why the Council is sometimes referred to as the Council of Ministers. The Council is led by the office of President, which rotates to a different country every six months. The President's work is supported by the General Secretariat, which is led by the Secretary General. The work of the Council is assisted by a group of twenty-seven ambassadors composing the Committee of Permanent Representatives (COREPER), which prepares Council agendas. Council responsibilities include approving the EU budget and laws with the Parliament, as well as matters arising from the first pillar, where the EU has full competence.

Process

The Council develops the EU's Common Foreign and Security Policies, mainly through its General Affairs and External Relations Council. The General Affairs and External Relations Council deals with foreign affairs and is composed of foreign ministers. It regularly issues "Council Conclusions" on a variety of subjects (often related to human rights and sometimes religious freedom), expressing the opinion of the Council of the European Union about a specific issue of concern. For these conclusions and CFSP decisions, unanimity is required. Two-thirds can decide to act together on behalf of the EU, but it would not reflect a consensus EU position.

The High Representative for the Common Foreign and Security Policy coordinates and aids in the development of CFSP and can speak on behalf of the EU when a common position has been unanimously approved. The High Representative also works with the European Commission's Commissioner on External Affairs, which can cause confusion about who is speaking on behalf of the EU. The position is held by the Council's Secretary General, Javier Solana of Spain, who was previously the Secretary General of NATO.

The High Representative's office does have a concentration on human rights issues, as human rights promotion is a CFSP position, and the High Representative has also appointed a Personal Representative for Human Rights. The High Representative is also assisted by ten EU Special Representatives who focus generally on specific countries or regions. The EU Special Representatives currently cover the following: Afghanistan, the African Great Lakes Region, Bosnia and Herzegovina, Central Asia, the former Yugoslav Republic of Macedonia, Kosovo, the Middle East, Moldova, the South Caucasus, and Sudan.

Should the European Constitution ever be approved, the Council would experience many changes. The six-month rotating presidency would be replaced with a five-year term. The High Representative would be upgraded to the position of EU Foreign Minister.

Lastly, the Council of the European Union should not be confused with the European Council. The European Council convenes four times a year between all twenty-seven heads of state and the President of the European Commission. The purpose of the European Council is to establish the general political trajectory of the EU and to settle disputes that their ministers could not resolve. If issues of religious freedom arise during their discussions, the venue is very difficult for religious freedom advocates to access.

Advocacy Actions

The EU has three mechanisms at its disposal to express concern about human rights and religious freedom violations—declarations by the President or High Representative, démarche, or sanctions. Religious freedom advocates should forward information about religious freedom abuses occurring outside the EU to the Council for consideration in their Council Conclusions and other decisions. In addition to meeting with Council representatives, advocates should also contact the office of the High Representative for the Common Foreign and Security Policy. The High Representative and office staff, the Personal Representative for Human Rights, and the Special Representatives follow religious freedom issues through the prism of human rights

---

CONTACT INFORMATION

Council of the European Union
http://www.consilium.europa.eu/
Rue de la Loi 175
B-1048 Brussels
Belgium
Tel: +32 2 281 61 11
Fax: +32 2 281 69 34

Javier Solana, High Representative for Common Foreign and Security Policy
http://www.consilium.europa.eu/App/Solana
Rue de la Loi 175
B-1048 Brussels
Belgium
Tel: +32 2 281 56 60
Fax: +32 2 281 56 94
presse.cabinet@consilium.europa.eu

Personal Representative of the High Representative for Human Rights
http://www.consilium.europa.eu/cms3_fo/showPage.
asp?id=849&lang=EN
Rue de la Loi 175
B-1048 Brussels
Belgium
Tel: +32 2 281 61 11
Fax: +32 2 281 69 34

EU Special Representatives
http://www.consilium.europa.eu/cms3_fo/showPage.
asp?id=263&lang=EN

and would be interested in violations occurring outside the EU. Advocates can request that the concerns be raised bilaterally or through declarations. Advocates should maintain contact with the permanent representatives of EU member states assigned to the Committee of Permanent Representatives. Diplomats at COREPER meet regularly to discuss human rights and country situations. Advocates should also work to establish contact with diplomats representing the upcoming EU presidency.

EU Enlargement and Other Programs

Policymakers

While not directly concerning religious freedom, the EU enlargement process has proven effective in moving governments to change problematic policies. Respect for human rights, and also religious freedom, is a prerequisite for interested applicants. Since 2004, the Union has grown from fifteen to twenty-seven members. The most recent entrants, Bulgaria and Romania, had to undertake many reforms to bring their laws and policies into conformity with European Union standards. The current candidate countries are Turkey, Croatia, and Macedonia. The European Commission maintains offices in each capital to liaise with the government about reform efforts.

The standards for entry are high and are referred to as the "Copenhagen Criteria":

1. democracy, the rule of law, human rights;
2. functioning market economy;
3. application of the EU's rules and policies (known as the *acquis communautaire*).

The lure of joining the EU and having unhindered access to its market is an incredibly powerful incentive for reform. For instance, the negotiations with Turkey have resulted in religious freedom improvements, with several reforms of Turkish law improving the ability of non-Muslim religious communities to obtain legal status and operate more freely. While many limitations on religious freedom remain unaddressed, these initial religious reforms only came to pass because of EU accession pressure.

Another program that works with the accession process is the Stabilization and Association Process (SAP), which aids the countries of Southeast Europe in developing and strengthening their commitment to democratization and human rights. If these criteria are met, this engagement could lead to a future candidacy for full EU membership. Six Balkan countries currently participate—Albania, Bosnia and Herzegovina, Croatia, Macedonia, Montenegro, and Serbia. The SAP has also resulted in important governmental reforms.

The European Neighbourhood Policy (ENP) focuses on countries not seeking EU membership. Initiated in 2004, it provides financial and technical support to promote democracy and human rights in countries neighboring the European Union. Countries participating in the ENP include Algeria, Armenia, Azerbaijan, Belarus, Egypt, Georgia, Israel, Jordan, Lebanon, Libya, Moldova, Morocco, the Palestinian Authority, Syria, Tunisia, and Ukraine. However, human rights reforms are not as likely through the ENP process as through other programs, since the leverage of EU membership is not present.

The EU also maintains Partnership and Cooperation Agreements (PCAs) that assist Eastern European and Central Asian governments with their transition from authoritarian systems to functioning democracies that respect human rights. These agreements span ten years and establish the political, economic, and trade relationships between the country in question and the EU. PCAs are in effect with Armenia, Azerbaijan, Belarus, Georgia, Kazakhstan, the Kyrgyz Republic, Moldova, Tajikistan, Turkmenistan, Ukraine, and Uzbekistan. While also lacking the lure of EU membership to spur reforms, the EU will threaten to revoke PCAs to encourage human rights improvements. For instance, the PCA with Uzbekistan was temporarily suspended in 2005 after the government indiscriminately fired into a crowd of protesters. PCAs have never been enacted with Belarus and Turkmenistan due to their poor human rights records.

Advocacy Actions

Considering the influence of the EU enlargement process, advocates should work with the Commissioner for Enlargement and the offices in candidate countries to provide information about policies and/or laws limiting religious freedom, as well as provide recommendations for reform. Similar information can be offered regarding SAP countries. Religious freedom advocates should also provide information to the Commissioner for External Relations and European Neighbourhood Policy regarding countries in the ENP or PCA programs, urging increased EU attention on matters of concern.

EUROPEAN UNION ANNUAL REPORT ON HUMAN RIGHTS

Monitoring Body

In 1999, the European Union began issuing a report on human rights. Jointly prepared by the EU Presidency, the European Commission, and the Council Secretariat, the annual report covers the work of the EU in encouraging respect for human rights for a twelve-month period from July to June. Unlike the human rights report issued by the U.S. Department of State, the EU report does not document the human rights record of every country in the world. Instead, it reviews EU activities generally and addresses specific countries in the context of the various EU engagement programs, providing only the briefest of statements about the human rights situation there. If religious freedom is referenced, it will occur in this context. Also of interest is the annex, which lists the projects funded under EIDHR and the recipient organizations.

European Commission
http://ec.europa.eu/commission_barroso/president/
European Commission
1049 Brussels
Belgium
Tel: +32 2 298 81 55
sg-web-president@ec.europa.eu

EUROPEAN UNION AGENCY FOR FUNDAMENTAL RIGHTS

Monitoring Body

In March 2007, the European Monitoring Centre on Racism and Xenophobia (EUMC) was upgraded to a human rights agency and became the EU Agency for Fundamental Rights (FRA). Based in Vienna, Austria, the FRA monitors human rights in all twenty-seven EU member states but does not investigate individual complaints. The FRA is led by a Director, who is selected and supervised by a Management Board comprised of independent experts from each member state.

Process

The FRA is tasked with assisting member states with the implementation of the provisions of the European Charter of Human Rights. While following all human rights, the FRA pays particular attention to the "phenomena of racism, xenophobia and anti-Semitism," as well as the protection of minorities and gender equality. To fulfill its monitoring activities, the FRA collects data from each country, analyzes the information, and publishes an annual report on fundamental freedoms in the EU, as well as periodic thematic reports. For instance, it has published separate reports on anti-Semitism and Islamophobia in the EU. The FRA is also empowered to provide unsolicited reports to member states about compliance.

The former EUMC, to facilitate its monitoring activities, established the European Information Network on Racism and Xenophobia (RAXEN), composed of National Focal Points in each member state. The National Focal Points gathered information at the local level and shared it through the network with the EUMC, and also disseminated EUMC and EU materials locally. RAXEN was the backbone of the EUMC's monitoring activities, and the new FRA will maintain this valuable network.

FRA's new Fundamental Rights Platform displays an increased commitment to working closely with nongovernmental organizations and civil society on human rights issues, beyond what was done by the former EUMC. The Platform is intended to be a "mechanism for the exchange of information and pooling of knowledge" between the FRA and NGOs (FRA Web site). Participants will be encouraged to provide suggestions for action and information about violations. Notably, churches and religious organizations are specifically mentioned among the enumerated list of groups able to participate with the Platform.

Advocacy Actions

With the recent reconstitution, it is too soon to evaluate whether the Agency for Fundamental Rights will continue its predecessor's full monitoring activities. The FRA Web site notes that the new founding statute places more emphasis on working with civil society and public education than the regulations for the EUMC, which may signal a reduction in its level of monitoring. Regardless, religious freedom advocates should submit information to FRA and to the National Focal Points in the RAXEN network about violations of religious freedom under the Charter and situations of religious discrimination. European advocates should also apply for membership in the Fundamental Rights Platform.

CONTACT INFORMATION

European Union Agency for Fundamental Rights (FRA)
http://fra.europa.eu/
Schwarzenbergplatz 11
AT-1040 Vienna
Austria
Tel: +43 1 580 30 60
Fax: +43 1 580 30 699
information@fra.europa.eu

4

COUNCIL OF EUROPE

The Council of Europe (CoE) is the oldest regional organization in Europe, established in 1949 by the Treaty of London with ten founding members. The CoE was originally envisioned as a way to build European identity after World War II. Open to all European democracies, the CoE expanded significantly after the end of the Cold War, and its membership overlaps with both the European Union and the Organization for Security and Cooperation in Europe. The CoE now stretches into Eastern Europe and beyond, with members including the Russian Federation, Armenia, Azerbaijan, and Georgia. Today, the number of participating countries totals forty-seven, plus six observers (Belarus, Canada, the Holy See, Japan, Mexico, and the United States).

> **Council of Europe members**
> Albania, Andorra, Armenia, Austria, Azerbaijan, Belgium, Bosnia and Herzegovina, Bulgaria, Croatia, Cyprus, Czech Republic, Denmark, Estonia, Finland, France, Georgia, Germany, Greece, Hungary, Iceland, Ireland, Italy, Latvia, Liechtenstein, Lithuania, Luxembourg, Malta, Moldova, Monaco, Montenegro, Netherlands, Norway, Poland, Portugal, Romania, Russian Federation, San Marino, Serbia, Slovakia, Slovenia, Spain, Sweden, Switzerland, Macedonia, Turkey, Ukraine, United Kingdom

Headquartered in Strasbourg, France, the purpose of the CoE is to promote human rights, democratization, and rule of law in all member countries. Considering the wide array of countries and traditions brought into the CoE after the postcommunism expansion, the CoE focuses heavily on ensuring all members uphold their legally binding commitments to human rights and democratization. The CoE has several important bodies that the religious freedom advocate should be aware of—the European Court of Human Rights, the Committee of Ministers, the Commissioner for Human Rights, and the European Commission against Racism and Intolerance, as well as the Parliamentary Assembly.

Nongovernmental Involvement

The Council of Europe system is open to NGOs and advocacy groups. Advocates wishing to engage the CoE effectively should obtain "participatory status" by applying to the CoE Secretary General. Their letter must demonstrate that they are an international nongovernmental organization "particularly representative" in their area of expertise and operating on a European level, as opposed to just a national level. NGOs granted participatory status may observe the work of the various CoE bodies and submit reports, and they will be invited to ad hoc CoE conferences. No accreditation is required for NGOs to file cases with the European Court, other than demonstrating that they are the representatives of the alleged victim.

Religious Freedom Commitments

The essential document for the Council of Europe is the Convention for the Protection of Human Rights and Fundamental Freedoms, also known as the European Convention on Human Rights, which was adopted in 1950 and entered into force in 1953. Acceptance has become a prerequisite for applicant countries wishing to join the CoE. Predating the UN International Covenant on Civil and Political Rights, the European Convention represented the first attempt to make legally binding the aspirational rights highlighted in the UN Universal Declaration of Human Rights.

Article 9 of the Convention protects the religious freedom of individuals residing in CoE countries. Following a similar formula to the UDHR, it specifically recognizes the freedom of the individual to "change his religion or belief." Article 9 also recognizes the dual rights of individuals and communities to manifest their religion through worship, education, and practice. Subsection 2 of Article 9 does contain a limitation clause on manifestations of religious belief, but restrictions must meet a rigorous test to pass muster.

Article 10 protects all forms of expression, including religious speech, and Article 14 also forbids discrimination based on religion. Notably, and unlike in other regional and international covenants, the European Convention does not protect freedom of religion from derogations in times of emergency. There is also no limitation on religious freedom on grounds of "national security."

Article 9 – Freedom of thought, conscience and religion
1.Everyone has the right to freedom of thought, conscience and religion; this right includes freedom to change his religion or belief and freedom, either alone or in community with others and in public or private, to manifest his religion or belief, in worship, teaching, practice and observance.

2. Freedom to manifest one's religion or beliefs shall be subject only to such limitations as are prescribed by law and are necessary in a democratic society in the interests of public safety, for the protection of public order, health or morals, or for the protection of the rights and freedoms of others.

Convention for the Protection of Human Rights and Fundamental Freedoms

Many additional protocols have been added to the Convention to expand its scope on a variety of issues. However, the greatest developments (especially for religious freedom) have come through the rulings of the European Court of Human Rights, which was established by the European Convention.

EUROPEAN COURT OF HUMAN RIGHTS

Complaint Recourse Mechanism

The European Court represents the most advanced and developed international human rights judicial system in the world, as all forty-seven Council of Europe members have submitted themselves to the Court's jurisdiction. The number of cases sent to the court is very large and increases each year. In 1981, roughly four hundred applications were filed, whereas in 2001 close to fourteen thousand were submitted. The Court is therefore extremely active, hearing a wide range of cases based on the various articles of the European Convention for Human Rights. In its various rulings, the Court has repeatedly emphasized that the freedom of thought, conscience, and religion is one of the foundations of a democratic society and must be protected. The Court's religious freedom jurisprudence will not be discussed here, but there are many resources easily accessible describing the various rulings and their impact.

Like domestic court systems, the wheels of justice turn slowly at the European Court. However, its judgments are legally binding and are often viewed as authoritative to other nations outside Europe. The number of judges serving at the court is equal to the number of member countries—currently forty-seven.

Judges serve in their individual capacities for a six-year term and are elected by the CoE Parliamentary Assembly with the possibility of reelection. Judges may not be involved in conduct "incompatible" with their independence or impartiality. However, they may sit on tribunals overseeing cases involving their home countries—an apparent conflict of interest the Council does not see.

Complaint Admissibility

The court is open to individuals who allege a violation of their rights under the European Convention. Until the entry into force of Protocol 11 in 1998, individuals did not have direct recourse and had to confront a complicated two-tiered system, first petitioning the Commission on Human Rights, with surviving complaints then forwarded to the court. However, Protocol 11 in effect merged the Commission into an expanded court (the Commission no longer exists as a distinct body), gave individuals the right for direct petition, and revised court procedures to quicken the response time (from five to six years to two to three years).

Article 35 – Admissibility Criteria
1. The Court may only deal with the matter after all domestic remedies have been exhausted, according to the generally recognised rules of international law, and within a period of six months from the date on which the final decision was taken.

2. The Court shall not deal with any application submitted under Article 34 that
    a) is anonymous; or
    b) is substantially the same as a matter that has already been examined by the Court or has already been submitted to another procedure of international investigation or settlement and contains no relevant new information.

3. The Court shall declare inadmissible any individual application submitted under Article 34 which it considers incompatible with the provisions of the Convention or the protocols thereto, manifestly ill-founded, or an abuse of the right of application.

4. The Court shall reject any application which it considers inadmissible under this Article. It may do so at any stage of the proceedings.

Convention for the Protection of Human Rights and Fundamental Freedoms

The Court is open to adjudicate conflicts between member states or rule on petitions brought by individuals, NGOs, or groups of individuals claiming to be the victims of a breach in the European Convention by a member state. Complaints cannot be brought against individuals. Admissibility requirements include the following:

- exhaustion of domestic remedies
- case initiated within six months of a final ruling
- petitions cannot be anonymous (upon request, the court can consent to keep the names of petitioners confidential)
- petitions cannot be before another international tribunal
- petitions cannot be "manifestly ill-founded."

Complaint Procedure

To hear cases, petitioners must write the court in Strasbourg alleging a violation of the European Convention. Violations do not have to concern state action, as the Court has ruled against governments for failing to take action against nonstate actors. The court Registry will send an application, which should be returned promptly with a signature and summary of the allegations and supporting facts, a listing of violated Convention rights, and copies of domestic decisions regarding the case.

The court has three levels of review—three judge committees, seven judge Chambers, and seventeen judge Grand Chambers. Committees review all applications and strike those that are clearly inadmissible. Their action is not reviewable. Petitions are next considered by a Chamber, which will again decide on admissibility, and if in the affirmative, the merits of the case. The Grand Chamber acts as a final court of appeals where applicants can appeal Chamber decisions.

It generally takes one year for a Chamber to decide on the admissibility question. An expedited process is available for cases involving a threat of imminent physical harm. The Court can take "interim measures" in such situations, in which it requests the offending government to take steps to prevent an action that could result in irreparable harm. For instance, in a case concerning the inappropriate extradition of Chechens from the Republic of Georgia to Russia, the Court issued interim measures directing Georgia not to extradite the individuals until the case was heard.

Remedies

For controversies found to be admissible, a Chamber will first strive to find a "friendly settlement" between the parties, so as to avoid actual litigation. However, if that is not possible, the trial process will initiate, with a Chamber receiving briefs with legal arguments from the applicants. Legal representation is not required but is recommended, as proceedings transpire through the writing of legal briefs and court hearings. A legal aid mechanism does exist for those who cannot afford proper representation. The vast majority of cases end at the Chamber level.

Chamber decisions can be appealed to the Grand Chamber. The Grand Chamber, however, will only hear those cases that involve "serious question affecting the interpretation of the Convention" or where the Chamber decision might have a "result inconsistent with a judgment previously delivered by the Court." Member states generally abide by final decisions.

Decisions can come either as awards of "just satisfaction" for monetary damages or lawyer's fees, or through "individual" or "general measures" that order a state to comply with its Council obligations through a specific act (i.e., registering a church). Notably, the Court is not empowered to annul national laws. In addition, unlike in common law systems in the United States and the United Kingdom, there is no *stare decisis*. However, the Court is moving in that direction, as it often recognizes precedents from previous rulings. Notably, the Court is not responsible for overseeing the execution of its judgments—this responsibility falls to the Committee of Ministers of the Council of Europe. The Committee will oversee government compliance and ensure that compensation is paid or specific actions are taken.

Advocacy Actions

The European Court of Human Rights is the most influential international human rights judicial body and can rule on religious freedom violations. Advocates should consider bringing cases on behalf of victims to the European Court asking for compensation or specific action, while also being prepared to participate in legal proceedings spanning several years. Advocates must be willing and able to meet the many submission requirements and maintain active involvement over the course of the lengthy process.

CONTACT INFORMATION

European Court of Human Rights
http://www.echr.coe.int/echr/
Council of Europe
67075 Strasbourg-Cedex
France
Tel: +33 3 88 41 20 18
Fax: +33 3 88 41 27 30

COMMITTEE OF MINISTERS OF THE COUNCIL OF EUROPE

Policymakers

The Committee of Ministers is the Council's primary decision-making body. It is composed of foreign ministers or their deputies from every member state. As mentioned above, the Committee is the enforcement arm of the Court— Article 46 of the European Convention, as amended by Protocol 11, gives the Committee the responsibility for supervising the execution of Court decisions. To fulfill this mandate, the Committee will meet six times a year to discuss these matters. Decisions taken in the form of resolutions during these meetings, as well as the Annotated Agenda and the Order of Business, are available publicly.

The Committee of Ministers can also speak to issues touching on religious freedom through the holding of conferences or symposia. For example, during San Marino's chairmanship of the Committee in 2007, it convened a special conference on "The Religious Dimension of Intercultural Dialogue." The conference provided an opportunity for member states to discuss good practices and ways to foster dialogue between different religious communities, as well as between religious groups and governments.

Advocacy Actions

Generally, the Committee of Ministers is a difficult body to access. However, advocates should forward information about failures of CoE countries to implement European Court decisions. Advocates should also participate in conferences touching on religious freedom, which could provide another forum for raising awareness about problematic situations.

CONTACT INFORMATION

Committee of Ministers
http://www.coe.int/t/cm/
Council of Europe
Palais de l'Europe
Avenue de l'Europe
F-67075 Strasbourg Cedex
France
Tel: +33 3 88 41 20 00
Fax: +33 3 88 41 27 81

COMMISSIONER FOR HUMAN RIGHTS

Monitoring Body

The Council of Europe Commissioner for Human Rights was established in 1999 after the closing of the Commission for Human Rights under the Protocol 11 reforms. The Commissioner is an independent institution that promotes respect for human rights in all CoE member countries. The current Commissioner, Thomas Hammarberg of Sweden, began his nonrenewable six-year term in 2006.

Process

While in a sense replacing the Commission on Human Rights, the Commissioner plays a different role within the CoE. The position was specifically chartered as a "non-judicial institution," so the Commissioner plays no role in the vetting of applications to the European Court of Human Rights, and he may not bring cases to the Court or advocate for individual cases. However, upon the universal ratification by all Council members of Protocol 14, the Commissioner will be empowered to submit written comments and participate in cases before the European Court. As of this writing, all member states except the Russian Federation have ratified the protocol.

Currently, the Commissioner is empowered to identify "possible shortcomings in the law and practice of member States concerning the compliance with human rights." Once identified, the Commissioner may work to promote the "effective implementation of these standards" by assisting in efforts to address these deficiencies. To fulfill this mandate, the Commissioner can travel to member countries to meet with high-ranking officials and parliamentarians to discuss issues of concern, as well as meet with nongovernmental organizations. These trips produce a public report that analyzes the human rights situation and provides recommendations, which are presented to the Committee of Ministers and the Parliamentary Assembly. A few years after the initial visit, the Commissioner or his office may conduct a follow-up visit to evaluate progress made on employing the recommendations. A follow-up report is also issued.

When deemed appropriate, the Commissioner is free to issue recommendations on a specific human rights case in a member state without visiting, as well as provide unsolicited opinions on draft legislation or specific policies. The Commissioner is also tasked with promoting general awareness of human rights and supporting national human rights institutions.

Advocacy Actions

The Commissioner plays an important advocacy role in the Council of Europe system, so advocates should provide the Commissioner with information about shortcomings in the practices of CoE countries and suggestions for reform regarding religious freedom. This information can be used either in Commissioner reports or to encourage increased engagement with a state over an issue of concern. Advocates can also attempt to meet with the Commissioner during country visits, as well as arrange meetings with victims of religious freedom violations. Once Protocol 14 is ratified by all CoE member states, advocates could approach the Commissioner about cases before the European Court and provide additional information and legal arguments.

Contact Information

Thomas Hammarberg, Commissioner for Human Rights
http://www.coe.int/t/commissioner/
Office of the Commissioner for Human Rights
Council of Europe
F-67075 Strasbourg Cedex
France
Tel: + 33 3 88 41 34 21
Fax: + 33 3 90 21 50 53
commissioner@coe.int

Venice Commission

Monitoring Body

The Venice Commission, officially known as the European Commission for Democracy through Law, is an independent consultative body of the Council of Europe. Founded in 1990 and headquartered in Venice, Italy, it is charged with upholding Europe's constitutional heritage of democracy, human rights, and rule of law. The Venice Commission is composed of highly regarded independent experts versed in law or political science. The roster of experts therefore includes scholars, judges, and parliamentarians, appointed to four-year terms, all acting in their personal capacity.

Process

These experts review domestic legislation regarding constitutions or other laws potentially impacting human rights, in light of CoE agreements and international standards. The Venice Commission is empowered to draft guidelines on its own initiative and issues opinions in response to requests from CoE countries or organs. Importantly, the work of the Venice Commission is not limited to CoE members: it may issue opinions to any requesting country. Venice Commission members include all CoE countries, as well as Kyrgyzstan, Chile, South Korea, and Montenegro under its Enlarged Agreement.

The Venice Commission has been active on issues relating to religious freedom. For instance, it issued a strong opinion on a pending religion law in Romania, correctly criticizing the highly discriminatory registration scheme. While nonbinding, the importance and respectability of the Venice Commission requires governments to give its assessments serious attention.

Advocacy Actions

The Venice Commission is a prestigious international body that has spoken on the issue of religious freedom. While it is not possible for individuals or advocates formally to file petitions requesting Venice Commission review, they can send information to the Commission and approach individual commissioners about problematic laws or draft legislation that would benefit from Commission review.

CONTACT INFORMATION

European Commission for Democracy through Law
http://www.venice.coe.int/
Secretariat of the Venice Commission
Council of Europe
F-67075 Strasbourg Cedex
France
Fax: +33 3 88 41 37 38
venice@coe.int

EUROPEAN COMMISSION AGAINST RACISM AND INTOLERANCE

Monitoring Body

Originally created in 1993 and strengthened in 2002 with a new statute, the European Commission against Racism and Intolerance (ECRI) serves the Council as an independent human rights monitoring body. ECRI is led by an Executive Secretary and a support staff. Each CoE member state may appoint one expert and a deputy to serve in their individual capacities for a renewable five-year term.

ECRI is tasked with combating "racism, racial discrimination, xenophobia, antisemitism and intolerance in greater Europe," in light of the European Convention. While religious freedom is not specifically listed, ECRI will take action to combat "violence, discrimination and prejudice" based on religion. ECRI's activities in fulfilling its mandate fall into three categories of work: a country-by-country approach, work on general themes, and relations with civil society.

Process

Regarding the country-by-country approach, ECRI is charged with generating country reports that focus on the phenomena of racism, racial discrimination, xenophobia, anti-Semitism, and intolerance in each member state. These reports review the effectiveness of member state legislation and policies in combating racism and provide constructive recommendations for improved action. Each year, ECRI reports on ten to twelve countries, which begins a four- to five-year cycle of reporting. The third round of reporting focuses less on documenting problems, concentrating instead on whether previous ECRI recommendations have been successfully implemented, and if so, to what extent.

The reporting process begins when ECRI rapporteurs visit a country to meet with NGOs and government officials. Their visit will result in a draft report, which will be shared confidentially with the government for feedback. After the conclusion of this dialogue, the final report is adopted and transmitted by the Committee of Ministers to the government concerned. The report is made available to the public about six to ten months after transmission, unless the government in question objects. The reports will address religious freedom concerns, if serious problems are present in the country.

ECRI's work on general themes provides examples of "best practices" in combating these forms of intolerance in all member states. ECRI will also issue General Policy Recommendations, which can touch on the treatment of religious groups. For instance, General Policy Recommendation Number 5 reported on "Combating intolerance and discrimination against Muslims" and Number 9 reported on "The fight against anti-Semitism." ECRI's civil society work is focused on supporting positive relations between civil society and member states.

Advocacy Actions

ECRI's extensive reporting and monitoring system offers a valuable avenue for additional advocacy on religious freedom. Advocates should forward to ECRI information about instances of discrimination or intolerance based on religion. Advocates should try to meet with ECRI Rapporteurs when they conduct a country visit and provide information and recommendations.

CONTACT INFORMATION

European Commission against Racism and Intolerance
http://www.coe.int/t/E/human_rights/ecri/
Council of Europe
F-67075 Strasbourg Cedex
France
Fax: +33 3 88 41 39 87

Parliamentary Assembly of the Council of Europe

Policymakers

The Parliamentary Assembly of the Council of Europe (PACE), located in Strasbourg, France, is composed of 630 parliamentarians (315 representatives and 315 substitutes) elected or appointed from national legislatures. Each of the forty-seven CoE countries is allowed to determine who may serve in the Parliamentary Assembly. PACE is led by a president elected from the body, who can serve up to three one-year terms.

Process

While not having the authority of a national legislature or the European Parliament, the Parliamentary Assembly is active on human rights issues. PACE regularly sends teams of parliamentarians on fact-finding missions to member states and observer countries. The Parliamentary Assembly can also pass nonbinding resolutions, which are often effective in shaming an offending government into action. The Parliamentary Assembly has also begun writing an annual report on the state of human rights and democracy in Europe.

PACE does maintain twelve standing committees that focus on a range of issues. The Committee on the Honouring of Obligations and Commitments by member states of the Council of Europe would focus on CoE member compliance. For instance, this committee has been engaged with Armenia over the issue of conscientious objection to military service based on religious beliefs. The Committee on Legal Affairs and Human Rights and its Subcommittee on Human Rights would most naturally address religious freedom issues in countries not participating in the Council of Europe. The Committee on Political Affairs and its three subcommittees on the Middle East, External Relations, and Belarus could also address religious freedom concerns.

Advocacy Actions

The Parliamentary Assembly, with its vast membership, represents an expansive parliamentary forum to push for religious freedom. Advocates should provide individual parliamentarians, relevant committees, and the Parliamentary

Assembly President with information about violations of religious freedom and request their involvement. Advocates should also attend PACE meetings and observe discussions from the gallery, as well as participate in any special meetings concerning religious freedom. Advocates should also try to arrange meetings between victims and PACE delegations conducting country visits. To attend PACE meetings, advocates will need to obtain "participatory status" from the CoE Secretary General.

Contact Information

Parliamentary Assembly
http://assembly.coe.int/
http://assembly.coe.int/ASP/Committee/
PACECommitteesInfoListing_E.asp
Council of Europe
Avenue de l'Europe
F-67075 Strasbourg Cedex
France
Tel: +33 388 41 20 00
Fax: +33 388 41 27 81
pace.com@coe.int

5

Organization for Security and Cooperation in Europe

The Organization for Security and Cooperation in Europe (OSCE) is an important institution for advocacy in Europe and Eurasia. Encompassing North America, Europe, Russia, and the successor states emerging from the former Soviet Union, the fifty-six-member OSCE is the largest regional security organization in the world. Religious freedom has been an integral part of the OSCE process, which over the past thirty years has developed some of the most sophisticated commitments on religious freedom at the international level. From the Helsinki Final Act, to the Vienna and Copenhagen Concluding Documents, OSCE participating States have repeatedly affirmed the freedom of thought, conscience, religion, or belief as a fundamental human right.

> **OSCE participating states**
> Albania, Andorra, Armenia, Austria, Azerbaijan, Belarus, Belgium, Bosnia and Herzegovina, Bulgaria, Canada, Croatia, Cyprus, Czech Republic, Denmark, Estonia, Finland, France, Georgia, Germany, Greece, Holy See, Hungary, Iceland, Ireland, Italy, Kazakhstan, Kyrgyzstan, Latvia, Liechtenstein, Lithuania, Luxembourg, Macedonia, Malta, Moldova, Monaco, Montenegro, Netherlands, Norway, Poland, Portugal, Romania, Russian Federation, San Marino, Serbia, Slovak Republic, Slovenia, Spain, Sweden, Switzerland, Tajikistan, Turkey, Turkmenistan, Ukraine, United Kingdom, United States of America, Uzbekistan

The body originated in 1975 with the signing of the Helsinki Final Act, a politically binding agreement between NATO, Warsaw Pact, and neutral and non-aligned nations that focused on three "baskets" of issues—security matters, economic concerns, and the "human dimension." The human dimension is OSCE parlance for human rights, and under this rubric falls religious freedom.

During the Cold War era, the OSCE (then known as the Conference on Security and Cooperation in Europe) provided a valuable forum for dialogue between adversaries, as well as a place to discuss human rights issues. With the end of the Cold War and the emergence of new countries from the remains of the Soviet Union, the geographic scope of the OSCE shifted east and now reaches into Central Asia. All of the countries formerly under communist governments have acceded to the Helsinki Final Act and subsequent OSCE agreements. Importantly, unlike with other international systems, no reservations may be taken in the OSCE system, so these new members completely accepted all previous commitments.

Nongovernmental Involvement

The OSCE is perhaps the most open to NGO involvement of any of the international organizations discussed. Unlike the UN system, the OSCE maintains no accreditation process for nongovernmental organizations. For advocates to participate in public OSCE meetings, they must simply submit the registration form before the announced deadline. Registration will entitle them to speak during plenary sessions, provide documents, and convene side events. NGOs will only be prohibited from participating if they have been involved with or promoted acts of violence.

RELIGIOUS FREEDOM COMMITMENTS

OSCE participating States are not legally obligated to uphold their Helsinki commitments, but are rather politically committed. Consequently, these commitments are not actionable domestically like other international legal conventions. Nations have nevertheless politically promised to uphold these rights, and the OSCE provides several forums to review the performance of member countries. The eleven OSCE partner countries from the Mediterranean basin and Asia have not pledged to uphold OSCE commitments and only participate as observers.

OSCE commitments on religious freedom are very specific. Below are the key themes that are central to the protection of religious freedom in the OSCE system:

- freedom to profess and practice a religion alone or in community with others
- freedom to change one's religion
- freedom to meet with and exchange information with coreligionists regardless of frontiers
- freedom to present freely to others and discuss religious views
- elimination and prevention of discrimination based on religious grounds in all fields of civil, political, economic, social, and cultural life

- noninterference in the affairs of religious communities, such as selection of personnel
- right of parents to ensure religious education of their children in line with their own convictions.

The limitation clause follows customary international standards.

There are three key OSCE documents regarding religious freedom—the founding Helsinki Final Act, the Vienna Concluding Document, and the Copenhagen Concluding Document. The relevant portions of each are presented below.

Basket I Section VII Respect for human rights and fundamental freedoms, including the freedom of thought, conscience and religion or belief

The participating States will respect human rights and fundamental freedoms, including the freedom of thought, conscience, religion or belief, for all without distinction as to race, sex, language or religion.

Within this framework the participating States will recognize and respect the freedom of the individual to profess and practice, alone or in community with others, religion or belief acting in accordance with the dictates of his own conscience.

Helsinki Final Act

---

(16) In order to ensure the freedom of the individual to profess and practice religion or belief, the participating State will, inter alia,

(16.1) –take effective measures to prevent and eliminate discrimination against individuals or communities on the grounds of religion or belief in the recognition, exercise and enjoyment of human rights and fundamental freedoms in all fields of civil, political, economic, social and cultural life, and to ensure the effective equality between believers and non-believers;

(16.2) –foster a climate of mutual tolerance and respect between believers of different communities as well as between believers and non-believers;

(16.3) –grant upon their request to communities of believers, practicing or prepared to practice their faith within the constitutional framework of their States, recognition of the status provided for them in the respective countries;

(16.4) –respect the right of these religious communities to
  - establish and maintain freely accessible places of worship or assembly
  - organize themselves according to their own hierarchical and institutional structure

Continued from page 77

- select, appoint and replace their personnel in accordance with their respective requirements and standards as well as with any freely accepted arrangement between them and their States
- solicit and receive voluntary financial and other contributions.

(16.5) —engage in consultation with religious faiths, institutions and organizations in order to achieve a better understanding of the requirements of religious freedom;

(16.6) —respect the right of everyone to give and receive religious education in the language of his choice, whether individually or in association with others;

(16.7) —in this context respect, inter alia, the liberty of parents to ensure the religious and moral education of their children in conformity with their own convictions;

(16.8) —allow the training of religious personnel in appropriate institutions;

(16.9) —respect the right of individual believers and communities of believers to acquire, possess, and use sacred books, religious publications in the language of their choice and other articles and materials related to the practice of religion or belief;

(16.10) —allow religious faiths, institutions and organizations to produce, import and disseminate religious publications and materials;

(16.11) —favorably consider the interest of religious communities to participate in public dialogue, including through the mass media.

(17) The participating States recognize that the exercise of the above mentioned rights relating to the freedom of religion or belief may be subject only to such limitations as are provided by law and consistent with their obligations under international law and with their international commitments. They will ensure in their laws and regulations and in their application the full and effective exercise of the freedom of thought, conscience, religion or belief.

(32) They will allow believers, religious faiths and their representatives, in groups or on an individual basis, to establish and maintain direct personal contacts and communication with each other, in their own and other countries, inter alia, through travel, pilgrimages and participation in assemblies and other religious events. In this context and commensurate with such contacts and events, those concerned will be allowed to acquire, receive and carry with them religious publications and objects related to the practice of their religion or belief.

(68) They will ensure that persons belonging to national minorities or regional cultures on their territories can give and receive instruction on

their own culture, including instruction through parental transmission of language, religion and cultural identity to their children.

Vienna Concluding Document

(9.1) [The participating States reaffirm that] everyone will have the right to freedom of expression including the right to communication. This right will include freedom to hold opinions and to receive and impart information and ideas without interference by public authority and regardless of frontiers. The exercise of this right may be subject only to such restrictions as are prescribed by law and are consistent with international standards.

(9.4) [The participating States reaffirm that] everyone will have the right to freedom of thought, conscience, and religion. This right includes freedom to change one's religion or belief and freedom to manifest one's religion or belief, either alone or in community with others, in public or in private, through worship, teaching, practice and observance. The exercise of these rights may be subject only to such restrictions as are prescribed by law and are consistent with international standards.

Copenhagen Concluding Document

CHAIRMAN-IN-OFFICE AND THE PERMANENT COUNCIL

Policymakers

The OSCE is headquartered in Vienna, Austria, where each participating State has accredited diplomats. Leadership comes from the Chairman-in-Office position, which is held by a different participating State each year. When a country assumes the Chairmanship, its foreign minister is the nominal head of the OSCE. In addition to speaking for the OSCE, during the standard year term the Chairman-in-Office can shape OSCE policies and visit OSCE countries to raise human rights concerns.

The Chairman also oversees the main meeting of the year, the Ministerial Council, where foreign ministers convene to discuss the political priorities of the OSCE, as well as the Human Dimension Implementation Meeting and the three Supplementary Human Dimension Meetings. The Chairman can also select the topics of the three Supplementary meetings, in consultation with other OSCE members. For instance, the Dutch Chairmanship in 2003 convened a special Supplementary Human Dimension Meeting specifically on religious freedom.

On a daily basis, the Chairman-in-Office works with the Permanent Council, also seated in Vienna, where accredited ambassadors meet weekly in private plenary sessions to discuss various issues facing the region. Considering that the OSCE's primary focus is human rights, these issues are often raised at the Permanent Council. There is also a special committee of the Permanent Council that handles human rights questions.

The OSCE also has a Secretary General, who leads the OSCE Secretariat. Appointed for three years and also based in Vienna, the Secretary General is not analogous to the UN Secretary General. The position has fewer powers and cannot speak for the Organization, but rather represents the Chairman-in-Office and is the chief administrative officer of the OSCE. While some human rights functions are under the supervision of the Secretary General, none relate to religious freedom.

Advocacy Actions

Both the Permanent Council and the human rights committee are closed to the public and nongovernmental organizations. However, advocates should send information to the office of the Chairman-in-Office, as well as to sympathetic delegations, and ask that serious situations be raised formally during Permanent Council or human rights committee meetings. In addition, should the Chairman visit a country with a problematic religious freedom record, advocates should facilitate a meeting between the Chairman and victims.

CONTACT INFORMATION

Chairman-in-Office
http://www.osce.org/
Organization for Security and Cooperation in Europe
Wallnerstrasse 6
1010 Vienna
Austria
Tel: + 43 1 514 36 60 00
Fax: +43 1 514 36 69 96

OFFICE FOR DEMOCRATIC INSTITUTIONS AND HUMAN RIGHTS

Monitoring Body

The Office for Democratic Institutions and Human Rights (ODIHR) is the special arm of the Organization, concentrating solely on human rights and democracy building. Headquartered in Warsaw, Poland, ODIHR is led by a Director, who is usually an ambassador appointed from an OSCE country for a term of five years. ODIHR assists participating States in carrying out and consolidating their democratic systems, through election monitoring, technical assistance on the drafting of laws, and convening regional meetings to discuss various human rights topics. For instance, ODIHR has held two meetings in Central Asia on religious freedom-related issues and has provided critiques of draft religion laws. ODIHR is also responsible for organizing the annual human rights review conference, which is discussed later.

Process

ODIHR has broken its work down into distinct units that focus on a range of issues—Democratization, Elections, Gender Equality, Human Rights, Roma and Sinti, and Tolerance and Non-Discrimination. Under the current organization of responsibilities, religious freedom matters are dealt with by the Tolerance and Nondiscrimination Unit and not the Human Rights Unit. Established in 2004, the Tolerance and Nondiscrimination Unit has limited monitoring capacities and so mainly works with religious communities and nongovernmental organizations.

The unit approaches religious freedom from two angles: first, the more traditional rights view, examining whether individuals or communities are prevented from exercising their fundamental rights; and second, whether groups or individuals are being discriminated against because of their religious beliefs. OSCE countries have agreed to periodically forward statistical information to ODIHR about hate crimes, which include crimes motivated by religious bias. ODIHR staff can raise issues of concern with participating States, but there are no formal procedures and this is often done in private.

Advocacy Actions

The primary purpose of ODIHR is to promote human rights and democratization. Advocates should report individual religious freedom violations or more systemic abuses to ODIHR and the Tolerance and Nondiscrimination Unit. The Unit can potentially follow up with an offending government about these allegations or use the information to contrast the statistical data provided by the government on hate crimes. Advocates can also request that the ODIHR Director raise concerns specifically with an offending government.

CONTACT INFORMATION

ODIHR Tolerance and Nondiscrimination Unit
http://www.osce.org/odihr/20051.html
Office for Democratic Institutions and Human Rights
Aleje Ujazdowskie 19
00-557 Warsaw
Poland
Tel: +48 22 520 06 00
Fax: +48 22 520 06 05

ADVISORY PANEL OF EXPERTS ON FREEDOM OF RELIGION OR BELIEF

Monitoring Body and Policymakers

ODIHR has established and manages the Advisory Panel of Experts on Freedom of Religion. The Advisory Panel of Experts serves as a consultative body on trends affecting the freedom of religion and advises ODIHR on actions that would support and advance this right. The Advisory Panel is composed of two bodies, the Council and the Panel, totaling roughly sixty experts and representatives of various religious faiths. The Council is composed of approximately fifteen individuals, selected by the ODIHR Director from academia or nonprofit organizations, who serve in their personal capacities. The Panel has a much wider membership, as every participating State may appoint two individuals. There is not a defined term of service for Advisory Panel members on either the Council or the broader Panel. Advisory Panel activities are supported by the ODIHR Tolerance and Nondiscrimination Unit.

Process

To request Advisory Panel assistance, participating States can make a request through their ambassadors to the OSCE or through an OSCE Mission (discussed below), should one be operating on their territory. OSCE Missions can also independently request Advisory Panel assistance. In response, members of the Council will author technical critiques on laws or legislation affecting religion or belief for the Advisory Panel. These comprehensive legal critiques provide recommendations on how to bring draft legislation into conformity with OSCE commitments on religious freedom. The Advisory Panel also published "Guidelines for Review of Legislation Pertaining to Religion or Belief," which is a resource for legislators and NGOs on how to ensure that emerging legislation upholds international commitments to freedom of religion, as well as the "Toledo Guiding Principles on Teaching about Religions and Beliefs in Public Schools." The Advisory Panel can also conduct less-formal consultations with legislators and officials working on these issues.

There is no formal complaint procedure to the Council. However, the Advisory Panel has responded to complaints from religious communities. Religious communities can request Council assistance either through the ODIHR Tolerance and Nondiscrimination Unit or by approaching Council members directly. For instance, the Advisory Panel publicly condemned the bulldozing of a Hare Krishna commune in 2006 by Kazakhstani authorities.

Advocacy Actions

The Advisory Panel is an accessible mechanism that can address legal shortcomings affecting the freedom of religion. Advocates should request the attention of the Panel to situations in which legislation or government action is infringing upon religious freedom, by forwarding information about problematic laws or draft legislation through the ODIHR Tolerance and Nondiscrimination Unit. Advocates should also consider attending ODIHR meetings where Advisory Panel members are speaking, to raise concerns directly.

CONTACT INFORMATION

Advisory Panel of Experts on Freedom of Religion or Belief
http://www.osce.org/odihr/20056.html
c/o ODIHR Tolerance and Nondiscrimination Unit
Aleje Ujazdowskie 19
00-557 Warsaw
Poland
Tel: +48 22 520 06 00
Fax: +48 22 520 06 05
tolerance@odihr.pl

HIGH COMMISSIONER ON NATIONAL MINORITIES

Monitoring Body

The Office of the OSCE High Commissioner on National Minorities (HCNM) was created in 1992 to "identify and seek early resolution of ethnic tensions that might endanger peace, stability or friendly relations between OSCE participating States."[1] Located in The Hague, Netherlands, the High

Commissioner is appointed for a three-year term, which can be renewed once. The HCNM can address religious freedom issues only if the national minority is recognized as a religious minority. For example, the High Commissioner could raise with Turkey the limitations placed upon ethnic Greeks, who are Turkish citizens living in Turkey, in enjoying their Greek Orthodox religious practices. The intersection between religious freedom advocacy and the HCNM is narrow, but could be useful for certain religious communities.

Advocacy Actions

If the religious community of concern is considered a national minority, advocates should establish contact with the High Commissioner and his office, provide information, and request his involvement. If the HCNM visits the country in question, advocates should also work to arrange a meeting with the victimized community.

CONTACT INFORMATION

High Commissioner on National Minorities
http://www.osce.org/hcnm/
Office of the OSCE High Commissioner on National Minorities
Prinsessegracht 22
2514AP The Hague
Netherlands
Tel: +31 70 312 55 00
Fax: +31 70 363 59 10

PERSONAL REPRESENTATIVES OF THE CHAIRMAN-IN-OFFICE

Policymakers

One area of particular influence for the Chairman-in-Office is the power to create and appoint "personal representatives." OSCE modalities permit the creation of these positions at the Chairman's discretion in response to a "crisis or a conflict" for the duration of the term. However, the positions are often extended by subsequent Chairmen, allowing the positions to work for longer periods.

In 2003, the then-Bulgarian Chairman-in-Office created three positions to deal with tolerance-related issues:

- Personal Representative on Combating anti-Semitism
- Personal Representative on Combating Intolerance and Discrimination against Muslims
- Personal Representative on Combating Racism, Xenophobia and Discrimination, also focusing on Intolerance and Discrimination against Christians and Members of Other Religions

These mandates have been renewed each year and the positions reappointed. These positions were designed to liaise with governments about issues of concern within their mandate. The ODIHR Tolerance and Nondiscrimination Unit provides some logistical support for these individuals, to aid their work.

Advocacy Actions

All three Personal Representatives potentially touch on different aspects of religious freedom affecting different groups. Advocates should consider approaching the Personal Representatives through the ODIHR Tolerance and Nondiscrimination Unit with information about an issue of concern relevant to their mandate and request their engagement.

CONTACT INFORMATION

Chairman-in-Office Representatives to Promote Tolerance
http://www.osce.org/about/19257.html
c/o ODIHR Tolerance and Nondiscrimination Unit
Aleje Ujazdowskie 19
00-557 Warsaw
Poland
Tel: +48 22 520 06 00
Fax: +48 22 520 06 05

OSCE FIELD OPERATIONS

Monitoring Body

OSCE institutions play an important role in human rights advocacy, as well. The OSCE maintains field missions in Southeast Europe, Eastern Europe, the Caucasus, and Central Asia.

These missions represent an on-the-ground presence by the OSCE in a number of countries where religious freedom may not be fully respected.

These missions are headed by an ambassador from a participating State and a small staff. Missions will regularly meet with NGOs and religious groups to collect information and report their findings to the Permanent Council.

OSCE field operations

Southeast Europe
OSCE Presence in Albania
OSCE Mission to Bosnia and Herzegovina
OSCE Mission to Croatia
OSCE Mission to Montenegro
OSCE Mission to Serbia
OSCE Mission in Kosovo
OSCE Spillover Monitor Mission to Skopje

Eastern Europe
OSCE Office in Minsk
OSCE Mission to Moldova

OSCE Project Coordinator in Ukraine

Caucasus
OSCE Office in Baku
OSCE Mission to Georgia
OSCE Office in Yerevan

Central Asia
OSCE Centre in Almaty
OSCE Centre in Ashgabad
OSCE Centre in Bishkek
OSCE Project Coordinator in Uzbekistan
OSCE Centre in Dushanbe

Advocates should be mindful that missions in countries with a problematic human rights record usually have the least influence with the host government, so the assistance they can offer is often limited. Still, heads of mission do have the ability to raise directly with host governments problems that come to their attention.

Advocacy Actions

Advocates should meet with, or encourage coreligionists to meet with, OSCE Missions to share their concerns and provide information about abuses. Advocates should also consider requesting mission intervention in problematic situations.

CONTACT INFORMATION

http://www.osce.org/about/13510.html

HUMAN DIMENSION MEETINGS

The OSCE convenes four annual meetings to review the implementation of participating States of their "human dimension" commitments. Every fall the Human Dimension Implementation Meeting (HDIM) convenes in Warsaw,

Poland. This two-week meeting covers the entire gamut of human rights, with a special session specifically on protection of religious freedom. In addition, three Supplementary Human Dimension Meetings (SHDM) are held throughout the year, usually in Vienna, on topics selected by the Chairman-in-Office. The HDIM and SHDM meetings are open to the public, and nongovernmental organizations are encouraged to participate and speak.

With no accreditation process, advocates must simply register on time to attend the HDIM or an SHDM. In a surprisingly egalitarian arrangement, religious freedom advocates, religious groups, and NGO representatives may participate on the same level as member states at these meetings, giving statements (referred to as "interventions") in the main plenary sessions criticizing the very countries seated around the table. Advocates and their organizations can also request permission to convene smaller meetings, called "side events," to allow a more informal opportunity to discuss human rights issues among delegates and NGOs.

The HDIM and SHDMs play an important role in the creation of new politically binding commitments for all OSCE participating States. If advocates can build sufficient political will among OSCE countries during these meetings, then the recommendations emerging from these events can be forwarded to the annual December meeting of foreign ministers for consideration. Only a ministerial meeting can approve new, politically binding commitments.

Advocacy Actions

Advocates should attend the annual HDIM meeting and any relevant SHDM meetings. During these events, they should give interventions during plenary sessions highlighting specific abuses and consider holding side events. Advocates should also try to meet with delegations from participating States attending the SHDM/HDIM to brief them on situations and ask for their assistance.

CONTACT INFORMATION

Human Dimension Implementation Meeting
http://www.osce.org/odihr/16533.html

Supplementary Human Dimension Meetings
http://www.osce.org/odihr/16537.html

OSCE Parliamentary Assembly

Policymakers

Like the Council of Europe, the OSCE Parliamentary Assembly is composed of parliamentarians elected to national legislative bodies. With support staff based in Copenhagen, Denmark, the Assembly meets regularly throughout the year. Its winter meeting convenes annually in Vienna, Austria but is generally not attended by nongovernmental organizations. The annual summer session is the main meeting and is convened in a different city each year. During the summer session, the Assembly will divide into three committees to debate and pass nonbinding resolutions. The Third Committee considers human rights issues, also referred to as the "human dimension." These resolutions do not have the force of law but do provide parliamentarians with the opportunity to speak in unison on human rights concerns.

Advocates and their organizations may attend these summer meetings if they can find a delegation to sponsor their presence (which is usually not a problem). Speaking during committee and plenary sessions is limited to the parliamentarians, but advocates will be able to observe, convene side events to highlight issues of concern, and talk with parliamentarians on the margins of the meeting.

Advocacy Actions

Advocates should attend OSCE Parliamentary Assembly meetings and meet with legislators from countries of concern. In addition, advocates should brief parliamentarians from more sympathetic nations on actions needed elsewhere in the region to promote religious freedom. Advocates should also work with delegations on language to add to resolutions about specific instances of religious freedom violations, as well as consider holding a side event on issues of concern. Advocates will need to find a delegation sponsor to attend the annual session.

Contact Information

OSCE Parliamentary Assembly
http://www.oscepa.org/
Rådhusstræde 1
1466 Copenhagen K
Denmark
Tel.: +45 33 37 80 40
Fax: +45 33 37 80 30
osce@oscepa.dk

6

ORGANIZATION OF AMERICAN STATES

The Organization of American States (OAS) is a regional organization for the countries of North, Central, and South America and the Caribbean. All thirty-five countries in the Western Hemisphere are members, but only thirty-four are allowed to participate—Cuba is excluded. Headquartered in Washington, D.C. (just one block from the White House), the OAS claims to be the oldest regional organization in the world, tracing its origins to the 1889 First International Conference of American States. However, the founding document for the modern organization, the Charter of the Organization of American States, was signed in 1948 and entered into force in 1951 at the Ninth International Conference.

> **Organization of American States members**
> Antigua and Barbuda, Argentina, Bahamas, Barbados, Belize, Bolivia, Brazil, Canada, Chile, Colombia, Costa Rica, Cuba,* Dominica, Dominican Republic, Ecuador, El Salvador, Grenada, Guatemala, Guyana, Haiti, Honduras, Jamaica, Mexico, Nicaragua, Panama, Paraguay, Peru, Saint Kitts and Nevis, Saint Lucia, Saint Vincent and the Grenadines, Suriname, Trinidad and Tobago, United States of America, Uruguay, Venezuela

The Organization of American States is also commonly referred to as the Inter-American System. The relevant institutions for advancing religious freedom are the Inter-American Commission on Human Rights, the Inter-American Court of Human Rights, and the Inter-American Institute of Human Rights.

Nongovernmental Involvement

The OAS welcomes the participation of nongovernmental organizations, and registered groups may attend OAS conferences and meetings, make presentations, and provide information and advice. NGOs are referred to as "civil society organizations," which are defined as any national or international institutions or organizations of a nongovernmental nature. Interested groups must send a complete application to the Secretary General, who will refer it to the Permanent Council's Committee on Civil Society Participation in OAS Activities for consideration. The Committee will make a recommendation to the Permanent Council, which will make the final decision.

Application to participate

  a. The name(s) of its directors and legal representative(s).

  b. Its primary areas of activity and their relationship to the activities of the OAS organs, agencies, and entities in which it wishes to participate.

  c. Reasons why it believes its proposed contributions to OAS activities would be of interest to the OAS.

  d. Identification of the OAS work areas in which it proposes to support ongoing activities or to make recommendations on the best way to achieve OAS objectives.

  e. The application shall be accompanied by the following documents:
    • Charter or constitution • Statutes • Most recent annual report • Institutional mission statement • Financial statements for the previous fiscal year, including reference to public and private sources of financing

---

Religious Freedom Commitments

The OAS Charter declares the organization's core principles to be the promotion of hemispheric peace, security, and representative democracy. While silent to the specific issue of religious freedom, it does affirm the fundamental rights of the individual. (It also supports the vague principle of the "spiritual unity of the continent . . . based on respect for the cultural values of the American countries.") In similar fashion to the UN Charter, which also only touches upon human rights, the OAS Charter relies on a separate declaration to provide a catalogue of fundamental rights.

American Declaration of the Rights and Duties of Man

The American Declaration of the Rights and Duties of Man provides this enumeration and was approved in 1948 by the same conference that established the OAS. The American Declaration predates the UN Universal Declaration by six months and was therefore the first human rights document on the international scene. The American Declaration covers a range of civil and political rights, as well as economic and social rights. In addition to declaring fundamental freedoms, it sets forth corresponding duties for individuals to achieve and establishes the Inter-American Commission on Human Rights. The Article III language on religious freedom is minimal, offering fewer protections than the Universal Declaration and other international human rights treaties. Article XXII also provides protection from religiously based discrimination.

> Article III – Every person has the right freely to profess a religious faith, and to manifest and practice it both in public and in private.
>
> Article XXII – Every person has the right to associate with others to promote, exercise and protect his legitimate interests of a political, economic, religious, social, cultural, professional, labor union or other nature.
>
> **American Declaration of the Rights and Duties of Man**

Importantly, both the Inter-American Commission on Human Rights and the Inter-American Court of Human Rights (both discussed below) have ruled that the American Declaration is legally binding on all OAS countries. Member states may disagree with this assessment, as the American Declaration was originally adopted as a nonbinding agreement (like the Universal Declaration). These rulings are significant for advocates, as it binds all OAS members to an enforceable standard of human rights—even those countries that have not ratified the more comprehensive American Convention on Human Rights (such as Canada and the United States). However, countries will object to any procedures brought under this ruling, making compliance with any judgments all the more difficult to obtain.

American Convention on Human Rights

The American Convention on Human Rights followed the Declaration but is a legally binding document for all countries that have ratified the agreement. (Approximately one-fourth of OAS member states have yet to ratify.) For those contracting states, the American Convention is the primary document concerning human rights and religious freedom. Adopted in 1969 and entering into force in 1978, it built upon the American Declaration by enumerating a more detailed set of human rights. It also strengthened the Inter-American Commission on Human Rights and created the Inter-American Court of Human Rights.

The very first article of the American Convention prohibits religiously based discrimination. The religious freedom provisions are found later, in Article 12, and are quite strong. Unlike the UN International Covenant on Civil and Political

Rights, the American Convention expressly states in two separate subclauses that individuals have the right to change their religious beliefs and no governmental restrictions should impair this right. Article 12 follows international custom when discussing the right to meet together in public or private.

Article 12 – Freedom of conscience and religion

1. Everyone has the right to freedom of conscience and of religion. This right includes freedom to maintain or to change one's religion or beliefs, and freedom to profess or disseminate one's religion or beliefs, either individually or together with others, in public or in private.

2. No one shall be subject to restrictions that might impair his freedom to maintain or to change his religion or beliefs.

3. Freedom to manifest one's religion and beliefs may be subject only to the limitations prescribed by law that are necessary to protect public safety, order, health, or morals, or the rights or freedoms of others.

4. Parents or guardians, as the case may be, have the right to provide for the religious and moral education of their children or wards that is in accord with their own convictions.

American Convention on Human Rights

The Article 12(3) limitation clause does not affect personal beliefs, but rather only external displays of religion. As with the ICCPR, religious freedom is not viewed as absolute, but the reasons for limiting are very narrowly construed and only for exceptional circumstances. Article 27 addresses "Suspension of Guarantees," and religious freedom and ten other rights are specifically protected from derogations during a time of war or other public emergency.

Article 12 also guarantees the right of individuals to "profess or disseminate" their religious beliefs. This is further supported in the following article that addresses "Freedom of Thought and Expression." The Article 13 language on the "freedom to seek, receive, and impart information and ideas of all kinds" protects religiously motivated speech.

General Assembly and Supporting Organs

Policymakers

The main body of the OAS is the General Assembly, which convenes all the hemisphere's foreign affairs ministers in an annual session to decide the priorities and direction of the Organization. The implementing body for these decisions is the Permanent Council, which is composed of ambassadors accredited to the OAS. The Permanent Council holds regular public meetings on the first and third Wednesdays of each month, reports to the General Assembly, and is directed by the office of the Chairman, which rotates to a different country every three months.

The Permanent Council is divided into several committees, with the Committee on Judicial and Political Affairs tasked with human rights issues. Both the Committee and the Permanent Council can consider the reports of the Inter-American Commission on Human Rights and the Inter-American Court of Human Rights. The Committee can forward recommendations to the Permanent Council, and the Permanent Council can forward recommendations to the General Assembly.

The OAS is also led by a full-time international public servant, the Secretary General, who oversees the work of the OAS General Secretariat. The General Assembly elects the Secretary General for a five-year term. The former Chilean Interior and Foreign Minister José Miguel Insulza was elected to the post in 2005.

Advocacy Actions

Because the General Assembly is composed of heads of state, it can be challenging for advocates to access. Instead, they should provide information on infringements of religious freedom to sympathetic delegations at the Permanent Council, the Committee on Judicial and Political Affairs, and the Secretary General. Advocates should provide recommendations for General Assembly actions to counter violations of religious freedom.

Contact Information

Permanent Council
http://www.oas.org/consejo/
17th Street & Constitution Ave., N.W.
Washington, D.C. 20006
Tel: (202) 458-3000
csecretario@oas.org

Inter-American Commission on Human Rights

Complaint Recourse Mechanism and Monitoring Body

The Inter-American Commission on Human Rights (IACHR) is an autonomous unit of the OAS, originally established by the Charter and later strengthened by the American Convention. Its purpose is to investigate complaints of specific instances of human rights abuse, monitor the overall human rights situation in member states, and assist member states in strengthening their laws and policies to protect human rights. The IACHR is composed of a body of seven independent human rights experts, elected to four-year terms by the OAS General Assembly. The IACHR is led by one of the seven experts who serves as President and is supported by an Executive Secretariat. Headquartered in Washington, D.C., it convenes six weeks a year and all member states are subject to its jurisdiction.

The two most valuable IACHR mechanisms to religious freedom advocates are the petition process concerning human rights abuses and the on-site visit procedure. Individuals and NGOs can actively participate in both proceedings. In addition, the Commission annually submits a report to the General Assembly reviewing human rights throughout the Americas, as well as giving recommendations for specific state action.

Complaint Admissibility

Through the Commission's quasi-judicial petition process, it can receive complaints from any individual, group of individuals, or nongovernmental organization from any member state alleging a violation of rights found under the American Declaration or American Convention. The petition can concern a situation involving the complainant or a third party. Importantly, the following guidelines apply to petitions:

- the petition must allege either abuse by a member state or failure to prevent an abuse by a private actor
- the petition must establish the exhaustion of all domestic remedies
- the petition must be filed within six months of exhaustion
- the petition must be in one of the four OAS languages (Spanish, Portuguese, French, or English).

In urgent situations where "irreparable harm to persons" is possible, as a safeguard the Commission can request that the member state involved adopt precautionary measures to prevent such an outcome.

Article 28 – Requirements for the consideration of petitions

Petitions addressed to the Commission shall contain the following information:

  a. the name, nationality and signature of the person or persons making the denunciation; or in cases where the petitioner is a nongovernmental entity, the name and signature of its legal representative(s);
  b. whether the petitioner wishes that his or her identity be withheld from the State;
  c. the address for receiving correspondence from the Commission and, if available, a telephone number, facsimile number, and email address;
  d. an account of the act or situation that is denounced, specifying the place and date of the alleged violations;
  e. if possible, the name of the victim and of any public authority who has taken cognizance of the fact or situation alleged;
  f. the State the petitioner considers responsible, by act or omission, for the violation of any of the human rights recognized in the American Convention on Human Rights and other applicable instruments, even if no specific reference is made to the article(s) alleged to have been violated;
  g. compliance with the time period provided for in Article 32 of these Rules of Procedure [petitions lodged within a period of six months following the date on which the alleged victim has been notified of the exhaustion of domestic remedies];
  h. any steps taken to exhaust domestic remedies, or the impossibility of doing so as provided in Article 31 of these Rules of Procedure; and,
  i. an indication of whether the complaint has been submitted to another international settlement proceeding as provided in Article 33 of these Rules of Procedure.

Rules of Procedure for the Inter-American Commission on Human Rights

Complaint Procedure

The first evaluation of whether petitions meet the requirements for consideration is conducted by the Executive Secretariat. If a petition is lacking, the Executive Secretariat will contact the petitioner and ask for additional information. The IACHR will review all applications deemed not meeting the requirements for consideration before rejection. If more than one petition alleges similar facts, the Commission may join them into one complaint.

Once a case is determined to meet these basic requirements, the Commission will open the case and request a response from the offending government within two months, unless urgent circumstances necessitate an immediate reply. The identity of the petitioner will not be disclosed. After evaluating their response, the petition, and observations received from third parties, the IACHR can issue a public report on admissibility or accept the case and address admissibility in the final judgment.

If deemed admissible, the Commission will initiate proceedings on the merits and give the petitioner two months to submit additional information and the offending government(s) two months to respond. Each party will have the opportunity to answer the other's assertions. The Commission may also conduct on-site visits to evaluate further the situation, request specific information, and hold hearings in which each side can present its facts and legal arguments. In urgent cases where the "life or personal integrity of a person is in imminent danger,"[1] the offending government will be requested to respond as soon as possible. Before rendering its decision, the Commission will provide an opportunity for a friendly settlement between parties.

Remedies

If the IACHR finds a violation by an offending government, it will prepare a private report for the government with proposals and recommendations of remedial actions and a deadline for their adoption. The Commission has no enforcement arm and cannot require specific actions or the awarding of damages. However, if there is no compliance, the Commission has two options. One is to issue a second private report again requesting action by a certain deadline. If the state again fails to comply, the Commission may make the second report public. The other option, if the offending government has submitted itself to the jurisdiction of the Inter-American Court of Human Rights, is for the Commission to forward the case to the court for review (if the petitioner agrees).

Monitoring Process

Commission hearings are not limited to the petition process but may be convened regarding follow-up to its recommendations, as well as to review precautionary measures or to initiate an independent effort to receive information about human rights abuses in a member state. It may also conduct on-site visits not in conjunction with a review proceeding. For a site visit to occur, a Special Commission will be formed and an invitation will be requested. Visits can be in response to new human rights concerns or, for some countries, can occur annually or biannually. After the visit is completed, the Special

Commission will issue a report. These visits can shine a light on abuses, and NGOs and concerned groups can participate as well. Advocates can call the Commission to learn about the dates of scheduled country visits.

The Commission may also establish permanent rapporteurs on topics relating to rights under the American Declaration or American Convention. While no position exists for religious freedom, in 1997 the Commission established the Special Rapporteur for Freedom of Expression. Catalina Botero Marino of Venezuela was elected in 2007, and she may issue reports and respond directly to individual petitions alleging violations by a member state. While the Special Rapporteur mainly focuses on media freedoms, journalistic independence, and political speech, the right to religious expression, including proselytizing, would fall under its mandate.

Advocacy Actions

The Inter-American Commission on Human Rights provides a useful avenue for advocates to pursue remedies for religious freedom violations. Advocates must be willing to meet the various requirements of the complaint mechanism and have the resources to stay engaged throughout the process. Advocates should request IACHR country visits and meet with the Special Commission during any such trip. Advocates should also directly petition the Special Rapporteur for Freedom of Expression regarding situations in which religious speech is limited.

CONTACT INFORMATION

Inter-American Commission on Human Rights
http://www.cidh.org/
1889 F Street, N.W.
Washington, D.C., 20006
Fax: (202) 458-3992

INTER-AMERICAN COURT OF HUMAN RIGHTS

Complaint Recourse Mechanism

The Inter-American Court of Human Rights was established by the American Convention and is based in San José, Costa Rica. It is an independent judicial system overseeing the application and interpretation of the American Convention. Similar to the European Court of Human Rights before its 1998 reforms, the Court is part of a two-tiered system. It only takes referrals from the Inter-American Commission, and the Commission appears in all contentious cases before the Court. Because individuals do not enjoy direct recourse, the Court's caseload is much smaller than the European Court of Human Rights: in 2006 the Court convened seven times and issued twenty-three decisions.

Nations under the jurisdiction of the Court
Argentina, Barbados, Bolivia, Brazil, Colombia, Costa Rica, Chile, Dominica, Ecuador, El Salvador, Granada, Guatemala, Haiti, Honduras, Jamaica, Mexico, Nicaragua, Panama, Paraguay, Peru, Dominican Republic, Suriname, Trinidad and Tobago, Uruguay, Venezuela

---

The Court consists of seven judges, who are nominated by member states. The judges can be from any country in the Americas, even if their country did not sign the American Convention, but no two may be from the same country. One judge is elected President by the Court for a renewable two-year term. The Court holds public hearings in Costa Rica but can also conduct field hearings and site visits. Currently, the Court has jurisdiction over twenty-five countries that have ratified or adopted the American Convention on Human Rights.

Complaint Procedure

There are two different kinds of jurisdiction over cases: advisory and contentious. Advisory opinions do not concern specific cases but rather are interpretations of any human rights treaties in force in the hemisphere or the compatibility of domestic law with OAS commitments. Any OAS member, regardless of whether they have adopted the OAS Charter, may make submissions.

Contentious cases are between a contracting state and the Commission over an active dispute of a specific issue that was not successfully resolved through the Commission's procedures. When an application is accepted in a contentious case, the procedures are similar to domestic courts, with both sides submitting written briefs containing pleadings, motions, and evidence. While not permitted directly to approach the Court, the alleged victims and their representatives are permitted directly to participate and submit evidence throughout. When there are similar fact patterns in common between cases, the Court can combine these into one complaint.

Remedies

If the Court finds a violation of the rights or freedoms under the American Convention, its decree will require the taking of appropriate remedies and the paying of compensation to the aggrieved party. Decisions are rendered publicly. In "cases of extreme gravity and urgency,"[2] the Court has the ability to enact provisional measures to prevent "irreparable damage to persons" at its own initiative, or at the request of the Commission, alleged victims, or their representatives.

While not having an enforcement mechanism, member states generally show high regard for the Court's decisions. Its rulings serve as a guide throughout the Americas, with domestic courts sometimes referencing court decisions. The Court will also provide an annual report of its activities and judgments to the General Assembly, as well as highlight countries not complying with its judgments and provide recommendations for follow-up action.

Advocacy Actions

While advocates cannot directly access the Court, they can work with the Commission to ensure that unresolved cases are considered. If a case is referred to the Court, advocates can provide additional documents and legal arguments on behalf of the victims they represent. Advocates can also work with the Court, the Commission, and offending governments to ensure that rulings are fully implemented and compensation awarded.

CONTACT INFORMATION

Inter-American Court of Human Rights
http://www.corteidh.or.cr/
P.O. Box 6906-1000
San José
Costa Rica
Tel: (506) 2234 0581
Fax: (506) 2234 0584
corteidh@corteidh.or.cr

INTER-AMERICAN INSTITUTE OF HUMAN RIGHTS

Monitoring Body

Created in 1980, the Inter-American Institute of Human Rights was established as an independent research facility dedicated to the promotion of human rights and the strengthening of the principles of the American Convention. Based in San José, Costa Rica, it supports more than fifty projects with nongovernmental organizations to educate the public about human rights. It does not investigate individual cases, monitor government actions, or present cases to the Commission or the Court, but rather works to facilitate dialogue between governments and civil society.

The Institute currently focuses on four themes: justice and security; political participation; education in human rights; and the effective exercise of economic, social, and cultural rights. In addition, the Institute has initiated a focus on freedom of expression. As with the Special Rapporteur, this is more focused on journalistic freedoms, but it too would intersect with limitations on religious speech.

Advocacy Actions

Advocates should provide information to the Inter-American Institute of Human Rights about cases of religious freedom violations. Advocates can also request Institute assistance in facilitating dialogue between problematic governments and victimized groups, as well as provide information to the freedom of expression focus group regarding limitations of religious speech.

CONTACT INFORMATION

Inter-American Institute of Human Rights
http://www.iidh.ed.cr/
P.O. Box 10081-1000
San José
Costa Rica
Tel: (506) 234 04 04
Fax: (506) 234 09 55
instituto@iidh.ed.cr

7

AFRICAN UNION

The African Union (AU) is the youngest of the region systems—its founding agreement, the Constitutive Act of the African Union, was approved in 2000 and entered into force in 2001. Comprising fifty-three member states, it represents all of the countries of the African continent both north and south of the Sahara Desert (except Morocco), and it is headquartered in Addis Ababa, Ethiopia. The AU is, however, the successor organization to the Organization of African Unity (OAU) and can therefore trace its origins back to 1963 and the passing of the Charter of the Organization of African Unity.

African Union members
Algeria, Angola, Benin, Botswana, Burkina Faso, Burundi, Cameroon, Cape Verde, Central African Republic, Chad, Comoros, Democratic Republic of the Congo, Republic of the Congo, Côte d'Ivoire, Djibouti, Egypt, Equatorial Guinea, Eritrea, Ethiopia, Gabon, Gambia, Ghana, Guinea, Guinea-Bissau, Kenya, Lesotho, Liberia, Libya, Madagascar, Malawi, Mali, Mauritania, Mauritius, Mozambique, Namibia, Niger, Nigeria, Rwanda, Western Sahara (SADR), São Tomé and Príncipe, Senegal, Seychelles, Sierra Leone, Somalia, South Africa, Sudan, Swaziland, Tanzania, Togo, Tunisia, Uganda, Zimbabwe

---

To understand the AU, one must first understand the history of the Organization of African Unity. The OAU was originally focused on ending apartheid and colonial control on the continent. The founding charter made only passing mention of human rights, pledging its members to have "due regard" for the Universal Declaration, and contained no mention of religious freedom. As the OAU matured, concerns were raised about a perceived double standard, where the OAU would criticize nonmembers but would be silent on the human rights abuses committed by its own. Consequently, the OAU worked through the 1960s and 1970s to create specific human rights commitments for all members, which resulted in the African Charter on Human and Peoples' Rights in 1981.

The African Charter concretized basic human rights and religious freedom, and also established the African Commission on Human and Peoples' Rights. These reforms led to further discussions in the 1990s about how to improve the ability of African countries, working in unison, to promote fundamental freedoms, peace, and security. This culminated in the 1999 Sirte Declaration in which OAU members agreed to create a new pan-African organization. The Constitutive Act of the African Union followed in 2000 and entered into force in 2001, thus establishing the African Union.

The transition from the Organization of African Unity to the AU is ongoing and, as of this writing, is not complete. While the agreement establishing the AU does increase the importance of human rights, the AU still retains as key objectives other issues such as defending the sovereignty, territorial integrity, and independence of its members; working to build partnerships between governments and civil society; and focusing on integrating the continent economically and socially. Time will tell whether the AU will improve continental respect for human rights protection over the former OAU.

Nongovernmental Involvement

NGOs can play an important role in the work of the African Union. "Observer status" is required for those groups wishing to engage the African Commission on Human and Peoples' Rights. The same status is also required for those groups petitioning the African Court of Human and Peoples' Rights. The requirements for observer status are straightforward, and NGOs must send their request and supporting documentation to the Secretariat of the African Commission.

Chapter 1

All organisations applying for observer status with the African Commission shall consequently:
- Have objectives and activities in consonance with the fundamental principles and objectives enunciated in the OAU Charter and in the African Charter on Human and Peoples' Rights;
- Be organisations working in the field of human rights
- Declare their financial resources

To this effect, such an Organisation shall be requested to provide:
- A written application addressed to the Secretariat stating its intentions, at least three months prior to the Ordinary Session of the Commission which shall decide on the application, in order to give the Secretariat sufficient time in which to process the said application.

- Its statutes, proof of its legal existence, a list of its members, its constituent organs, its sources of funding, its last financial statement, as well as a statement on its activities.
- The statement of activities shall cover the past and present activities of the Organisation, its plan of action and any other information that may help to determine the identity of the organisation, its purpose and objectives, as well as its field of activities.
- No application for Observer Status shall be put forward for examination by the Commission without having been previously processed by the Secretariat.
- The Commission's Bureau shall designate a rapporteur to examine the dossiers. The Commission's decision shall be notified without delay to the applicant NGO.

Resolution on the Criteria for Granting and Enjoying Observer Status to Non-Governmental Organisations Working in the Field of Human Rights with the African Commission on Human and Peoples' Rights

RELIGIOUS FREEDOM COMMITMENTS

The Constitutive Act of the African Union does not speak specifically to religious freedom but does contain stronger references and commitments to human rights than does the original OAU Charter. Article 3 of the Constitutive Act speaks to the objectives of the AU. Subarticle (e) takes "due account" of the Universal Declaration, and Subarticle (h) goes further by establishing as objectives the promotion and protection of "human and peoples' rights in accordance with the African Charter" and other human rights instruments. Article 4, outlining the AU's principles, further bolsters this commitment by declaring that the AU will function in accordance with "respect for democratic principles, human rights, the rule of law and good governance."

The previously mentioned African Charter on Human and Peoples' Rights represents the principal document for the continent concerning human rights, as all fifty-three AU members have ratified it. Sometimes labeled as the Banjul Charter, a reference to where it was adopted in 1981, the Charter entered into force in 1986. The Charter is distinctive, as in addition to covering basic civil and political rights, it addresses economic rights and places a large emphasis on the role of the community in development and security. It also speaks to the duties of individuals to the community.

Considering the far-reaching nature of the document, the Article 8 religious freedom provision is surprisingly limited. While speaking to the right to practice religion freely, it does not follow the more specific language found

in other international documents. It also is silent about the question of changing one's religion. Other relevant articles concerning religious freedom are
Article 9(2), which supports religious speech by guaranteeing the "right to
express and disseminate" one's opinions, and Article 2, which prohibits religious discrimination.

> **Article 8**
> Freedom of conscience, the profession and free practice of religion shall be
> guaranteed. No one may, subject to law and order, be submitted to mea-
> sures restricting the exercise of these freedoms.
>
> **African Charter on Human and Peoples' Rights**

The Assembly, the Executive Council, and the Permanent Representatives Committee

Policymakers

The three main organs of the African Union have been constituted and have
begun working—the Assembly, the Executive Council, and the Permanent
Representatives Committee. The Assembly leads the AU and is composed of
heads of state. Acting as the "supreme organ," the Assembly establishes the
decisions of the Union and monitors the implementation of those policies
by member states. The Assembly meets once a year and is led by the Chairman, a head of state elected by his peers for a one-year term of office. In
January 2007, President John Kufuor of Ghana was elected Chairman in a
contentious race against President Omar Hasan Ahmad al-Bashir of Sudan.
President al-Bashir lost due to Sudan's poor human rights record and inac-
tion in quelling the violence in Darfur. In electing President Kufuor, the AU
signaled that human rights abuses will not be ignored, as was common with
the former OAU.

The Assembly is supported by all the foreign ministers sitting in the
Executive Council, which meets twice a year. The Executive Council oversees
implementation of Assembly decisions and may make its own decisions on
issues of mutual concern. Notably, human rights are not an enumerated area
in which the Executive Council can act. Preparing the work of the Executive Council is the Permanent Representatives Committee, where accredited
ambassadors discuss the daily work of the AU.

Advocacy Actions

Of these forums, the best for engagement is the Permanent Representatives Committee, where advocates can raise issues of concern with ambassadors. Advocates should also forward issues of concern to the AU Chairman, requesting his intervention. NGO participation at the annual Assembly meetings varies, depending in part on the visa policies of the host country each year regarding the entrance of foreign NGOs. However, even if NGOs are allowed to attend, the level of their inclusion is limited.

CONTACT INFORMATION

African Union Chairman / Permanent Representatives Committee
http://www.africa-union.org/
African Union Headquarters
P.O. Box 3243
Roosevelt Street
(Old Airport Area)
W21K19
Addis Ababa
Ethiopia
Tel: (251) 11 551 77 00
Fax: (251) 11 551 78 44

AFRICAN UNION COMMISSION

Policymakers

The African Union Commission functions somewhat like the European Commission—it is led by a Chairperson and supported by eight Commissioners responsible for separate departments focusing on different issue portfolios. It also serves as the secretariat for the organization, addressing the day-to-day administrative needs. The Chairman and Commissioners are appointed by the Assembly. The Commission represents the AU and defends its policies, while also developing strategic plans for the Executive Council to consider.

The Department of Political Affairs covers human rights, as well as democracy promotion, refugee issues, and external AU relations. Since 2003, the current Commissioner for Political Affairs has been Julia Dolly Joiner, a high-ranking government official from The Gambia.

Advocacy Actions

The African Union Commission plays an important role in the running of the organization and can raise concerns about religious freedom violations with member states. Advocates should make the Commissioner for Political Affairs and the Commission Chairperson aware of violations of religious freedom and ask for their intervention. Advocates should also work to arrange meetings with victims when the Commissioner visits a country of concern.

Contact Information

Jean Ping, Chairman
http://www.africa-union.org/root/au/index/index.htm
African Union Commission
Addis Ababa
Ethiopia
Tel: (251) 11 5514554
Fax: (251) 11 5513036
chairperson@africa-union.org

Julia Dolly Joiner, Commissioner for Political Affairs
http://www.africa-union.org/root/au/index/index.htm
African Union Commission
Addis Ababa
Ethiopia
Tel: (251-115) 52 58 59
Fax: (251-115) 52 58 56
jdollyj@yahoo.com

African Commission on Human and Peoples' Rights

Monitoring Body and Complaint Recourse Mechanism

The African Commission on Human and Peoples' Rights (ACHPR) was established under the African Charter for Human and Peoples' Rights, and so opened its doors in 1987 after the Charter entered into force. The headquarters of the ACHPR are located in Banjul, The Gambia. The ACHPR is composed of eleven Commissioners acting in their individual capacities who serve renewable six-year terms. One of the Commissioners serving as Chairman oversees the two ten-day meetings held in the spring and fall. Observer status allows NGOs to participate in the two annual meetings.

Monitoring Process

The African Charter authorizes the ACHPR to promote and protect human rights and to "collect documents, undertake studies and researches on African problems in the field of human and peoples' rights, organize seminars, symposia and conferences, disseminate information, encourage national and local institutions concerned with human and peoples' rights, and should the case arise, give its views or make recommendations to Governments" (Article 45). Contracting parties to the African Charter are also obligated to submit reports to the Commission on their compliance, to which the ACHPR will respond following evaluation. The ACHPR will work with NGOs and civil society during this process and accept information and suggested recommendations for country improvement. However, state compliance is poor.

Complaint Admissibility

The ACHPR is specifically authorized to receive complaints and to conduct investigations through its communication procedure, which is a quasi-judicial procedure through which individuals, groups of individuals, and nongovernmental organizations can formally submit allegations of human rights violations. States may also submit complaints to the ACHPR concerning violations of the Charter by other member countries, but this is rarely done. To be considered, the complaint must meet the admissibility requirements and a majority of the Commissioners must agree to review it. To be admissible, the communication must conform to the following criteria:

- it must not be anonymous (although the complainant can request anonymity);
- it must concern violations of rights falling under the African Charter;
- it must demonstrate the exhaustion of all domestic remedies;
- it must be submitted in a reasonable time after exhaustion.

Complaint Procedure

Petitioners will receive an initial confirmation of receipt, but offending governments will not be notified until the ACHPR decides affirmatively to review the claims. For petitions under review, the ACHPR will first attempt to find an amicable solution between the parties. If that is not possible, the ACHPR will request information from offending governments in response to the allegations and additional arguments from the petitioner. These can be in writing, or either party can make oral presentations.

Remedies

After considering the information, the ACHPR will issue nonbinding recommendations with its findings to both parties and forward its recommendations to the annual meeting of heads of state at the Assembly. Notably, if the Assembly approves, then the states are legally bound to the recommendations. The recommendations are initially private, but they can be made public if the government in question does not object.

The African Charter did not give the ACHPR a follow-up or enforcement mechanism to ensure compliance. From 1987 to 2003, the ACHPR completed 122 complaints through its communications procedure—sixty-three were declared inadmissible, five were settled amicably, two were cleared, eight were withdrawn, and forty-four countries were found to be in violation. As the ACHPR is not able to track compliance, an independent study found that of the forty-four countries out of compliance, only six fully implemented the ACHPR's recommendations.

If the ACHPR finds that a "series of serious or massive violations of human and peoples' rights" has transpired, it shall immediately bring these findings to the attention of the Assembly. The Assembly has the option to approve or reject the findings by a majority vote. There have been instances in which member countries have gathered enough votes to block a report from obtaining Assembly approval. In addition, the Assembly can request that the ACHPR conduct an "in-depth study of these cases and make a factual report"[1] and submit its recommendations to the Assembly for consideration. For emergency situations in which the life of a victim is in danger, the ACHPR can invoke provisional measures requesting the offending government to delay any action until its review is complete.

Advocacy Actions

The oldest human rights body in the African system, the African Commission on Human and Peoples' Rights has much experience is assisting victims of human rights abuse. Therefore, despite the poor compliance rate with its recommendations, advocates should utilize the ACHPR's communication procedure, if they have the resources to stay actively engaged throughout the various levels of review and provide documentation and legal arguments. Advocates should also provide information to the ACHPR regarding religious freedom violations, as well as draft reports critiquing country submissions on their compliance with the African Charter.

Contact Information

African Commission on Human and Peoples' Rights
http://www.achpr.org/
48 Kairaba Avenue
P.O. Box 673
Banjul
The Gambia
Tel: (220) 4392 962
Fax: (220) 4390 764
achpr@achpr.org

African Court on Human and Peoples' Rights

Complaint Recourse Mechanism

The AU is developing a continental court, the African Court on Human and Peoples' Rights, in response to the poor compliance to the ACHPR complaint process. When the African Charter was originally under discussion, the drafters did not believe Africa was ready for a supranational court like those found in Europe or the Americas. It was not until 1998 that the OAU approved a protocol to the African Charter to establish the Court to reinforce and supplement the human rights work of the ACHPR. The protocol entered into force in 2005.

While twenty-one countries have agreed to the Court's jurisdiction, the Court is still developing, as its statute has not been promulgated. In addition, in 2004, the AU determined the Court should be merged with the African Court of Justice (which has not entered into force). However, until that court comes into being, the African Court on Human and Peoples' Rights will continue to develop its own structure and standards.

Countries under Court jurisdiction
Algeria, Burkina Faso, Burundi, Côte d'Ivoire, the Comoros, Gabon, The Gambia, Ghana, Kenya, Lesotho, Libya, Mali, Mauritius, Mozambique, Niger, Nigeria, Rwanda, Senegal, South Africa, Togo, and Uganda

The Court will be seated in Arusha, Tanzania. Unfortunately, this will create an expensive logistical challenge for its sister body, the ACHPR, headquartered on the opposite side of the continent. The Assembly elected the Court's first panel of eleven judges in 2006. Judges can only be nominated by countries party to the protocol, and judges will work independently and autonomously. They serve a six-year term and may only be reelected once. The Court elects its own President for a two-year term.

There are several remarkable features to the Court. First, its jurisdiction is very broad—it covers the African Charter and the protocol, as well as "any other relevant Human Rights instrument ratified by the States concerned."[2] The Court will therefore be able to interpret any UN treaty that a country is a party to, regardless of whether that particular treaty has any judicial mechanism. The Court will in effect serve as a judicial arm of the UN, improving the implementation of those treaties beyond their application elsewhere in the world.

Second, member states and AU organs may ask for advisory opinions. The protocol also provides this same ability to any organization recognized by the AU. Nongovernmental organizations with observer status could therefore request the Court to review problematic laws, policies, actions, or draft legislation in countries that have ratified the protocol.

Lastly, individuals and NGOs have standing to make complaints directly to the Court. However, for this to be possible, a country ratifying the protocol must specifically accept the Court's competence to receive these types of cases. The Court therefore falls short of the European Court of Human Rights, where individuals automatically have this right, but exceeds the Inter-American Court of Human Rights, where individual cases can only be brought by the Inter-American Commission on Human Rights on behalf of a victim.

Complaint Admissibility

For the Court to accept a complaint from a non-state actor residing in a country over which it has jurisdiction, it must first make a determination on the admissibility of the case. The ACHPR will be asked to give an opinion, and the Court will use the same admissibility criteria established by the African Charter and used by the ACHPR. The petition must meet the following criteria:

- it must not be anonymous (although the complainant can request anonymity);
- it must concern violations of rights falling under the African Charter;
- it must demonstrate the exhaustion of all domestic remedies;
- it must be submitted in a reasonable time after exhaustion.

The Court can either accept the case or transfer it to the ACHPR for review. The Court may also issue provisional measures in emergency situations threatening the life of an individual.

Complaint Procedure

For accepted cases, the Court will first try to find an amicable settlement. If no settlement is possible, a public court proceeding will begin, during which representatives of the alleged victim and offending government will make their arguments. The exact details of the process will be clarified once its rules of procedure are established.

Remedies

If the Court finds violations of human rights, it will "make appropriate orders to remedy the violation, including the payment of fair compensation or reparation."[3] Its decisions will be read publicly in court and sent to all AU members and the African Union Commission. The Executive Council will be responsible for monitoring the implementation of a decision.

Advocacy Actions

If it lives up to its statute and if it can avoid the compliance problems plaguing the ACHPR, the African Court could become a highly valuable tool for religious freedom advocacy. Once operational, advocates should submit complaints to the Court regarding situations of religious freedom violations in countries agreeing to the Court's jurisdiction and allowing individual complaints. Advocates should also be aware of other international conventions that member countries have ratified and consider bringing complaints under those provisions, if they exceed the protections of the African Charter. Court advisory opinions requested by advocacy groups with observer status could also be useful in combating problematic laws and policies limiting religious freedom.

CONTACT INFORMATION

No information is available as of this writing.

PAN-AFRICAN PARLIAMENT

Policymakers

The Pan-African Parliament, also known as the African Parliament, was created by the Constitutive Act of the African Union, along with the other organs of the AU. It is the legislative body of the AU and is seated in Midrand, South Africa. Its first session was in 2004, and it will operate under limited modalities for its first five years. During this initial period, the 265 parliamentary representatives will be selected by the legislatures of each AU member state. Eventually, these representatives will be directly elected in their home countries. In addition, during the inaugural five-year period, the parliament will only have oversight, advisory, and consultative powers. In 2009, the African Parliament is scheduled to obtain full legislative powers.

One of the stated goals of the African Parliament is to "promote the principles of human rights and democracy in Africa."[4] It is also envisioned that civil society groups will be very involved as partners in its oversight and legislative functions. The African Parliament has ten standing committees, one of which is the Committee on Justice and Human Rights. The African Parliament is led by a president, currently Dr. Amb. Gertrude I. Mongella from Tanzania.

Advocacy Actions

Advocates should not ignore the promising potential of the Pan-African Parliament in offering additional advocacy routes to pursue. Advocates should approach parliamentarians representing countries with problematic records concerning religious freedom, as well as provide information to sympathetic delegations, making them aware of the violations occurring elsewhere. Advocates should also provide information to the Committee on Justice and Human Rights, as well as to the President of the African Parliament, and request their intervention.

CONTACT INFORMATION

Pan-African Parliament
http://www.pan-africanparliament.org/
Gallagher Estate
Private Bag X16
Midrand 1685
Johannesburg
Republic of South Africa
Tel: +27(0) 11 545 5000
Fax: +27(0) 11 545 5136
secretariat@panafricanparliament.org

8

UNITED STATES BODIES AND INSTITUTIONS

Many countries protect religious freedom. However, due to the unique history of the United States and its exceptional commitment to religious freedom, this chapter will specifically examine the various U.S. government agencies and offices that engage on international religious freedom issues.[1]

As many early immigrants came to the United States fleeing religious persecution in Europe, the importance of protecting religious liberties was enshrined in the First Amendment to the U.S. Constitution, guaranteeing that "Congress shall make no law respecting an establishment of religion, or prohibiting the free exercise thereof." These promises were made binding at both the state and federal level through the Fourteenth Amendment.

The transition from domestic protection to international promotion of religious freedom, and human rights generally, did not emerge until the 1970s and 1980s. As these new foreign policy priorities developed, the U.S. Congress believed the State Department could more vigorously promote religious liberty and passed the International Religious Freedom Act (IRFA) in 1998. In its findings, IRFA juxtaposed the international standard guaranteeing religious freedom against the poor compliance by many countries, noting that more than one-half of the world's population lived under regimes that severely restricted the religious freedoms of their citizens. IRFA established religious freedom as a priority in all bilateral and multilateral talks and created new institutions, foremost of which is a special office within the State Department to monitor religious freedom worldwide, headed by the Ambassador-at-Large for International Religious Freedom. If religious freedom advocates can successfully mobilize the State Department, it will be a force multiplier to their efforts.

IRFA also created the U.S. Commission on International Religious Freedom (USCIRF) to act as a watchdog to the State Department's handling of religious freedom concerns. Other bodies exist within the panoply of U.S.

government agencies—in the European and Eurasian context, the U.S. Commission on Security and Cooperation in Europe, also known as the Helsinki Commission, monitors respect for human rights and religious freedom in Europe and the former Soviet Union. The Congressional-Executive Commission on China also follows a range of political developments in China, including religious freedom. These institutions all represent places where advocates can advance their concerns and push for real action. Congress itself is another valuable venue, with its members and committees engaged on questions of religious persecution.

STATE DEPARTMENT OFFICE FOR INTERNATIONAL RELIGIOUS FREEDOM

Policymakers and Monitoring Body

Because the United States has a diplomatic presence in almost every country in the world, the State Department has the ability to engage globally on religious freedom issues. The International Religious Freedom Act created new institutions to combat religious freedom violations and persecution. Foremost is the Office for International Religious Freedom (IRF Office) within the State Department, headed by a high-level diplomat, the Ambassador-at-Large for International Religious Freedom.

The Ambassador-at-Large leads a cadre of Foreign Service Officers and civil servants who monitor religious freedom globally and devise strategies to reduce abuses. The IRF Office works with other offices within the State Department to ensure that religious freedom concerns are included in discussions with foreign governments. The IRF Office regularly interacts with "desk officers," Foreign Service Officers who cover specific countries and act as liaisons between the State Department bureaucracy and a particular U.S. embassy.

Playing a critical role in the collection of information are the U.S. embassies and consulates abroad. All U.S. embassies have at least one Foreign Service Officer detailed to cover human rights and religious freedom issues, and these individuals make field visits and meet with individuals and governmental representatives. Foreign Service Officers will often raise human rights and religious freedom concerns with the host government, lending credibility to the concerns and also putting officials on notice that the proper resolution is of interest to the United States. These civil servants also generate the first draft of the annual religious freedom and human rights reports.

The Ambassador-at-Large and his staff also meet directly with private individuals, religious groups, and foreign officials about religious freedom concerns, either in the field or in Washington. The activities of the ambassador and the office lead up to the *Annual Report on International Religious Freedom*, which each year covers a twelve-month period from July to June. Exceeding eight hundred pages, the report assesses the state of religious freedom in every country in the world, except the United States. U.S. embassies compile the information and write the first draft, focusing on religious freedom violations, changes since the previous report, and embassy activities to promote religious freedom. The embassy submits its draft to the IRF Office for its country experts to edit further. All the religious freedom reports are posted on the State Department's Web site and are translated and posted on U.S. embassy Web sites as well.

The religious freedom report is utilized for policy decisions. IRFA provides a calibrated list of actions the State Department can take in response to religious freedom violations, be they mild or severe. The Act created a new designation for the worst countries, found to be committing "particularly severe violations of religious freedom"—Country of Particular Concern (CPC) status. "Particularly severe violations" are defined as "systematic, ongoing [and] egregious," listing examples such as torture and imprisonment. Congress gave teeth to the new office and the status it created; if a country is designated with CPC status, there is a menu of sanctions available to motivate recalcitrant governments to improve religious freedom conditions. The CPC designation will last until removed.

> The term "particularly severe violations of religious freedom" means systematic, ongoing, egregious violations of religious freedom, including violations such as –
>
> (A) torture or cruel, inhuman, or degrading treatment or punishment;
> (B) prolonged detention without charges;
> (C) causing the disappearance of persons by the abduction or clandestine detention of those persons; or
> (D) other flagrant denial of the right to life, liberty, or the security of persons.
>
> **Section 3, International Religious Freedom Act**

Technically, the Secretary of State can make a determination at any time, but in practice these determinations occur soon after the release of the religious freedom report. The list makes up a "who's who" of worst violators, and the

Ambassador-at-Large and the IRF Office play a crucial role in recommending to the Secretary of State which countries should be designated. At the time of writing, current countries designated as CPC are Burma, Democratic People's Republic of Korea (North Korea), Eritrea, Iran, People's Republic of China, Saudi Arabia, Sudan, and Uzbekistan.

Advocacy Actions

Advocates should build relationships with the Ambassador-at-Large and IRF Office staff and brief them on situations of concern by providing actionable information that contains specific details about religious freedom violations. Advocates should advocate for CPC designations and urge the State Department to act, as well as make coreligionists in other countries aware of the IRF Office. Advocates can also request IRF Office assistance in having the State Department raise concerns directly with government officials or foreign embassies.

CONTACT INFORMATION

Office of International Religious Freedom
http://www.state.gov/g/drl/irf/
2201 C Street, N.W.
Washington, D.C. 20520
Main Switchboard: (202) 647-4000
TTY: (800) 877-8339

STATE DEPARTMENT AND THE BUREAU OF DEMOCRACY, HUMAN RIGHTS, AND LABOR

Policymakers and Monitoring Body

The International Religious Freedom Office works within the State Department's Bureau of Democracy, Human Rights, and Labor (DRL). In support of the stated foreign policy objective of supporting human rights, the State Department has steadily increased the amount of resources dedicated to human rights issues. Today, State Department efforts to press for human rights are made primarily through DRL.

Headed by an Assistant Secretary of State, this bureau follows a variety of human rights issues on a day-to-day basis through the reporting from U.S. embassies and consulates abroad and through contact with nongovernmental organizations and foreign embassies in Washington. Like the IRF Office, DRL also interacts with country desk officers. While DRL is the primary office within the State Department to raise concerns about human rights, it also works with an array of boutique offices that follow specific issues, such as refugees, Holocaust-era property restitution issues, anti-Semitism, trafficking in persons, and religious freedom.

Like the religious freedom report, there is an annual report on human rights that follows each calendar year. Overall responsibility for the *Country Reports on Human Rights Practices* falls to DRL, and the report assesses the state of human rights in every country in the world, other than the United States. Initial drafts are created at the embassies and sent to DRL for refinement, and like the religious freedom report, the finished product is available online. These comprehensive reports are a tremendous resource for documenting abuses or tracking improvements, and they cover a multitude of human rights issues, from democracy standards to torture to press freedom. Reporting on the calendar year and including a section on religious freedom, the report is an important tool for policymakers when determining a course of action in regard to a particular country, as by law, security assistance may be limited for any country that "engages in a consistent pattern of gross violations of internationally recognized human rights."[2]

Advocacy Actions

Advocates should provide DRL with detailed information about specific religious freedom concerns to help ensure that the human rights report is complete and accurate. Advocates should meet with U.S. Embassy staff (and/or recommend coreligionists meet) to ensure embassy personnel receive current information to report or act upon. Advocates can also request that DRL or embassies raise concerns directly with government officials or foreign embassies.

CONTACT INFORMATION

Bureau of Democracy, Human Rights and Labor
http://www.state.gov/g/drl/
2201 C Street, N.W.
Washington, D.C. 20520
Main Switchboard: (202) 647-4000
TTY: (800) 877-8339
U.S. Embassies: http://usembassy.state.gov/

U.S. Commission on International Religious Freedom

Policymakers and Monitoring Body

The U.S. Congress also created the U.S. Commission on International Religious Freedom (USCIRF) through IRFA to serve as a watchdog over State Department activities, to help ensure that the historic American commitment to religious freedom was firmly entrenched in U.S. foreign policy. USCIRF does not conduct diplomacy with foreign governments. It is led by nine private-sector commissioners: three appointed by the President, three by Senate leadership, and three by the House of Representatives leadership. The Ambassador-at-Large for International Religious Freedom serves as an ex-officio commissioner.

USCIRF's monitoring role is mainly exercised through the annual nomination of countries for CPC status and the issuance of country reports with policy recommendations for the President, Secretary of State, and the Congress. These recommendations outline actions USCIRF believes the United States should take toward countries with problematic policies. The State Department is not bound to these nominations or recommendations, but to date all designated countries have been nominated by USCIRF. The Commission can also hold public hearings on different countries of concern, as well as hold more informal briefings at their offices.

Commission staff follow religious freedom issues worldwide, in a sense shadowing the activities of the IRF Office, but pay particular attention to CPC countries and other countries they believe should be designated as such in the future. Staffers are active in monitoring religious freedom abuses, often traveling to countries to conduct fact-finding missions either with Commissioners or alone. They are also open to meeting with advocates visiting Washington.

Advocacy Actions

Advocates should supply reliable information and recommendations to USCIRF to help ensure that issues are addressed in their annual reports, focusing primarily on CPC countries or countries possibly meeting the definition. Advocates should also contact Commissioners directly and provide material regarding possible CPC countries to aid their deliberations.

CONTACT INFORMATION

U.S. Commission on International Religious Freedom
http://www.uscirf.gov
800 N. Capitol Street, N.W., Suite 790
Washington, D.C. 20002
Tel: (202) 523-3240
Fax: (202) 523-5020
communications@uscirf.gov

U.S. COMMISSION ON SECURITY AND COOPERATION IN EUROPE (HELSINKI COMMISSION)

Policymakers and Monitoring Body

Established in 1976 by Congress, the U.S. Commission on Security and Cooperation in Europe, also known as the Helsinki Commission, monitors the compliance of the Helsinki Final Act and the other commitments under the Organization for Security and Cooperation in Europe (OSCE). A U.S. government commission, its staff monitors all fifty-six member countries in North America, Europe, and Eurasia concerning their human rights and religious freedom commitments. The Commission also plays a think-tank type role, working with the State Department on the formulation of U.S. foreign policy as it relates to the OSCE.

The Helsinki Commission is unique, in that it has twenty-one Commissioners representing two branches of government; eighteen from Congress and three from the executive branch. Congressional Commissioners are bipartisan and evenly divided between the House and Senate. The remaining three Commissioners represent the Departments of State, Commerce, and Defense, which reflect the three "baskets" of the Helsinki Process. Notwithstanding the executive branch relationship, the Helsinki Commission follows the lead of their congressional Commissioners, and the Chair rotates between the House and Senate every two years with each new Congress. Because of the direction provided by its congressional leadership, the Commission functions much like a congressional committee, but with no legislative oversight.

A professional staff supports Commissioners by following specific countries and thematic issues, one of which has traditionally been religious freedom. The Helsinki Commission can convene congressional hearings and briefings on various human rights topics, which can focus or touch upon religious freedom-related matters. Helsinki Commission staff are also fully integrated with State Department delegations to OSCE meetings, and they travel on behalf of the Commission to OSCE participating States to discuss issues of concern with NGOs and government officials. These trips often result in public reports regarding implementation of OSCE commitments and possible congressional follow-up.

Advocacy Actions

Advocates should provide detailed information to Helsinki Commission staff on various concerns in Europe and Eurasia about specific violations of OSCE commitments on religious freedom. Advocates can request Commission action on an issue, which can take the form of letters from members of Congress or Congressional Record statements. Advocates should also attend Helsinki Commission hearings and briefings and provide documentation of abuses, when appropriate. Commission staff can also provide advice on ways to utilize OSCE mechanisms effectively to raise situations of concern.

CONTACT INFORMATION

U.S. Commission on Security and Cooperation in Europe (Helsinki Commission)
http://www.csce.gov
234 Ford House Office Building
3rd and D Streets, S.W.
Washington, D.C. 20515
Tel: (202) 225-1901
Fax: (202) 226-4199
info@csce.gov

CONGRESSIONAL-EXECUTIVE COMMISSION ON CHINA

Policymakers and Monitoring Body

The Congressional-Executive Commission on China (CECC) was created by Congress in 2000 to monitor and report on human rights and the development of the rule of law in China. The CECC emerged from the debate that year on whether to give China Permanent Normal Trade Relations with the U.S. Until 2000, the Congress would regularly debate China's human rights record before deciding on whether to grant temporary trade preferences. Not wanting to lose that opportunity, many members of Congress were only willing to grant permanent trade relations if the China Commission were created to monitor these very important issues.

Similar to the Helsinki Commission, the CECC has Commissioners from both branches—nine Senators, nine members of the House of Representatives, and five administration officials appointed by the President. The CECC works to encourage improvement by the Chinese government in respecting its own laws, constitution, and international agreements. Notably, the legislation establishing the China Commission specifically outlines religious freedom as an area of focus. Religious freedom is defined as more than just the ability to meet for worship, but to worship "free of involvement of and interference by the government."[3]

The China Commission's main activity is the writing of an annual report to the President and Congress about human rights and the rule of law in China, with recommendations for legislative or executive action. The CECC also maintains a list of prisoners jailed or detained because of human rights activities, including for religious reasons. Importantly, its founding statute also declares that the CECC will "seek out and maintain contacts" with nongovernmental organizations and receive information from these groups.

The CECC staff is composed of U.S. experts on China, with their expertise covering the range of issues outlined in their founding statute. To gather information for their annual reports, the CECC will convene hearings and informal roundtables, undertake fact-finding missions, and meet with Chinese officials, scholars, and academics.

Advocacy Actions

Advocates should provide detailed information and recommendations to China Commission staff on religious freedom violations for submission in their annual report. Advocates should also send the China Commission names of individuals jailed on account of their religious beliefs. Advocates should also attend China Commission hearings and informal roundtables and provide documentation of abuses.

CONTACT INFORMATION

Congressional-Executive Commission on China
http://www.cecc.gov/
242 Ford House Office Building
Washington, D.C. 20515
Tel: (202) 226-3766
Fax: (202) 226-3804
infocecc@mail.house.gov

CONGRESS

Policymakers

The U.S. Congress plays an energetic role in advocating for religious freedom. Individual members of Congress continually engage on international religious freedom issues, as their committee hearings consistently testify. Consequently, "the Hill" offers an open door for advocacy groups to raise concerns about specific situations.

The passage of the International Religious Freedom Act vividly demonstrated Congress' ability to respond legislatively to concerns about religious freedom in significant ways. More often, however, the Congress has spoken through nonbinding resolutions. For instance, in 2006 both the House and Senate passed a resolution on religious freedom in the Russian Federation. It had no legal effect but did express the opinion of the Congress on the treatment of religious freedom in Russia.

Members of Congress and Senators, acting in their independent capacity, can meet heads of state and ambassadors accredited to the United States and raise their concerns about limitations on religious practice. Most ambassadors will find time to meet with members or respond to their letters, as well as convey these concerns back to their capitals. This activism is not limited to those members serving on the committees dealing with foreign affairs. Members who have little or no interest in international issues will often engage on issues of international religious freedom, either because of their own personal faith perspective or because of the urging of their constituents.

In addition to individual action, congressional committees play an important role through their various hearings. Hearings are important, as they express congressional interest in a subject to both the country concerned and the State Department. Members are action oriented, and they will use hearings to search for concrete steps that can be taken.

In addition, usually after the release to Congress of the religious freedom report by the State Department, the House Foreign Affairs Committee (HFAC) will convene an oversight hearing to review the findings and to discuss countries with problematic policies. HFAC also holds country-specific hearings during which issues of religious freedom can also be raised. For instance, during a general hearing on Afghanistan in 2003, panelists spent time discussing whether the new constitution would limit or facilitate religious freedom for non-Muslims. HFAC also maintains a special subcommittee that focuses specifically on human rights—the Subcommittee on International Organizations, Human Rights, and Oversight—and religious freedom concerns often arise. Congressmen also maintain the Tom Lantos Human Rights Commission, as well as the Taskforce on International Religious Freedom.

House Foreign Affairs Subcommittees
Subcommittee on Africa and Global Health
Subcommittee on Asia, the Pacific, and the Global Environment
Subcommittee on Europe
Subcommittee on International Organizations, Human Rights, and Oversight
Subcommittee on the Middle East and South Asia
Subcommittee on Terrorism, Nonproliferation, and Trade
Subcommittee on the Western Hemisphere

Senate Foreign Relations Subcommittees
Subcommittee on Western Hemisphere, Peace Corps, and Narcotics Affairs
Subcommittee on Near Eastern and South and Central Asian Affairs
Subcommittee on African Affairs
Subcommittee on East Asian and Pacific Affairs
Subcommittee on International Operations and Organizations, Democracy and Human Rights
Subcommittee on European Affairs
Subcommittee on International Development and Foreign Assistance, Economic Affairs, and International Environmental Protection

---

In the Senate, the Foreign Relations Committee (SFRC) also addresses human rights and religious freedom concerns. The committee does not have a thematic subcommittee dedicated to human rights, but its regional subcommittees often focus on religious freedom concerns within a country context.

For both houses, the appropriations committees have considerable clout over issues concerning foreign affairs. Funding both the State Department and foreign aid programs, appropriators can either increase monies for U.S. government programs supporting religious freedom, or look to limit, condition, or cut aid to governments that are religious freedom violators.

Advocacy Actions

American advocates should contact their Representatives and Senators regarding religious freedom violations either through letter, e-mail, or personal meetings. Advocates from other countries can also conduct similar awareness campaigns. While also looking to meet directly with members of Congress, advocates should present information in an easily accessible format to staff in personal offices and relevant committees. Actions that advocates can pursue include requesting meetings with a representative of the government in question, writing to the head of state, raising the issue at hearings or through legislation, or pushing the State Department to act.

CONTACT INFORMATION

U.S. Congress
http://www.house.gov/
http://www.senate.gov/

House Foreign Affairs Committee (HFAC)
http://www.internationalrelations.house.gov/
2170 Rayburn House Office Building
Washington, D.C. 20515
Tel: (202) 225-5021

House Committee on Appropriations
http://appropriations.house.gov/
Room H-218, The Capitol
Washington, D.C. 20515
Phone: (202) 225-2771

Senate Committee on Foreign Relations
http://foreign.senate.gov/
Dirksen Senate Office Building
Washington, D.C. 20510-6225
Majority Phone: (202) 224-4651
Minority Phone: (202) 224-6797

Senate Committee on Appropriations
http://appropriations.senate.gov/
The Capitol, S-131
Washington, D.C. 20510
Tel: (202) 224-7363

9

NONGOVERNMENTAL ORGANIZATIONS

The guidebook has thus far described the relevant international mechanisms available to religious freedom advocates. In utilizing these mechanisms, however, advocates rarely act as individuals. More commonly, they conduct their advocacy through the work of nongovernmental organizations (NGOs) to which they belong, including both religiously based organizations and secular groups. This chapter will provide a practical overview of NGOs, explaining the diverse roles they play in advocating for religious freedom.

NGO OVERVIEW

Identity and Motivation

Though widely varied in structure and function, religious freedom NGOs share a common nongovernmental identity that affords them several general advantages. First, they maintain a significant amount of autonomy in the strategies and methodologies they employ to advocate for religious freedom, unconstrained by many of the political and bureaucratic limitations of national or international bodies. This autonomy allows them to speak more frankly, act more quickly, and innovate more freely than can international bodies and governments. In addition, NGOs typically can more easily access and gain the trust of persecuted faith communities, especially if they are coreligionists, as persecuted groups are often suspicious of governmental agencies because of past mistreatment.

Their nongovernmental status is not the only commonality among NGOs; they also share a commitment to religious freedom as a fundamental human right and a deep compassion for victims of religious persecution. The reasons for this commitment vary widely, however. One common motivation is the religious identity of the organizations themselves. Many religious groups form NGOs specifically dedicated to the freedom of their faith internationally. These organizations are typically staffed by adherents to the faith and are motivated by shared religious beliefs and concern for their coreligionists around the world.

One might expect that the differences in religious identities of these NGOs would hinder their ability to collaborate in promoting religious freedom internationally. However, faith-based religious freedom NGOs typically acknowledge that improved religious freedom benefits all faith communities, both their own and others', and there are many positive examples of interfaith collaboration in the field. Notably, the 1998 International Religious Freedom Act was passed in large part through the joint efforts of faith-based religious freedom NGOs lobbying the U.S. Congress. These NGOs ranged from the Religious Action Committee of Reform Judaism, to the National Spiritual Assembly of the Baha'is of the United States, to the National Association of Evangelicals, to the Uighur-American Association (representing the largely Muslim Uighur people in China).

Faith-based NGOs possess certain advantages. Because of shared beliefs with victims, they often more easily gain victims' trust and are able to obtain detailed testimonies of abuses that victims may otherwise be too frightened or suspicious to share with nonbelievers. In addition, these NGOs' religious identity connects them to an international network of fellow faith adherents, providing a ready base of contacts around the world from whom to obtain information.

However, the same religious identity that wins trust in the field can bring about suspicion from foreign governments. Faith-based NGOs may be suspected of funneling financial or religious resources to their coreligionists, or using their human rights work as a guise under which to conduct proselytizing activities. These NGOs may also have difficulty working with Western governments, secular human rights organizations, and international bodies. These entities are often careful not to compromise their secular identities by supporting religious work through funding or partnerships.

Religious belief is not the only motivation behind religious freedom NGOs. Many advocates possess a deeply held commitment to human rights with no religious affiliation, and many human rights organizations are avowedly secular, such as Amnesty International and Human Rights Watch. This secular identity helps such organizations avoid skepticism about a hidden religious agenda, erecting fewer barriers to collaboration with secular entities, and allows them to work with all victims of persecution rather than those of a particular faith group. Furthermore, they have easier access to partnerships and funding from nonreligious sources, including large philanthropic foundations and governments.

A final motivation for religious freedom advocacy is commitment to a complementary cause. For example, in some areas, large numbers of women convert to Christianity because it promises them greater social status. An NGO that works for gender equality in this area may necessarily become involved in advocating for religious freedom for these new female converts. Similarly, socioeconomic development among communities of religious minorities is often hampered by their governments' discrimination against them. Development NGOs may need to address religious freedom issues in order to effectively improve the socioeconomic conditions of these communities. In these examples, the NGOs may conduct their advocacy directly through the channels described in this book, or they may partner with religious freedom NGOs so that their work supports one another. Thus, religious freedom work may be carried out by NGOs with seemingly disparate missions, whose motivation for advocacy is neither religious belief nor human rights, but commitment to a related issue. Other issues that may overlap with religious freedom in a given context include press freedom, property rights, and ethnic minority rights, among many others. (Conversely, religious freedom NGOs sometimes find that they must address complementary issues, such as development or education, in order to effectively advocate for religious freedom in a given context.)

Structure and Function

Religious freedom NGOs are typically governed by boards of directors, which can range in size from several to dozens of members. They vary just as widely in organizational structure. An NGO may be as small as just a few employees and on-the-ground contacts, or it may be a subset of a large, international organization with vast financial and human resources.

TYPES OF NGO ACTIVITIES

NGO functions—embodied in the NGOs' unique visions, missions, and methodologies—are as varied as their structures. Below are descriptions of common functions; organizations may perform one, several, or all of these as part of their advocacy. Because of the great variety that exists, this list is not exhaustive, and many overlaps occur.

Gathering and Disseminating Information

In repressive climates, where speech and press freedoms are also restricted, information about religious freedom abuses is often difficult to obtain. Many religious freedom NGOs work with on-the-ground contacts—including government officials, aid workers, and coreligionists—to obtain such information. NGOs must take steps to determine the veracity of the information they receive. For example, victims' testimonies are often more reliable when obtained through face-to-face contact, using a trusted translator (i.e., provided by the NGO rather than the government). Many repressive governments monitor correspondence, e-mail, and phone calls, making contacts less likely to share information openly over these channels. Concurrent reports from multiple trusted sources can validate these first-person testimonies. Such steps are important in filtering false or exaggerated claims, which some religious adherents may make accidentally or purposefully (to bring attention, funds, or followers to their cause). A religious freedom NGO risks its own credibility by perpetuating such claims, whether intentionally or through carelessness.

After obtaining reliable testimony, NGOs disseminate information about abuses in a number of formats: e-mail campaigns, public presentations, reports, press releases, editorials, and consultations with relevant government agencies and international bodies (described in previous chapters). Those who receive the information may then use it to augment and support their own advocacy efforts.

Most religious freedom NGOs perform this function in some capacity, often as a foundation for their programs. They may also rely on the information gathered by other NGOs to verify and enhance their own findings.

Examples of NGOs that gather and disseminate information include Christian Solidarity Worldwide, Compass Direct, and Open Doors.

Generating Pressure and Influencing Policy

NGOs can also attempt to generate pressure against repressive governments in hopes of bringing about changes to policies affecting religious freedom. This pressure is often overt, designed to embarrass foreign countries that violate religious freedom. Such embarrassment threatens repressive regimes in several ways. First, shame is a powerful tool in many non-Western cultures, where concepts such as "saving face" are highly valued. Second, public embarrassment may embolden dissidents within the regime, as they perceive global public opinion to be sympathetic to their cause. These dissidents' protests may undermine the government's ability to maintain order and thus threaten their hold on power. Finally, many repressive governments are in developing countries, where favorable relations with powerful Western countries are important for economic growth and international aid. These governments fear that negative attention will lead Western countries to alter favorable policies. For these reasons, the threat of public shaming can be sufficient to elicit accommodations (albeit sometimes minimal) in religious freedom policies.

NGOs apply pressure to offending governments through such means as press releases, editorials, Web sites, e-mail campaigns, petitions, phone calls to government officials and representatives, testimonies to international organizations and domestic government bodies, and public protests. These activities draw attention to governments' poor religious freedom records, in hopes of creating widespread public concern and influencing leaders to take action against unfavorable policies. Such policies may include, among others, demarching a capital to raise concerns, designating a country as a Country of Particular Concern (described in detail in Chapter 8), denying normal trade relations, withdrawing diplomatic representation or severing diplomatic relations, imposing sanctions, or failing to support bids to join international bodies such as the World Trade Organization.

Most religious freedom NGOs include some of these policy activities in their work and have one or several employees who liaise with government officials and international bodies about religious freedom issues.

Examples of such NGOs include Amnesty International, Human Rights Watch, World Evangelical Alliance's Religious Liberty Commission, Jubilee Campaign, Human Rights First, International League for Human Rights, and the Hudson Institute's Center for Religious Freedom.

Informing Foreign Policy

As the previous section indicated, many NGOs seek to influence the policies of their governments in response to religious freedom abuses by other countries. Another aspect of influencing policy, however, is working to make religious freedom a more prominent issue in foreign policy considerations. The passage of the International Religious Freedom Act in 1998 made significant advances toward this goal in the United States, guaranteeing religious freedom's prominent role in American foreign policy. However, many Western policymakers remain generally uninformed about religious freedom and, more basically, about the role of religion in international affairs, a topic that is generally avoided in traditional foreign service courses. For this reason, some NGOs are working to increase the understanding of the importance of religion and religious freedom in foreign affairs. This work may take the form of journal articles, lecture series, conferences, and dialogues that highlight the importance of religious freedom in foreign policy considerations.

Examples of NGOs that perform this function include the Institute on Religion and Public Policy, the International Center for Religion and Diplomacy, and the Council on Faith and International Affairs.

Assisting Victims of Persecution

Some religious freedom NGOs focus their efforts on supplying aid to victims of persecution. This aid can take many forms: legal aid to assist victims in filing claims with relevant agencies and courts; material assistance to families of victims who have been imprisoned or killed; medical or mental care for a religious believer who has been tortured; religious resources, including sacred texts and teaching materials, that are illegal or too expensive to obtain normally; assisting religious refugees with documentation, referrals, sponsorship, and resettlement; or other types of assistance. This kind of work is often carried out by faith-based NGOs concerned about the plight of coreligionists in hostile areas. Their assistance may also take more abstract forms, such as organizing moments of silence or days of prayer dedicated to those persecuted for the faith.

Although these activities may seem less political than those described in previous sections, they are often viewed with suspicion or hostility by foreign governments and local communities. Traditional societies sometimes view religious minorities as traitors who have adopted a foreign culture, undermining indigenous culture and power structures. When these believers then receive aid from foreign organizations, this view is reinforced, confirming suspicions and creating resentment. Providing religious resources can be controversial, as it can jeopardize the safety of the recipients and, in some cases, violate the laws of the state.

Examples of NGOs that aid victims of persecution include Voice of the Martyrs, International Christian Concern, Christian Solidarity International, Iranian Christians International, Christian Freedom International, and Physicians for Human Rights.

Mediating Religious Freedom Conflicts

Some NGOs seek to mediate conflicts between religious communities and the governments that repress them. These NGOs seek to persuade governments to protect religious freedom, and to persuade religious believers to act in ways that do not unnecessarily provoke government suspicion or trigger a reaction. In persuading governments, a straightforward appeal to human dignity and justice is rarely effective. While a repressive government may value these concepts, it has already shown through its religious freedom violations that it values other interests more—such as social stability, cultural preservation, or maintaining power. Thus, persuasion must appeal to some aspect of governmental self-interest.

This kind of work is typically more quiet and gradual than those types described in previous sections. Public shaming and covert activities can be counterproductive strategies if they engender suspicion rather than trust. Instead, by seeking to respect national sovereignty, NGOs can quietly build relationships with key leaders and create a climate of trust. This relationship will allow the NGO to offer direct critiques of government actions at strategic moments, many of which will be private conversations rather than public meetings. NGOs may also host nonthreatening events, such as scholarly conferences and policy forums, in which non-Western scholars and practitioners subtly argue the importance of religious freedom. Such strategies give governments ownership of the concepts of religious freedom, helping them to understand its importance and implement it in ways that are tailored to their unique social context. NGOs hope that such ownership will lead to long-term change, not only in laws and policies, but in the mindset of the government. Religious freedom will thus be embraced, rather than merely tolerated in order to appease foreign governments and reduce international pressure.

These NGOs must also work closely with religious groups, being careful not to alienate them through an inappropriately close relationship with the government. Their interactions with these communities may vary widely, depending on the circumstances. NGOs may use trusted faith leaders to help educate others in the community about their rights under international or national laws, to encourage culturally sensitive practices that are less threatening to the government (without compromising core beliefs), or to counsel against activities that only exacerbate the problem, such as paying bribes in exchange for government protection. NGOs may also sponsor dialogue

between faith leaders and their communities or governments, aimed at recon-
ciling disputes and correcting misperceptions. They may even promote seemingly unrelated activities, such as theological or literacy training for uneducated
believers, in order to prevent the emergence of radical leaders who pervert the
faith to persuade people to take violent action against the state.

This kind of quiet work is unconventional, and thus NGOs conducting it
are far less common than those described above. One example is the Institute
for Global Engagement.

Developing and Promoting Rule of Law

Many countries that repress religious freedom do not have a well-developed
legal system and tradition of rule of law. As a result, laws and treaties protecting religious freedom are sometimes ignored or arbitrarily interpreted in
whatever way officials choose, often in accordance with security concerns or
cultural biases. When religious freedom violations occur, victims rarely have
access to legal representation, and if they do, they cannot be guaranteed a fair
trial. As a result, strengthening countries' legal systems and providing legal
assistance is important to improving religious freedom in the long term as a
right that is firmly upheld in law. Some religious freedom NGOs work primarily in this field, using a variety of strategies.

One common strategy is filing lawsuits on behalf of victims in international tribunals or in the domestic courts of offending countries. These lawsuits
not only provide expert legal representation to victims who might otherwise
not have access; they also raise the profile of such cases, leveraging popular
opinion against the government and thus indirectly applying pressure.

Another strategy is to work from within to develop the legal system's
capacity. Activities may include assisting in curriculum development at local
law schools, providing training for lawyers and judges, or working with
national lawmakers to develop religious freedom laws that are in accordance
with international standards. The final activity is often best done through neutral third parties rather than through a Western NGO. For example, an NGO
may facilitate a meeting or conference between regional lawmakers and legal
scholars, including those who the NGO knows are committed to religious
freedom. These non-Western scholars are able to influence their counterparts
in more repressive regimes, convincing them of the merits of religious freedom and helping them to codify it into domestic law.

Examples of this kind of NGO include the Becket Fund for Religious Liberty and Advocates International.

Advocacy Actions

The above descriptions of NGO functions are a starting point for understanding the types of work that religious freedom advocates can do. Despite their differences, these functions are most effective when applied together, building momentum toward greater religious freedom through a wide variety of complementary strategies. The first step for the would-be advocate is to decide not which strategy is superior, but which NGO is a good fit with one's own beliefs, education, and skills. Appendix V contains a list of religious freedom NGOs and contact information to help advocates begin their research.

Once one or several NGOs are selected, opportunities for advocacy include volunteering office time (answering phones, delivering mail, filing), participating on event-planning committees, raising funds or contributing financially, educating others about the work of the NGO and the issue of religious freedom, making strategic introductions to connect the NGO with relevant contacts, providing pro bono legal work, or pursuing employment.

10

CASE STUDY I—TURKMENISTAN

The following case study provides a useful example of how many of the previously discussed international institutions and bodies can be activated successfully for religious freedom concerns. Case Study I focuses on the Central Asian country of Turkmenistan, which has arguably the worst record on human rights in the entire fifty-six-nation OSCE region. The Turkmenistan case study is instructive, as between 2002 and 2005 religious freedom advocates utilized many of the previously highlighted offices and institutions of policymakers, monitoring bodies, and complaint recourse mechanisms with varying degrees of success.[1]

Gaining independence after the fall of the Soviet Union, the Turkmen people "elected" as president in 1992 their former communist boss, Saparmurat Niyazov. Niyazov ruled Turkmenistan with an iron fist until his death in December 2006. Named "President for Life" and referring to himself as the Turkmenbashi, the father of all Turkmen, Niyazov created a pervasive cult of personality. His face adorned almost every government building, and the months of the year were renamed, one after himself and one after his deceased mother. Niyazov wrote his own spiritual book, the *Ruhnama*, a rambling collection of thoughts on morality that was required by law to be physically placed in mosques on the same level as the Koran. Niyazov also made the book required reading in schools and at government jobs, and it was incorporated into the driving test. These nonsensical policies, however, disguised a brutal regime that allowed no dissent and significantly limited religious freedom.

Under the Niyazov regime, only two religious groups were allowed to operate openly—the Russian Orthodox Church and Sunni Islam—but with significant government interference and control. For instance, Turkmen authorities selected imams (or preachers) for mosques and limited the number of Orthodox services. For other groups to obtain permission to enjoy basic religious freedoms, like meeting for corporate worship, a congregation had to prove that its membership exceeded five hundred adult citizens in the locality where it wished to meet—an impossible hurdle for small groups to overcome. Many risked government action and met "illegally." The repercussions could be severe; for example, Turkmen authorities had the Adventist church in the capital, Ashgabat, bulldozed to the ground in 1999.

Religious freedom advocates and representatives of religious communities struggling to operate in Turkmenistan during this period began meeting with U.S. State Department officials, in either Ashgabad, Washington, or Vienna at the U.S. Mission to the OSCE. In addition, advocates and coreligionists petitioned members of Congress and their staffs, asking offices to write to Niyazov and meet with the Turkmen ambassador to raise the possibility of reducing U.S. assistance to the country if improvements were not made. NGOs wrote letters to then-Secretary of State Colin Powell and to USCIRF, urging CPC designation, and also spoke out at the yearly HDIM meeting in Warsaw.

Governments and international institutions began to respond to these awareness-raising efforts. For instance, NGOs worked with the State Department and the European Union to utilize UN monitoring bodies further to pressure Turkmenistan. Working together in 2003, the United States and the European Union collaborated on a UN Commission on Human Rights resolution criticizing the repressive Turkmen policies and highlighting specific religious freedom abuses.[2] The Commission on Human Rights approved a similar resolution on Turkmenistan's human rights record the following year that again highlighted restrictions on religious freedom.[3] Also in 2004, the UN General Assembly spoke for the first time about religious freedom abuses in a resolution on human rights in Turkmenistan, which echoed the Commission's concerns.[4] In 2005, the General Assembly again passed a resolution on Turkmenistan that noted some improvements in the regime's record on religious freedom but continued to pressure the government for additional reforms.[5]

The U.S. Embassy in Ashgabat became engaged, in response to increasing reports of religious freedom violations brought forward by advocates. The Embassy offered protests to Turkmen authorities, making clear that the bilateral relationship could suffer because a CPC designation was a real possibility unless concrete steps were taken to relax the registration system and allow greater religious freedom.[6] State Department officials from the IRF Office, DRL, and the desk reinforced this message in Washington to Turkmen officials. Concern was also expressed by U.S. officials to the OSCE in Ashgabad and at the Warsaw HDIM.[7] Other participating states, religious freedom advocates, and NGOs also expressed their alarm at the HDIM.[8] (The OSCE Mission in Ashgabat could do little, as it was already on bad terms with the government.) The U.S. Commission on International Religious Freedom also nominated Turkmenistan for CPC designation in its annual report (which it has since done repeatedly).[9] A coalition of human rights groups also wrote to U.S. Secretary of State Condoleezza Rice to urge for CPC designation of Turkmenistan.[10]

Advocates were also successful in moving members of Congress to act, and many called upon the State Department to designate Turkmenistan as a Country of Particular Concern. Thirty-four members of the House and Senate wrote to Secretary Powell in October 2003, calling for the CPC designation of Turkmenistan, as well as of Vietnam and Saudi Arabia.[11] The next year, the Helsinki Commission and USCIRF held a joint congressional briefing to highlight the limits on religious freedom to members of Congress and their staff, and to push for change.[12] In addition, the Helsinki Commission sent President Niyazov a letter asking for improvements on religious freedom and for the release of the former grand mufti as well as six Jehovah's Witnesses jailed for conscientious objection.[13]

By successfully creating a confluence of pressure from the U.S. Embassy and State Department, USCIRF, the Helsinki Commission, Congress, and the UN, advocates were able eventually to move the strange and reclusive Niyazov to liberalize Turkmen policies. Initial attempts, however, fell short of the line set by the international community when the government issued "reforms" that were actually additional regulations to increase governmental control of religious practice. Not deceived by these paper promises, the United States maintained its insistence on real progress if Turkmenistan wanted to avoid CPC designation.

Finally, Niyazov issued a new presidential decree reducing the registration threshold from five hundred per locality to five individuals nationally and registered many communities. In addition, in response to the Helsinki Commission Chairman's letter, authorities released the six Jehovah's Witnesses after they had served more than two years in abysmal conditions for conscientious objection to military service. Religious groups reported that the climate had actually improved, with groups allowed to meet more freely without the continuous threat of policy harassment or jail time. While religious freedoms are still not fully enjoyed in Turkmenistan, minority religious communities have reported an improvement in the overall climate and a greater ability to enjoy their religious liberties. Consequently, these advances have been enough for the country to avoid CPC designation as of this writing.

While Turkmenistan represents a victory for religious freedom advocacy, it also shows how difficult achieving success can be. A tremendous amount of effort was needed to move the government to act, and despite these improvements, reports continue to surface of sporadic instances of police harassment of religious meetings and jailing of religious leaders. The government has also not reduced its control of Islamic institutions. Continued pressure will be necessary to ensure that the full respect of religious freedom is enjoyed in Turkmenistan.

11

CASE STUDY II—VIETNAM

As noted in chapter 9, nongovernmental organizations (NGOs) often enjoy certain advantages in flexibility and access when it comes to religious freedom advocacy. Pressure applied to a country via governmental mechanisms will sometimes be insufficient if NGOs are not simultaneously working creatively through channels of civil society in that nation to create the conditions needed to sustain religious freedom. Case study II illustrates these dynamics in Vietnam—specifically through the work of one religious freedom NGO, the Institute for Global Engagement (IGE).

IGE—a transparently faith-based NGO based in the U.S.—has from 2004 to 2008 sent its key staff to Vietnam six times, leading various delegations of American leaders. IGE has also hosted numerous delegations from Vietnam visiting the United States. In the past year, IGE has met with the prime minister of Vietnam and has met twice with its president. IGE was also the only international religious freedom NGO allowed access to the previously persecuted regions of the Central and Northwest Highlands, where hundreds of Protestant churches have been legally registered since IGE's involvement.[1] IGE has also catalyzed several unprecedented conferences in Vietnam examining how to advance religious freedom and the rule of law.

The story of how IGE achieved this kind of access and impact demonstrates the value that NGOs can add to the cause of religious freedom advocacy.[2] IGE did not act in a vacuum—the U.S. Ambassador-at-Large for Religious Freedom, John Hanford, played an instrumental role in persistently and patiently working with the Vietnamese government to help effect changes. However, instead of examining government-to-government engagement, this chapter will highlight NGO engagement with a government to bring about systematic improvements in religious freedom.

VIETNAM AND ECONOMIC DEVELOPMENT

Vietnam is a country in the middle of serious transition and strategic trans-formation. Intelligent and industrious, the Vietnamese people—both the government and citizens—have made the collective decision not only to par-ticipate in the world economy, but to join the global civil society as well.

Vietnam's economy, for example, grew at a rate of over eight percent from 2005 to 2008. This is a remarkable statistic considering that Vietnam's biggest trading partners are also former enemies (the Japanese, the French, the Ameri-cans, and the Chinese). As a result, the poverty rate has decreased from fifty-eight percent in 1993 to twenty percent in 2004, while per capita income has increased from $170 to $620 in the same time frame. As the World Bank states, "Vietnam is one of the best-performing developing economies in the world . . . It has the potential to be one of the great success stories in development."[3]

These trends and statistics indicate something beyond economic benchmarks. Most of all, they indicate a desire not to let the past—from previous military enemies to failed economic policies—influence the future. They also indicate a comprehensive and systematic desire to provide quickly the most basic of human rights—the right not to live in poverty—as the basis for civil society.

Vietnam has not, however, had a strong record on religious freedom. Its argument has been that it is difficult to be concerned about religious freedom when there is no bread on the table. The recent unprecedented progress in poverty reduction therefore helps create an opening to advance religious free-dom as a critically important component in deepening and maturing Viet-namese civil society and integrating Vietnam into global civil society.

U.S.-VIETNAM RELATIONS

Due to the war between the U.S. and Vietnam in the 1960s and 1970s, rela-tions were not normalized until 1995. Since that time, relations and trade have steadily improved and increased, but religious freedom remained a paramount concern for the American people. It was particularly difficult for Americans to see the ethnic minorities of the Central and Northwest Highlands—who had fought with the United States against North Vietnam during the war—being persecuted for their Christian faith.

By September 2004, the United States designated Vietnam as a Coun-try of Particular Concern (CPC) for its systematic, ongoing, and egregious violations of religious freedom. Washington did not, however, implement any of the sanctions allowed by the International Religious Freedom Act of 1998. Instead, the office of International Religious Freedom at the State Department and the National Security Council at the White House developed a "road map" through which the United States and Vietnam would work together to remove the CPC designation. This agreement, which was signed on May 5, 2005, laid out the necessary results that Vietnam had to achieve in order to be removed from the CPC list.

Vietnam was anxious to get off the list for two reasons. Beyond the international "black eye," being on the list prevented Vietnam from establishing Permanent Normal Trade Relations (PNTR) with the United States, which was needed for the Americans to support Vietnam's ascension to the World Trade Organization. Compared to the United States, Vietnam has a population that is one-third of the size (85 million), living on one-thirtieth of the land. Almost thirty percent of the population is under the age of fourteen, and more than half of the population has been born since the fall of Saigon in 1975. The situation of young people with increasingly less land and less economic opportunity is something about which all governments are concerned.

As a function of the Communist Party's 2003 directive, Vietnam began to reshape its approach toward religion in 2004 with the publishing of the governmental "Ordinance on Belief and Religion" on November 15. On February 1, 2005, Vietnam published "Instruction of the Prime Minister on Some Tasks Regarding Protestantism," and on March 1, 2005 the government published the "Government Decree on Guidance for Implementation of a Number of Articles of the Ordinance on Belief and Religion."[4]

Vietnam also released forty-five prisoners of conscience in 2005 and 2006 while making it easier for churches legally to register, meet, and worship in the Central and Northwest Highlands. Vietnam also hosted the first conference in Southeast Asian history on religion and the rule of law in Hanoi in September 2006. This conference featured a comparative discussion and analysis of different approaches to the relationship between religion and state. (Its sequel in 2007 deepened the discussion, laying a framework for an eventual law on religious freedom.)

In November of 2006, after President Bush's state visit to Hanoi (while Vietnam was hosting the Asia-Pacific Economic Cooperation forum), the United States lifted the CPC designation. In December, the United States granted Vietnam PNTR and fully supported Vietnam's desire to join the WTO (which it did in January 2007).

IGE Engagement—Getting Started

IGE practices what it calls "relational diplomacy," which emphasizes patient cultivation of respectful relationships and practical agreements to work toward religious freedom in ways that are consistent with the local culture and rule of law. IGE likes to say that its job is to be a friend to the issue of religious freedom, a friend to the government of the particular country it is engaging, and a friend to the U.S. government—fashioning a win-win-win solution. In this sense, IGE practices a "Track 1.5" form of relational diplomacy. If "Track 1" diplomacy is government-to-government relations, and "Track 2" diplomacy is people-to-people, IGE operates in the middle.

In May of 2004, IGE hosted a senior leader from Vietnam who handled religious affairs in the south. Through that visit, IGE met the Vietnamese embassy staff. At the end of that experience, a senior Vietnamese diplomat remarked that IGE staff were the first Americans he had ever met who did not immediately "give me a list and tell me what to do."[5] He confided that not all Vietnamese communists were atheists and that many worshipped their ancestors. A relationship was born.

In October 2004—just after the CPC designation by the U.S. government—IGE's president Chris Seiple flew to Hanoi from Beijing, where he had just attended a conference on religion and the rule of law. He met with various Vietnamese leaders, from the Ministry of Foreign Affairs, the National Parliament, and the Vietnamese Academy of Social Sciences. After some frank discussions, they agreed that Seiple could return and visit the Central Highlands and also agreed on the possibility of doing a conference together on religion and the rule of law.

The government's top priority at the time was social stability. For that, it needed jobs and a continuing increase in living standards. Outside relations, especially with the United States, were thus paramount. The government very much wanted Permanent Normal Trade Relations with the U.S. to be approved by Congress the following year, and they were hoping to mark the tenth anniversary of normalized U.S.-Vietnamese diplomatic relations with a U.S. visit by the prime minister. They were seeking to join the WTO. They had joined the Asia-Pacific Economic Forum in 1998 and would host the APEC summit in late 2006. In early 2006, the Communist Party Congress, which meets once every five years, would convene to celebrate and reconsider the twentieth anniversary of *doi moi* ("renovation," the Vietnamese *perestroika* that has slowly opened up the economy).

The common link among these trends and aspirations was the rule of law—that is, using laws instead of communist-style regulations to govern. There needed to be rule of law if there was to be the kind of economic advancement needed to produce jobs, to get normal trade relations with the U.S., to continue *doi moi*, to host a successful APEC summit, and most importantly, to join the WTO. In short, they needed international legitimacy if they were to achieve internal progress and stability. These conditions were conducive for IGE to make diplomatic inroads, because from the beginning it had articulated its agenda for religious freedom in terms of a rule-of-law progression that served the long-term self-interest of Vietnam.

IGE Engagement—Deepening the Relationship

In June of 2005, Seiple visited Hanoi again and then flew to Dak Lak and Gia Lai provinces in the Central Highlands, where he met with provincial governors and other officials, as well as Protestant pastors who had suffered persecution in the past. This was the only visit to the Central Highlands by a Western NGO since the September 2004 CPC designation, and thus it positioned IGE as the only voice equipped to compare that on-the-ground reality with the stereotypes of Vietnam back in the United States.

From this trip emerged a commitment to sign a transparent and public agreement about how IGE would work in Vietnam going forward. The agreement was signed by IGE and the General-Secretary of the Vietnam-USA Society (VUS), a government-organized entity that was a member of the Vietnam Union of Friendship Organizations (an organization with cabinet-level status that had responsibility for Vietnamese civil society through its fifty-one member organizations).

Since the agreement was unprecedented, and because NGOs do not sign agreements with governments—the agreement was called a "Letter of Intent," or "LOI." The LOI placed religious freedom in the larger context of the bilateral relations between the United States and Vietnam, and in the larger context of people-to-people initiatives:

> VUS and IGE agree to cooperate in facilitating people-to-people diplomacy, through promoting experts' dialogues and exchange in all fields—e.g.,

social, economic, political, cultural, etc., including religious freedom and human rights.

Principles of Cooperation

We will work together through consensus, mutually respecting:

- One another's cultural and historical context
- The rule of law and each country's legal system
- The need for timely consultation.[6]

Furthermore, the LOI called for three confidence-building steps to deepen trust. The first step took place from February 24 to March 4, 2006, when IGE hosted a delegation of Vietnamese religious and government leaders in Washington. For the first time in Vietnam's diplomatic history, the Vietnamese government allowed an outside party, IGE, to select the religious representatives in the delegation. The group engaged in off-the-record discussions with key U.S. leaders at the State Department and the National Security Council, and on Capitol Hill about Vietnam's religious freedom situation. The delegation also participated in the first academic conference of its kind on religious freedom and U.S-Vietnam relations (cosponsored by IGE, Georgetown University, and George Washington University).

The second step took place on June 5–15, 2006, when Vietnam hosted a delegation of U.S. scholars and evangelical Protestant leaders in Vietnam. The delegation visited four provinces in Vietnam's Central and Northwest Highlands, building relationships, highlighting recent progress, and addressing ongoing problems. It was the first time that a large group of pastors from the United States had ever met their fellow pastors in Vietnam.

Meanwhile, as relationships deepened and tangible progress was made on the ground, Seiple had the opportunity to testify before the U.S. Senate Finance Committee on July 12, 2006, where he advocated lifting the CPC designation and articulated expectations the U.S. government should have as a result.[7]

> I believe that the United States should honor Vietnam's good faith effort in religious freedom, lift CPC, and then establish PNTR.
>
> These two particular actions send the strong signal that we both *respect* the efforts made thus far by the Vietnamese government to establish the rule of law (especially the protection of religious freedom), and that we *expect* the government of Vietnam to continue creating the rule-of-law structure necessary to promote religious freedom and free trade in a sustainable manner.

If such efforts do not continue at a reasonable pace, the U.S. should be ready to quickly reinstate CPC designation, possibly with sanctions.[8]

In addition, he privately and repeatedly advocated this position with the State Department and the National Security Council.

The LOI's third step took place in September 2006 when IGE co-convened with the Vietnamese Academy of Social Sciences an international conference on "Religion and the Rule of Law in Southeast Asia" in Hanoi. (Other conference cosponsors included Emory University and Brigham Young University.) This conference offered a regional forum for scholars and lawyers to discuss religion, culture, national security, and law. The conference was also attended by an IGE-sponsored delegation of American church pastors who had spent the previous week meeting with Vietnamese pastors from the country's most persecuted regions.

IGE Engagement—Establishing the Framework for the Future

At the conference's conclusion, IGE signed a formal Memorandum of Understanding (MOU) with VUS further to promote religious freedom together. This MOU established an annual conference series on religion and rule of law in Southeast Asia, partnerships between Vietnamese and American communities to promote socioeconomic development, exchanges of analysis on religious discrimination reports, and dialogue between governmental and religious representatives on Vietnam's legal framework for religious freedom.

Since these three steps, IGE has deepened and expanded its relationship with Vietnam. For example, in June 2007, Vietnam's President Nguyen Minh Triet made his landmark visit to the United States, the first by a Vietnamese head of state since 1975. IGE and a small group of religious leaders met with President Triet in Washington, D.C., providing a rare opportunity to speak openly with the president about issues of religious freedom. (IGE was the only NGO to meet with President Triet during his thirty-six hours in D.C.)

In November 2007, the second annual conference on religion and the rule of law took place in Hanoi. At the conclusion of the conference, IGE signed a protocol (or subagreement) that provides guidance for further implementing the socioeconomic development work of Glocal Ventures, Inc. (GVI)—a church-based development NGO of Northwood Church in Dallas, Texas, that has been operating in the northwest region of Vietnam for over ten years.[9]

During this same trip, IGE and its delegation deepened the top-down dialogue on religious freedom through meetings with President Triet, the National Assembly, the Ministry of Foreign Affairs, the Ministry of Public Security, and the Committee on Religious Affairs. The delegation also traveled to Lao Cai province in the northwest, where it met with registered and unregistered church leaders as well as government leaders at the commune, district, and provincial levels.

In early December 2007, Seiple again testified before Congress, this time before the House of Representatives, about why the United States should grant normal trade relations with Vietnam. In June 2008, IGE helped organize the prime minister's visit to Washington, D.C., and in October 2008 IGE traveled to the Central Highlands again to celebrate publicly the sixty-fifth anniversary of the Protestant church in Gia Lai Province.

CONCLUSION

As was noted in chapter 9,

> [NGOs] maintain a significant amount of autonomy in the strategies and methodologies they employ to advocate for religious freedom, unconstrained by many of the political and bureaucratic limitations of national or international bodies. This autonomy allows them to speak more frankly, act more quickly, and innovate more freely than can international bodies and governments.

The experience of IGE in engaging Vietnam from 2004 to 2008 provides real-world illustrations of how these dynamics can operate. To be sure, the sticks and carrots that were used by government entities to try to influence Vietnam were important. Neither governmental nor nongovernmental approaches ever operate in isolation. In this case, synergies developed that created opportunities for IGE to help harness Vietnam's enlightened self-interest on behalf of religious freedom progress. Further, IGE's transparent faith-based identity, which could have been a liability in dealing with Communist officials in Vietnam, proved not to be an obstacle because IGE engaged via relational, "Track 1.5" diplomacy that engendered trust and respect.

12

CONCLUSION

This guidebook has been written by practitioners working in the field of international religious freedom advocacy. They represent the variety of opportunities available to would-be advocates, from drafting press releases for a small NGO to lobbying at the highest levels of international power. The book has covered the work of international bodies, U.S. government entities, and NGOs as they work together to advance religious freedom around the world.

But in reality, religious freedom advocacy is rarely as simple as carrying out the mission of an NGO, or utilizing a complaint mechanism of the UN, or lobbying a congressional representative. Though all of these actions are important, none can occur in isolation, and none can guarantee that a repressive government will enact long-term, sustainable change in its religion policies. To see that kind of change occur, the mechanisms described must be used in concert with one another over a period of time, by advocates who are creative, innovative, committed, and sensitive to the subtleties of international affairs. Timing of advocacy actions is important, ideally coinciding with momentum already in place in foreign governments. To meet these conditions, advocates must not only be earnest but also well informed and able to contextualize and empathize. They must understand not only how a government restricts religious freedom but also why. In today's world of religiously motivated terror, shifting economic power, and unprecedented movement of ideas, people, and goods, the reasons for repression are varied and complex, as are their solutions.

This trend will not change in the near future, as religiously based conflicts continue to arise. In these situations, religious freedom abuses often go beyond individual rights, as the repression of a religious community or the forceful application of religious dogma onto a minority group can transform a religious dispute into a larger political conflict and lead to widespread destabilization. As sociologist Peter L. Berger wrote in *The Desecularization of the World: Resurgent Religion and World Politics,* "the assumption we live in a secularized world is false.... The world today is as furiously religious as it ever was." Consequently, religious persecution against believers and nonbelievers alike will be a recurring problem in the twenty-first century.

Examples of these complexities abound, as this text has already shown in the case studies for Turkmenistan and Vietnam. Other examples arise from around the world:

- Western European countries, traditionally among the freest in the world, are violating religious freedom as they deal with an influx of Muslim immigrants. Some citizens and policymakers see these immigrants as a threat not only to national identity but potentially to national security, making displays of religiosity (such as the headscarf for Muslim women) extremely provocative. Countries' commitments to freedom are being tested in new ways, resulting in laws banning religious garments or inflammatory religious rhetoric.

- China has a contentious history with the majority-Muslim population of its western province of Xinjiang. Most Xinjiang Muslims belong to minority ethnic groups, such as Hui, Uighur, Tajik, and Kazakh. The province is home to a separatist movement that wants independence from China and has resorted to terrorist tactics in the past. The region also borders Central Asian states with their own terrorist networks, and Chinese authorities fear the influx of radical groups and ideologies across its borders. Stability in this region is not only important to combat the threat of terror and secession, but also to secure access to China's oil-rich western neighbors, a high priority in China's growing, energy-hungry economy. Even if the central government loosened its grip on Xinjiang's Muslims, the region is so remote and undeveloped that policies would still be logistically difficult to implement, and local officials' biases dictate local politics, raising the question of how policies would exacerbate existing tensions.

- Pakistan's North West Frontier Province (NWFP) is a study in contradictions. Its population is overwhelmingly conservative Muslim; it borders Afghanistan and Pakistan's lawless tribal areas; it is the birthplace of the Taliban and al Qaeda and is believed to be the hiding place of Osama bin Laden; and until recently it was governed by a conservative Islamist political party. Despite these conditions, the region has a history of religious tolerance with few incidents of violence against religious minorities. Even under Islamist rule, Christian minorities were protected, new churches built, and interfaith dialogues hosted. However, the region's religious minorities face a deeper, more subtle discrimination in the form of economic and educational disempowerment. Advocates' efforts to improve religious minorities' conditions are hindered by inhospitable terrain, depressed economic conditions, strong anti-Western sentiment, security risks, and the region's importance in the global war against terrorists.

In the examples above, considerations of security, economy, and identity seem to clash with the ideal of religious freedom, and one would encounter similarly complex motivations behind repressive policies in other repressive countries. Advocates must therefore act carefully and respectfully, understanding countries' concerns while subtly introducing alternative policies that better help them achieve their goals while protecting religious freedom. This work is the challenge that faces religious freedom advocates in a complex and changing world.

Appendix I

ACRONYMS

AU	African Union
ACHPR	African Commission on Human and Peoples' Rights (AU)
CECC	Congressional-Executive Commission on China (U.S.)
CFSP	Common Foreign and Security Policy (EU)
CoE	Council of Europe
COREPER	Committee of Permanent Representatives (EU)
CPC	Country of Particular Concern (U.S.)
DG	Directorate-General (EU)
DG RELEX	Directorate-General for the External Relations (EU)
DRL	State Department Bureau of Democracy, Human Rights, and Labor
ECOSOC	Economic and Social Council (UN)
ECRI	European Commission against Racism and Intolerance (CoE)
EIDHR	European Instrument for Democracy and Human Rights (EU)
ENP	European Neighbourhood Policy (EU)
EU	European Union
EUMC	European Monitoring Centre on Racism and Xenophobia (EU)
FRA	Agency for Fundamental Rights (EU)
HCNM	Office of the OSCE High Commissioner on National Minorities
HDIM	Human Dimension Implementation Meeting (OSCE)

HFAC	House Foreign Affairs Committee (U.S.)
IACHR	Inter-American Commission on Human Rights (OAS)
ICCPR	International Covenant on Civil and Political Rights (UN)
ICESCR	International Covenant on Economic, Social and Cultural Rights (UN)
IRF	State Department Office for International Religious Freedom (U.S.)
IRFA	International Religious Freedom Act (U.S.)
MEPs	Members of the European Parliament (EU)
NGO	Nongovernmental Organization
OAS	Organization of American States
OAU	Organization of African Unity
ODIHR	Office for Democratic Institutions and Human Rights (OSCE)
OHCHR	Office of the High Commissioner for Human Rights (UN)
OSCE	Organization for Security and Cooperation in Europe
PACE	Parliamentary Assembly of the Council of Europe
PCA	Partnership and Cooperation Agreement (EU)
RAXEN	European Information Network on Racism and Xenophobia (CoE)
SAP	Stabilization and Association Process (EU)
SFRC	Senate Foreign Relations Committee (U.S.)
SHDM	Supplementary Human Dimension Meetings (OSCE)
UDHR	Universal Declaration of Human Rights (UN)
UN	United Nations
USCIRF	U.S. Commission on International Religious Freedom

Appendix II

INDIVIDUAL COMPLAINTS AND MODEL QUESTIONNAIRE OF THE UNITED NATIONS SPECIAL RAPPORTEUR ON FREEDOM OF RELIGION OR BELIEF

The Human Rights Council and the General Assembly have encouraged the continuing efforts in all parts of the world of the Special Rapporteur to examine incidents and governmental actions that are incompatible with the provisions of the Declaration on the Elimination of All Forms of Intolerance and of Discrimination Based on Religion or Belief and to recommend remedial measures as appropriate (Human Rights Council resolution 6/37 and General Assembly resolution 61/161).

Therefore, the Special Rapporteur would like to reiterate her invitation to governmental and non-governmental organizations, religious or belief communities as well as individuals to submit any reliable information they may possess with regard to potential or actual violations of the right to freedom of religion or belief. Subsequently, the Special Rapporteur may raise her concerns about the incidents reported and request Governments to make observations and comments on the matter. Please note that, as a general rule, the existence and content of both urgent appeals and letters of allegation remain confidential until a summary of such communications and the replies received from the State concerned are included in the Special Rapporteur's report to the Human Rights Council.

In its resolution 6/37 of 14 December 2007, the Human Rights Council urged States:

> "(a) To ensure that their constitutional and legislative systems provide adequate and effective guarantees of freedom of thought, conscience, religion and belief to all without distinction, inter alia, by the provision of effective remedies in cases where the right to freedom of thought, conscience, religion or belief, or the right to practice freely one's religion, including the right to change one's religion or belief, is violated;

(b) To design and implement policies whereby education systems promote principles of tolerance and respect for others and cultural diversity and the freedom of religion or belief;

(c) To ensure that appropriate measures are taken in order to adequately and effectively guarantee the freedom of religion or belief of women as well as individuals from other vulnerable groups, including persons deprived of their liberty, refugees, children, persons belonging to minorities and migrants;

(d) To ensure that any advocacy of religious hatred that constitutes incitement to discrimination, hostility or violence is prohibited by law;

(e) To exert the utmost efforts, in accordance with their national legislation and in conformity with international human rights and humanitarian law, to ensure that religious places, sites, shrines and symbols are fully respected and protected and to take additional measures in cases where they are vulnerable to desecration or destruction;

(f) To review, whenever relevant, existing registration practices in order to ensure the right of all persons to manifest their religion or belief, alone or in community with others and in public or in private;

(g) To ensure, in particular, the right of all persons to worship or assemble in connection with a religion or belief and to establish and maintain places for these purposes and the right of all persons to write, issue and disseminate relevant publications in these areas;

(h) To ensure that, in accordance with appropriate national legislation and in conformity with international human rights law, the freedom of all persons and members of groups to establish and maintain religious, charitable or humanitarian institutions is fully respected and protected;

(i) To ensure that, on account of religion or belief or the expression or manifestation of religion or belief, no one within their jurisdiction is deprived of the right to life, liberty or security of person, subjected to torture or arbitrary arrest or detention, or denied the rights to work, education or adequate housing, as well as the right to seek asylum, and to bring to justice all perpetrators of violations of these rights;

(j) To ensure that all public officials and civil servants, including members of law enforcement bodies, the military and educators, in the course of their official duties, respect different religions and beliefs and do not discriminate on the grounds of religion or belief, and that all necessary and appropriate education or training is provided;

(k) To step up efforts in implementing the Declaration on the Elimination of All Forms of Intolerance and of Discrimination based on Religion or Belief;

(l) To take all necessary and appropriate action, in conformity with international standards of human rights, to combat hatred, intolerance and acts of violence, intimidation and coercion motivated by intolerance based on religion or belief, as well as incitement to hostility and violence, with particular regard to religious minorities, and devoting particular attention to practices that violate the human rights of women and discriminate against women, including in the exercise of their right to freedom of thought, conscience, religion or belief;

(m) To promote and encourage, through education and other means, including regional or international cultural exchanges, understanding, tolerance and respect in all matters relating to freedom of religion or belief;"

In the discharge of her mandate, the Special Rapporteur has developed this model questionnaire in order to facilitate the submission of information. Although communications are also considered when they are not submitted in the form of this model questionnaire, the Special Rapporteur would be grateful for receiving information tailored to her mandate. The objective of this questionnaire is to have access to precise information on alleged violations of freedom of religion or belief. If any information contained in the questionnaire should be kept confidential please mark "CONFIDENTIAL" beside the relevant entry. Please do not hesitate to attach additional sheets, if the space provided is not sufficient.

Please feel free to contact the Special Rapporteur, if you have any further questions concerning the completion of this form. She has also developed a framework for communications which details the applicable international legal standards. An online digest of this framework together with pertinent excerpts of the Special Rapporteurs' reports is available at www2.ohchr.org/ english/issues/religion/standards.htm.

Model questionnaire

The questionnaire below should be filled out and sent to:

Special Rapporteur on Freedom of Religion or Belief

c/o Office of the High Commissioner for Human Rights
United Nations at Geneva
8-14 Avenue de la Paix
CH-1211 Geneva 10
Switzerland
Fax: (+41) 22 917 90 06
E-mail: freedomofreligion@ohchr.org or urgent-action@ohchr.org (then
please include in the subject box: Special Rapporteur on Freedom of
Religion or Belief)

---

1. GENERAL INFORMATION

- Does the incident involve an individual or a group?
- If it involves a religious or belief group please state the number of people involved and the denomination of the group:
- Country(ies) in which the incident took place:
- Nationality(ies) of the victim(s):
- Does domestic law require (re-)registration of religious associations and if yes, what is the current status of the group in question?

2. IDENTITY OF THE PERSONS CONCERNED

Note: if more than one person is concerned, please attach relevant information on each person separately.

- Family name:
- First name:
- Denomination of his/her religion or belief:
- Place of residence or origin:
- Age:
- Sex:
- Nationality(ies):

3. INFORMATION REGARDING THE ALLEGED VIOLATION

- Date and time (approximate, if exact date is not known):
- Place (location and country/countries):
- Please provide a detailed description of the incident in which the alleged violation occurred, and respectively the nature of the governmental action:
- Please provide any indication which might lead to the conclusion that the victim(s) has been targeted because of his/her religion or belief:
- Identification of the alleged perpetrator(s), name(s) if known and/or function, suspected motive:
- Are the alleged perpetrator(s) known to the victim?
- Are State agents or non-State actors believed to be involved in the alleged violation?
- If the alleged perpetrators are believed to be State agents, please specify (police, military, security services agents, unit to which they belong, rank and functions, etc.), and indicate why they are believed to be responsible; be as precise as possible.
- If identification as State agents is not possible, why do you believe that the Government authorities or related persons are involved in the incident?
- If there are witnesses to the incident, indicate their names, age, relationship and contact address. If they wish to remain anonymous, indicate if they are relatives, passers-by, etc.; if there is evidence, please specify.

4. STEPS TAKEN BY THE VICTIM, HIS/HER FAMILY OR ANYONE ELSE ON HIS/HER BEHALF?

- Please indicate if complaints have been filed, when, by whom, and before which State authorities or competent bodies (i.e. police, prosecutor, court):
- Were any other steps taken?
- Steps taken by the authorities:
- Indicate whether or not, to your knowledge, there have been investigations by the State authorities; if so, what kind of investigations? Please indicate progress and status of these investigations as well as which other measures have been taken?
- In case of complaints submitted by the victim or its family, how have those authorities or other competent bodies dealt with them? What has been the outcome of those proceedings?

5. IDENTITY OF THE PERSON OR INSTITUTION SUBMITTING THIS FORM

- Family name:
- First name:
- Contact number or address (please indicate country and area code):
- Fax:
- Telephone:
- Email:
- Status: individual, group, non-governmental organization, religious or belief group, inter-governmental agency, Government. Please specify:
- Do you act with knowledge and/or on behalf of the victim(s)?
- Please state whether you want your identity to be kept confidential:

Date you are submitting this form:

_____

Signature of the author

Appendix III

GUIDELINES FOR THE SUBMISSION OF INFORMATION TO THE SPECIAL RAPPORTEUR ON THE PROMOTION AND PROTECTION OF THE RIGHT TO FREEDOM OF OPINION AND EXPRESSION

In order for the Special Rapporteur to be able to take action regarding a communication on a case or incident, the following information, as a minimum, must be received.

1. ALLEGATION REGARDING A PERSON OR PERSONS:

- As detailed a description of the alleged violation as possible, including date, location and circumstances of the event;
- Name, age, gender, ethnic background (if relevant), profession;
- Views, affiliations, past or present participation in political, social, ethnic or labour group/activity;
- Information on other specific activities relating to the alleged violation.

2. ALLEGATION REGARDING A MEDIUM OF COMMUNICATION:

- As detailed a description of the alleged infringement on the right as possible, including date, location and circumstances of the event;
- The nature of the medium affected (e.g. newspapers, independent radio); including circulation and frequency of publication or broadcasting, public performances, etc.;
- Political orientation of the medium (if relevant).

3. INFORMATION REGARDING THE ALLEGED PERPETRATORS:

- Name, State affiliation (e.g. military, police) and reasons why they are considered responsible;

- For non-State actors, description of how they relate to the State (e.g. cooperation with or support by State security forces);
- If applicable, State encouragement or tolerance of activities of non-State actors, whether groups or individuals, including threats or use of violence and harassment against individuals exercising their right to freedom of opinion and expression, including the right to seek, receive and impart information.

4. INFORMATION RELATED TO STATE ACTIONS:

- If the incident involves restrictions on a medium (e.g. censorship, closure of a news organ, banning of a book, etc.); the identity of the authority involved (individual and/or ministry and/or department), the legal statute invoked, and steps taken to seek domestic remedy;
- If the incident involves arrest of an individual or individuals, the identity of the authority involved (individual and/or ministry and/or department), the legal statute invoked, location of detention if known, information on provision of access to legal counsel and family members, steps taken to seek domestic remedy or clarification of person's situation and status;
- If applicable, information on whether or not an investigation has taken place and, if so, by what ministry or department of the Government and the status of the investigation at the time of submission of the allegation, including whether or not the investigation has resulted in indictments.

5. INFORMATION ON THE SOURCE OF THE COMMUNICATIONS:

- Name and full address;
- Telephone and fax numbers and e-mail address (if possible);
- Name, address, phone/fax numbers and e-mail address (if applicable) of person or organization submitting the allegation.

Note: In addition to the information requested above, the Special Rapporteur welcomes any additional comments or background notes that are considered relevant to the case or incident.

FOLLOW-UP

The Special Rapporteur attaches great importance to being kept informed of the current status of cases and thus very much welcomes updates of previously reported cases and information. This includes both negative and positive developments, including the release of persons detained for exercising their rights to freedom of opinion and expression and to seek, receive and impart information, or the adoption of new laws or policies or changes to existing ones that have a positive impact on the realization of the rights to freedom of opinion and expression and information.

ROOT CAUSES

In order to carry out his work regarding the root causes of violations, which is of particular importance to the Special Rapporteur, he is very much interested in receiving information on and/or texts of draft laws relating to or affecting the rights to freedom of opinion and expression and to seek, receive and impart information. The Special Rapporteur is also interested in laws or government policies relating to electronic media, including the Internet, as well as the impact of the availability of new information technologies on the right to freedom of opinion and expression.

COMMUNICATIONS

Where requested or considered necessary by the Special Rapporteur, information on the source of the allegations will be treated as confidential. Any information falling within this description of the mandate of the Special Rapporteur should be sent to:

Special Rapporteur on the Promotion and Protection of the Right to Freedom of Opinion and Expression
c/o Office of the High Commissioner for Human Rights
United Nations Office at Geneva
1211 Geneva 10
Switzerland
Fax: +41 22 917 9003
e-mail: urgent-action@ohchr.org

Appendix IV

MODEL COMPLAINT FORM

For communications under:

- Optional Protocol to the International Covenant on Civil and Political Rights
- Convention against Torture, or
- International Convention on the Elimination of Racial Discrimination

Please indicate which of the above procedures you are invoking:
Date:

I. INFORMATION ON THE COMPLAINANT:

- Name:
- First name(s):
- Nationality:
- Date and place of birth:
- Address for correspondence on this complaint:
- Submitting the communication:
- On the author's own behalf:
- On behalf of another person:

[If the complaint is being submitted on behalf of another person:]
Please provide the following personal details of that other person:

- Name:
- First name(s):
- Nationality:
- Date and place of birth:
- Address or current whereabouts:

- If you are acting with the knowledge and consent of that person, please provide that person's authorization for you to bring this complaint:
  Or
- If you are not so authorized, please explain the nature of your relationship with that person:
- and detail why you consider it appropriate to bring this complaint on his or her behalf:

II. STATE CONCERNED/ARTICLES VIOLATED

- Name of the State that is either a party to the Optional Protocol (in the case of a complaint to the Human Rights Committee) or has made the relevant declaration (in the case of complaints to the Committee against Torture or the Committee on the Elimination of Racial Discrimination):
- Articles of the Covenant or Convention alleged to have been violated:

III. EXHAUSTION OF DOMESTIC REMEDIES/APPLICATION TO OTHER INTERNATIONAL PROCEDURES

- Steps taken by or on behalf of the alleged victims to obtain redress within the State concerned for the alleged violation – detail which procedures have been pursued, including recourse to the courts and other public authorities, which claims you have made, at which times, and with which outcomes:
- If you have not exhausted these remedies on the basis that their application would be unduly prolonged, that they would not be effective, that they are not available to you, or for any other reason, please explain your reasons in detail:
- Have you submitted the same matter for examination under another procedure of international investigation or settlement (e.g. the Inter-American Commission on Human Rights, the European Court of Human Rights, or the African Commission on Human and Peoples' Rights)?
- If so, detail which procedure(s) have been, or are being, pursued, which claims you have made, at which times, and with which outcomes:

IV. FACTS OF THE COMPLAINT

- Detail, in chronological order, the facts and circumstances of the alleged violations. Include all matters which may be relevant to the assessment and consideration of your particular case. Please explain how you consider that the facts and circumstances described violate your rights.

Author's signature: _____

[The blanks under the various sections of this model communication simply indicate where your responses are required. You should take as much space as you need to set out your responses.]

V. CHECKLIST OF SUPPORTING DOCUMENTATION (COPIES, NOT ORIGINALS, TO BE ENCLOSED WITH YOUR COMPLAINT):

- Written authorization to act (if you are bringing the complaint on behalf of another person and are not otherwise justifying the absence of specific authorization):
- Decisions of domestic courts and authorities on your claim (a copy of the relevant national legislation is also helpful):
- Complaints to and decisions by any other procedure of international investigation or settlement:
- Any documentation or other corroborating evidence you possess that substantiates your description in Part IV of the facts of your claim and/ or your argument that the facts described amount to a violation of your rights:

If you do not enclose this information and it needs to be sought specifically from you, or if accompanying documentation is not provided in the working languages of the Secretariat, the consideration of your complaint may be delayed.

Appendix V

Contact Information for NGOs

Globally Focused Non-Governmental Organizations

Advocates International
http://www.advocatesinternational.org/
8001 Braddock Road, Suite 300
Springfield, VA 22151-2110
Tel: (703) 894-1084
Fax: (703) 894-1074
info@advocatesinternational.org

Amnesty International
http://www.amnesty.org/
http://www.amnestyusa.org/
Amnesty International USA
5 Penn Plaza
New York, NY 10001
Tel: (212) 807-8400
Fax: (212) 627-1451
aimember@aiusa.org

Barnabas Fund
http://www.barnabasfund.org/
9 Priory Row
Coventry
CV1 5EX

United Kingdom
Tel: +44 24 7623 1923
Fax: +44 24 7683 4718
info@barnabasfund.org

Becket Fund for Religious Liberty
http://www.becketfund.org/
1350 Connecticut Ave. N.W.
Suite 605
Washington, D.C. 20036
Tel: (202) 955-0095
Fax: (202) 955-0090

Christian Freedom International
http://www.christianfreedom.org/
215 Ashmun Street
Sault Ste. Marie, MI 49783
Tel: (800) 323-2273
info@christianfreedom.org

Christian Solidarity International
http://www.csi-int.org/
870 Hampshire Avenue, Suite T
Westlake Village, CA 91361
csi@csi-usa.org
Phone: (888) 676-5700
Fax: (805) 777-7508

Christian Solidarity Worldwide
http://www.csw.org.uk/
P.O. Box 99, New Malden
Surrey KT3 3YF
United Kingdom
Tel: +44 845 456 5464
Fax: +44 208 942 8802
admin@csw.org.uk

Center on Faith and International Affairs
http://www.globalengage.org/research
Institute for Global Engagement
P.O. Box 12205
Arlington, VA 22219-2205
Tel: (703) 527-3100
info@cfia.org

Evangelicals for Human Rights
http://www.evangelicalsfor
humanrights.org
P.O. Box 941338
Atlanta, GA 31141-1338
Tel: (770) 936-9835
ehr@nrcat.org

Hudson Institute—Center for Religious Freedom
http://crf.hudson.org/
1015 15th Street, N.W.
6th Floor
Washington, D.C. 20005
Tel: (202) 974-2400
Fax: (202) 974-2410
info@hudson.org

Human Rights Watch
http://www.hrw.org/
350 Fifth Avenue, 34th Floor
New York, NY 10118-3299
Tel: (212) 290-4700
Fax: (212) 736-1300
hrwnyc@hrw.org

Human Rights First
http://www.humanrightsfirst.org/
333 Seventh Avenue, 13th Floor
New York, NY 10001-5108
Tel: (212) 845-5200
Fax: (212) 845-5299
feedback@humanrightsfirst.org

Institute for Global Engagement
http://www.globalengage.org
P.O. Box 12205
Arlington, VA 22219-2205
Tel: (703) 527-3100
Fax: (703) 527-5965
info@globalengage.org

Institute on Religion and Public Policy
http://www.religionandpolicy.org
1620 I Street, N.W.
Suite LL10
Washington, D.C. 20006
Tel: (202) 835-8760
Fax: (202) 835-8764
irpp@religionandpolicy.org

International Center for Religion and Diplomacy
http://www.icrd.org/
1156 Fifteenth St., N.W., Suite 910
Washington, D.C. 20005
Tel: (202) 331-9404
Fax: (202) 872-9137

International Christian Concern
http://www.persecution.org
2020 Pennsylvania Ave. N.W.
Box 941
Washington, D.C. 20006-1846
Tel: 1-800-ICC-5441
Fax: (301) 989-1709
icc@persecution.org

International Justice Mission
http://www.ijm.org
P.O. Box 58147
Washington, D.C. 20037-8147
Tel: (703) 465-5495
Fax: (703) 465-5499
contact@ijm.org

International League for Human Rights
http://www.ilhr.org/
352 Seventh Avenue,
Suite 1234
New York, NY 10001
Tel: (212) 661-0480
Fax: (212) 661-0416
info@ilhr.org

International Religious Freedom Watch
http://www.international
religiousfreedomwatch.org/
73 Patchwork Lane
Fishersville, VA 22939
lauzzell@aol.com

International Religious Liberty Association
http://www.irla.org/
12501 Old Columbia Pike
Silver Spring, MD 20904
Tel: (301) 680-6686
Fax: (301) 680-6695
info@irla.org

Jacob Blaustein Institute for the Advancement of Human Rights
http://www.ajc.org/humanrights
American Jewish Committee
P.O. Box 705
New York, NY 10150
Tel: (212) 751-4000
Fax: (212) 891-1450

Jubilee Campaign USA
http://www.jubileecampaign.org/
9689-C Main Street
Fairfax, VA 22031
Tel: (703) 503-0791
Fax: (703) 503-0792
jubilee@jubileecampaign.org

**Karamah: Muslim Women Lawyers
for Human Rights**
http://www.karamah.org/
Washington, D.C.
Tel: (202) 234-7302
Fax: (202) 234-7304
karamah@karamah.org

Open Doors
http://www.opendoorsusa.org
P.O. Box 27001
Santa Ana, CA 92799
Tel: (888) 5-BIBLE-5
Fax: (949) 752-6442
usa@opendoors.org

Physicians for Human Rights
http://physiciansforhuman
rights.org/
1156 15th Street, N.W.
Suite 1001
Washington, D.C. 20005
Tel: (202) 728-5335
Fax: (202) 728-3053

Voice of the Martyrs
http://www.persecution.com
P.O. Box 443
Bartlesville, OK 74005
Phone: (877) 337-0302
Fax: (918) 338-0189

**World Evangelical Alliance—
Religious Liberty Commission**
http://www.worldevangelicals.org/
commissions/rlc/
No. 32, Ebenezer Place
Dehiwala 10350
Sri Lanka

wearlc@sltnet.lk
Tel: +94 777 302699
Fax: +94 112 718823

*Europe-Focused Non-
governmental Organizations*

**Christian Solidarity Worldwide—
EU Office**
http://www.csw.org.uk/
P.O. Box 90
B-1040 Brussels 4
Belgium
Tel: +32 2 742 2082
Fax: +32 2 742 2894
csw-eu@csw.org.uk

European Evangelical Alliance
http://www.europeanea.org/
186 Kennington Park Road
London SE11 4BT
United Kingdom
Tel: +44 20 7582 7276
Fax: +44 20 7582 2043
info@europeanea.org

**European Platform on Religious
Intolerance and Discrimination
(EPRID)**
Brussels, Belgium
eprid.office@gmail.com

Forum 18 News Service
http://www.forum18.org
Postboks 6603
Rodeløkka
N-0502 Oslo
Norway
f18news@editor.forum18.org

Human Rights and Democracy Network (HRDN)
http://www.act4europe.org/code/en/about.asp?Page=41
Brussels, Belgium
lscurfield@qcea.org
nrougy@clubmadrid.org

Human Rights Without Frontiers
http://www.hrwf.net/
11 Avenue Winston Churchill
1180 Brussels
Belgium
Tel: +32 2 34 56 145
Fax: +32 2 343 74 91
info@hrwf.net

International Association for Religious Freedom
http://www.iarf.net/
Essex Hall, 1-6 Essex Street
London WC2R 3HY
United Kingdom
Tel: +81 675 035 602
hq@iarf.net

International Federation of Human Rights Leagues—FIDH
http://www.fidh.org/
17, passage de la main d'or
75011 Paris
France
Fax: +33 1 43 55 18 80

Moscow Helsinki Commission
http://www.mhg.ru/
Bolshoy Golovin per.d. 22, str. 1
103045 Moscow
Russia
Tel: +7 495 607 6069, 607 0769, 607 15 72
Fax: +7 495 207 6065
mhg-main@online.ptt.ru

Norwegian Centre for Human Rights
http://www.humanrights.uio.no/
Norwegian Center for Human Rights, University of Oslo
P.O. Box 6706, St. Olavs plass
0130 Oslo
Norway
Tel: +47 22 84 20 01
Fax: +47 22 84 20 02
info@nchr.uio.no

The Oslo Coalition on Freedom of Religion or Belief
http://www.oslocoalition.org/
P.O. Box 6706 St. Olavs plass
No-0130 Oslo
Norway
Tel: +47 22 84 20 47
Fax: +47 22 84 20 02
office@oslocoalition.org

World Vision International— Middle East and Eastern Europe
http://meero.worldvision.org/
P.O. Box 28979
2084 Nicosia
Cyprus
Tel: +357 22 870 277
Fax: +357 22 870 204
maia_woodward@wvi.org

Asia-Focused Nongovernmental
Organizations

All India Christian Council
http://www.indianchristians.in/
P. O. Box 2174
Secunderabad
Andhra Pradesh 500003
India
Tel: +91 40 27868907
Fax: +91 40 27868908

Almaty Helsinki Committee
http://www.humanrights.kz/
Koktem-1, 29, apt. 17
480070 Almaty
Kazakhstan
Tel: +7 3272 69 50 65
Fax: +7 3272 69 50 61
office-ahc@nursat.kz

Asian Human Rights Commission
http://www.ahrchk.net/index.php
19/F, Go-Up Commercial Building,
998 Canton Road, Kowloon
Hong Kong, China
Tel: +852 2698 6339
Fax: +852 2698 6367
ahrc@ahrc.asia

Catholic Bishops' Conference of India
http://www.cbcisite.com/
1, Ashok Place, New Delhi—110 001
India
Tel/Fax: +91 11 2334 8423
cbcimo@bol.net.in

China Aid
http://www.ChinaAid.org
P. O. Box 8513
Midland, TX 79708
Tel: (432) 689-6985
Fax: (432) 686-8355

Christian Solidarity Worldwide
http://www.csw.org.uk/
P.O. Box 99, New Malden
Surrey KT3 3YF
United Kingdom
Tel: +44 845 456 5464
Fax: +44 208 942 8802
admin@csw.org.uk

Commonwealth Human Rights Initiative
http://www.humanrightsinitiative.org/
B-117, Second Floor, Sarvodaya Enclave
New Delhi—110 017
India
Tel: +91 11 2685 0523, 2652 8152, 2686 4678
Fax: +91 11 2686 4688
info@humanrightsinitiative.org

CHRI London Office
Institute of Commonwealth Studies
28, Russell Square
London WC1B 5DS
United Kingdom
Tel: +44 020 7 862 8857
Fax: +44 020 7 862 8820
chri@sas.ac.uk

Compass Direct News Service
http://www.compassdirect.org/
P.O. Box 27250
Santa Ana, CA 92799
Tel: (949) 862-0304
Fax: (949) 752-6536
info@compassdirect.org

Evangelical Fellowship of India
http://www.efionline.org/
805/92, Deepali Building, Nehru
Place
New Delhi 110019
India
Tel: +91 11 2643 1133
Fax: +91 11 2628 5350
mail@efionline.org

International Campaign for Tibet
http://www.savetibet.org/
1825 Jefferson Place N.W.
Washington, D.C. 20036
Tel: (202) 785-1515
Fax: (202) 785-4343
info@savetibet.org

Hindu American Foundation
http://www.hinduamerican
foundation.org/
5268G Nicholson Lane #164
Kensington, MD 20895
Tel: (301) 770-7835 /
(877) 281-2838
Fax: (301) 770-7837

Human Rights in China
http://www.hrichina.org/public/
index

350 Fifth Avenue, Suite 3311
New York, NY 10118
Tel: (212) 239-4495
Fax: (212) 239-2561
hrichina@hrichina.org

Kyrgyz Committee for Human Rights (KCHR)
http://www.kchr.org/
Jumabek Str 123
87 Bishkek
Kyrgyz Republic
Tel: +996 312 30 47 98, 30 48 35
Fax: +996 312 30 47 99
kchr@kchr.org

National Commission for Minorities
http://ncm.nic.in/
5th Floor, Lok Nayak Bhavan
Khan Market
New Delhi 110 003
India
Tel: +91 11 2461 8349
Fax: +91 11 2469 3302, 2464 2645,
2469 8410
ncm-mma@nic.in

National Human Rights Commission
http://nhrc.nic.in/
Faridkot House
Copernicus Marg
New Delhi, PIN 110001
India
Tel: +91 11 2338 4012
Fax: +91 11 2338 4863
covdnhrc@nic.in, ionhrc@nic.in

South Asia Human Rights Documentation Centre
http://www.hrdc.net/sahrdc/
B-6/6, Safdarjung Enclave Extension
New Delhi 110029
India
Tel/Fax: +91 11 2619 1120, 2619 2717, 2619 2706
hrdc_online@hotmail.com

United Sikhs
http://www.unitedsikhs.org/
426-B, Industrial Focal Point
Amritsar 143 021
Panjab, India
Tel: +91 981 8096 705
unitedsikhs-asia@unitedsikhs.org

Uyghur Human Rights Project
http://www.uhrp.org
1701 Pennsylvania Avenue, N.W.
Suite 300
Washington, D.C. 20006
Tel: (202) 349-1496
Fax: (202) 349-1491
info@uhrp.org

Working Group for an ASEAN Human Rights Mechanism
http://www.aseanhrmech.org/
Ateneo Human Rights Center
20 Rockwell Drive
Rockwell Center, 1200 Makati City
Manila, Philippines
Tel: +63 2 899 7691
Fax: +63 2 899 4342
info@aseanhrmech.org

World Vision International— Asia-Pacific
http://www.wvasiapacific.org
Bangkok Business Center Building
13th floor
29 Sukhumvit 63 (Ekamai Road)
Klongton Nua, Wattana Bangkok
Thailand
Tel: +66 2 391 6155/+66 2 381 8861
asiapacific@wvi.org

North and South America–Focused Organizations

Agua Buena Asociación de Derechos Humanos
http://www.aguabuena.org/
Apartado 366-2200
Coronado, Costa Rica
Tel/Fax: +506 280 3548

American Arab Anti-Discrimination Committee
http://www.adc.org
1732 Wisconsin Avenue, N.W.
Washington, D.C. 20007
Tel: (202) 244-2990
Fax: (202) 244-7968
legal@adc.org

Asociación Pro Derechos Humanos (APRODEH)
http://www.aprodeh.org.pe/
Jr. Pachacútec 980
Lima 11
Peru
Tel: +51 431 0482
Fax: +51 431 0477

Casa de los Derechos Humanos
http://www.apdhb.org/
Av. 6 de Agosto N° 548
La Paz, Bolivia
Tel: 2440611 / 2440624 / 2440651

Center for Justice and International Law (CEJIL)
http://www.cejil.org/

CEJIL Mesoamerica
225 metros Sur y 75 metros Este del
Centro Cultural Mexicano
Los Yoses, San José
Costa Rica
Tel: +506 280 7473/7608
Fax: +506 280 5280
mesoamerica@cejil.org

CEJIL Brasil
Franklin Roosevelt, 194 Sl. 906 cep.
20021-120 Centro
Rio de Janeiro, RJ, Brasil
Tel: +55 21 2533 1660
Fax: +55 21 2517 3280
brasil@cejil.org

CEJIL Sur
Esmeralda 517 2 A
C1007ABC
Buenos Aires, Argentina
Tel: +54 11 4328 1025
sur@cejil.org

Centro de Derechos Humanos (CDH)
http://www.cdh.uchile.cl/

Universidad de Chile
Santa María 076
Providencia, Santiago
Chile
Tel: +56 2 978 5271
Fax: +56 2 978 5366
cdh@derecho.uchile.cl

Comisionado Nacional de los Derechos Humanos de Honduras
http://www.conadeh.hn/
Colonia Florencia Norte
Boulevar Suyapa
Tegucigalpa, Honduras
Tel: +504 239 0483

Comisión Nacional de los Derechos Humanos México (CNDH)
http://www.cndh.org.mx/
Periférico Sur 3469
Col. San Jerónimo Lídice
Delegación Magdalena Contreras
C.P. 10200
Mexico
Tel: +52 55 56 81 81 25, 54 90 74 00

Comunidad de Derechos Humanos
http://www.comunidad.org.bo/
Av. Ecuador No. 2612 esquina Pedro Salazar
Piso 2, Sopocachi
La Paz, Bolivia
Tel/Fax: +591 2 411985
comunidad@comunidad.org.bo

Derechos Human Rights
http://www.derechos.org/
US Office
46 Estabrook Street
San Leandro, CA 94577
Tel: (510) 483-4005
hr@derechos.org

Equipo Nizkor
http://www.derechos.org/nizkor/
eng.html

Instituto de Derechos Humanos de la Universidad Centroamericana
http://www.uca.edu.sv/publica/
idhuca/
Final Bulevar "Los Próceres", UCA
San Salvador, El Salvador
Tel: +503 210 6600, exts. 410, 411, or 412
Fax: +503 210 6677
idhuca@idh.uca.edu.sv

Instituto de Derechos Humanos Santo Domingo
http://www.idhsd.org/
Av. 27 de Febrero No. 583
Suite 306
Los Restauradores
Santo Domingo
República Dominicana
Tel: +809 531 8181
Fax: +809 531 3332
webmaster@idhsd.org

Movimiento Ecuménico por los Derechos Humanos (MEDH)
http://www.derechos.net/medh/
Moreno 1785—1. piso
C 1093 ABG
Argentina
Tel: +54 11 4382 5957, 4381 5589
medh@arnet.com.ar

Movimento Nacional de Direitos Humanos
http://www.mndh.org.br/
Brazil
Tel: +55 61 3273 7320
mndh@mndh.org.br

Washington Office on Latin America
http://www.wola.org/
1666 Connecticut Ave., Suite 400
Washington, D.C. 20009
Tel: (202) 797-2171
Fax: (202) 797-2172

World Vision International—Latin America and Caribbean
http://www.visionmundial.org/
Apartado 133-2300
Edificio Torres del Campo
Torre 1, piso 1 Frente al Centro
Comercial El Pueblo
Barrio Tournón
San Jose, Costa Rica
Tel/Fax: +506 257 5151

Sub-Saharan Africa-Focused Non-governmental Organizations

African Centre for Democracy and Human Rights Studies
http://www.acdhrs.org/
P.O.Box 2728
Serrekunda
The Gambia
Tel: +220 446 2341
Fax: +220 446 2338
edir@acdhrs.org

All African Conference of Churches
http://www.aacc-ceta.org/
P.O. Box 14205
00800 Westalnds
Nairobi
Kenya
Tel: +254 20 444 1483
Fax: +254 20 444 3241

Comité pour le Respect des Libertés et des Droits de l'Homme en Tunisie
www.maghreb-ddh.sgdg.org
contact@maghreb-ddh.sgdg.org

Commonwealth Human Rights Initiatives
http://www.humanrightsinitiative.org/
CHRI Ghana Office
House No.9
Samora Machel Street
Accra, Ghana
Tel/Fax: +233 21 271170
chriafrica@humanrightsinitiative.org

Congolese Observatory for Human Rights
http://www.fidh.org
c/o Federation Internationale des Ligues des Droits de l'Homme
17, passage de la main d'or
75011 Paris, France
Tel: +33 1 43 55 25 18
Fax : +33 1 43 55 18 80
fidh@csi.com

Ethiopian Human Rights Council
http://www.ehrco.org/
P.O. Box 2432
Addis Ababa, Ethiopia
Tel: +25115 514489, 517704
Fax: +25115 14539
ehrco@ethionet.et

Foundation for Human Rights Initiative
http://www.fhri.or.ug/
P.O. Box 11027
Kampala, Uganda
Tel: +256 41 510498, 510263, 510267
Fax: +256 41 510498

Human Rights Institute of South Africa
http://www.hurisa.org.za/
41 De Korte Street, Braamfontein
Johannesburg
South Africa
Tel: +27 11 403 0850
Fax: +27 11 403 0855
info@hurisa.org.za

Human Rights Trust of Southern Africa
P.O. Box CY2448, Causeway
Harare
Zimbabwe
Tel: +263 4 339819, 333882
Fax: +263 4 339818

Inter African Network for Human Rights and Development (Afronet)
P.O. Box 31145, Rhodes Park
Lusaka, Zambia
Tel: +260 1 251814
Fax: +260 1 251776
afronet@zamnet.zm

Kenya Human Rights Commission
http://www.khrc.or.ke/
P.O. Box 41079-00100
Nairobi, Kenya
Tel: +254 020 3874998/9,
38746065/6
Fax: +254 020 3874997
admin@khrc.or.ke

National Society for Human Rights in Namibia
http://www.nshr.org.na/
P.O. Box 23592
Windhoek, Namibia

Tel: +264 61 236 183 / 253 447
Fax +264 61 234 286
nshr@nshr.org.na

World Vision International—Africa
http://wvafrica.org/
P.O. Box 50816
Karen Road, Off Ngong Road
Nairobi, Kenya
Tel: +254 20 883 941

Zimbabwe Human Rights Association (ZimRights)
P.O. Box 3951
Harare, Zimbabwe
Tel: +263 4 707278, 705898
Fax +263 4 707277
dmachingura@zimrights.co.zw

Middle East- and North Africa-Focused Nongovernmental Organizations

American Middle-Eastern Christian Association
http://www.middleeasternchristian.org/
1407 Foothill Boulevard #235
LaVerne, California 91750
Tel: (909) 392-1111
Fax: (909) 392-4422
Info@MiddleEasternChristian.Org

Arab Organization for Human Rights
http://www.aohr.org/
91, Al-Marghany Street
Heliopolis
Cairo, Egypt
Tel: +20 2 4181396, 4188378

Fax: +20 2 4185346
aohr@link.com.eg

Arab Program for Human Rights Activists
http://www.aphra.org/
Osama El Sadik St., behind El Serag Mall, 8th district, building No. 10, 7th floor, flat No. 16
Nasr City
Cairo, Egypt
Tel: +222753975, 227753985
Fax: +222878773

Association for Civil Rights in Israel
http://www.acri.org.il/
P.O. Box 34510
Jerusalem 91000
Israel
Tel: +972 2 6521218
Fax: +972 2 6521219
mail@acri.org.il

B'TSELEM—The Israeli Information Center for Human Rights in the Occupied Territories
http://www.btselem.org/
P.O. Box 53132
Jerusalem 91531
Israel
Tel: +972 2 6735599
Fax: +972 2 6749111
mail@btselem.org

Cairo Institute for Human Rights Studies
http://www.cihrs.org/
P.O. Box 117 (Maglis El-Shaab)

Cairo, Egypt
Tel: +20 2 7963059, 7951112
Fax: +20 2 7921913
info@cihrs.org

Compass Direct News Service
http://www.compassdirect.org/
P.O. Box 27250
Santa Ana, CA 92799
Tel: (949) 862-0304
Fax: (949) 752-6536
info@compassdirect.org

Egyptian Institute for Personal Rights
http://www.eipr.org/
8 Mohamed Ali Jinnah Street
Garden City, Apt. 9, 4th floor
Cairo, Egypt
Tel/Fax: +20 2 794 3606, 796 2682
eipr@eipr.org

Ibn Khaldun Center for Development Studies (ICDS)
http://www.eicds.org/
P.O. Box 13 Mokattam
Cairo
Egypt
Tel: +20 2 5081617, 5081030, 6670974
Fax: +20 2 6670973
info@eicds.org

Institute for Gulf Affairs
http://www.gulfinstitute.org/
1900 L Street N.W., Suite 309
Washington, D.C. 20036
Tel: (202) 466-9500
web@gulfinstitute.org

Iranian Christians International
http://www.iranchristians.org/
P.O. Box 25607
Colorado Springs, Colorado 80936
Tel: (719) 596-0010
Fax: (719) 574-1141
info@iranchristians.org

Middle East Concern
https://www.givengain.com/cgi-bin/
giga.cgi?c=1489/
P.O. Box 2, Loughborough
Leicestershire LE11 3BG
United Kingdom
Tel: +44 15092 39400
Fax: +44 87013 48312

Rabbis for Human Rights
http://www.rhr.israel.net/
Rehov Harekhavim 9
Jerusalem 93462
Israel
Tel: +972 2 648 2757
Fax: +972 2 678 3611
info@rhr.israel.net

Appendix VI

RATIFICATION OF HUMAN RIGHTS TREATIES

	ICCPR	ICCPR-OP1	EU Charter	European Convention	OSCE	American Declaration	American Convention	African Charter
Afghanistan	X							
Albania	X			X	X			
Algeria	X	X						X
Andorra	X	X		X	X			
Angola	X	X						X
Antigua and Barbuda						X		
Argentina	X	X				X	X	
Armenia	X	X		X	X			
Australia	X	X						
Austria	X	X	X	X	X			
Azerbaijan	X	X		X	X			
Bahamas						X		
Bahrain	X							
Bangladesh	X							
Barbados	X	X				X	X	
Belarus	X	X			X			
Belgium	X	X	X	X	X			
Belize	X					X		
Benin	X	X						X
Bhutan								

	ICCPR	ICCPR-OP1	EU Charter	European Convention	OSCE	American Declaration	American Convention	African Charter
Bolivia	X	X				X	X	
Bosnia and Herzegovina	X	X		X	X			
Botswana	X							X
Brazil	X					X	X	
Brunei Darussalam								
Bulgaria	X	X	X	X	X			
Burkina Faso	X	X						X
Burundi	X							X
Cambodia	X							
Cameroon	X	X						X
Canada	X	X			X	X		
Cape Verde	X	X						X
Central African Republic	X	X						X
Chad	X	X						X
Chile	X	X		X*		X	X	
China								
Colombia	X	X				X	X	
Comoros								X
Congo, Republic of the	X	X						X
Costa Rica	X	X				X	X	
Côte d'Ivoire	X	X						X
Croatia	X	X		X	X			
Cuba						X		
Cyprus	X	X	X	X	X			

* Venice Commission Expanded Agreement

	ICCPR	ICCPR-OP1	EU Charter	European Convention	OSCE	American Declaration	American Convention	African Charter
Czech Republic	X	X	X	X	X			
Democratic People's Republic of Korea	X							
Democratic Republic of the Congo	X	X						X
Denmark	X	X	X	X	X			
Djibouti	X	X						X
Dominica	X					X	X	
Dominican Republic	X	X				X	X	
Ecuador	X	X				X	X	
Egypt	X							X
El Salvador	X	X				X	X	
Equatorial Guinea	X	X						X
Eritrea	X							X
Estonia	X	X	X	X	X			
Ethiopia	X							X
Fiji								
Finland	X	X	X	X	X			
France	X	X	X	X	X			
Gabon	X							X
Gambia	X	X						X
Georgia	X	X		X	X			
Germany	X	X	X	X	X			
Ghana	X	X						X
Greece	X	X	X	X	X			

	ICCPR	ICCPR-OP1	EU Charter	European Convention	OSCE	American Declaration	American Convention	African Charter
Grenada	X					X	X	
Guatemala	X	X				X	X	
Guinea	X	X						X
Guinea-Bissau								X
Guyana	X	X				X		
Haiti	X					X	X	
Holy See					X			
Honduras	X					X	X	
Hungary	X	X	X	X	X			
Iceland	X	X		X	X			
India	X							
Indonesia	X							
Iran, Islamic Republic of	X							
Iraq	X							
Ireland	X	X	X	X	X			
Israel	X							
Italy	X	X	X	X	X			
Jamaica	X					X	X	
Japan	X							
Jordan	X							
Kazakhstan	X				X			
Kenya	X							X
Kiribati								
Kuwait	X							
Kyrgyzstan	X	X		X*	X			
Laos								
Latvia	X	X	X	X	X			
Lebanon	X							

* Venice Commission Expanded Agreement

	ICCPR	ICCPR-OP1	EU Charter	European Convention	OSCE	American Declaration	American Convention	African Charter
Lesotho	X	X						X
Liberia								X
Libya	X	X						X
Liechtenstein	X	X		X	X			
Lithuania	X	X	X	X	X			
Luxembourg	X	X	X	X	X			
Macedonia	X	X		X	X			
Madagascar	X	X						X
Malawi	X	X						X
Malaysia								
Maldives	X							
Mali	X	X						X
Malta	X	X	X	X	X			
Marshall Islands								
Mauritania								X
Mauritius	X	X						X
Mexico	X	X				X	X	
Micronesia								
Moldova	X			X	X			
Monaco	X			X	X			
Mongolia	X	X						
Montenegro	X			X	X			
Morocco	X							
Mozambique	X							X
Myanmar								
Namibia	X	X						X
Nauru								
Nepal	X	X						

	ICCPR	ICCPR-OP1	EU Charter	European Convention	OSCE	American Declaration	American Convention	African Charter
Netherlands	X	X	X	X	X			
New Zealand	X	X						
Nicaragua	X	X				X	X	
Niger	X	X						X
Nigeria	X							X
Norway	X	X		X	X			
Oman								
Pakistan								
Palau								
Panama	X	X				X	X	
Papua New Guinea								
Paraguay	X	X				X	X	
Peru	X	X				X	X	
Philippines	X	X						
Poland	X	X	X	X	X			
Portugal	X	X	X	X	X			
Qatar								
Republic of Korea	X	X		X*				
Romania	X	X	X	X	X			
Russian Federation	X	X		X	X			
Rwanda	X							X
Sahrawi Arab Democratic Republic								X
Saint Kitts and Nevis						X		
Saint Lucia						X		

* Venice Commission Expanded Agreement

	ICCPR	ICCPR-OP1	EU Charter	European Convention	OSCE	American Declaration	American Convention	African Charter
Saint Vincent and the Grenadines	X	X				X		
Samoa								
San Marino	X	X		X	X			
Sao Tome and Principe								X
Saudi Arabia								
Senegal	X	X						X
Serbia	X	X		X	X			
Seychelles	X	X						X
Sierra Leone	X	X						X
Singapore								
Slovakia	X	X	X	X	X			
Slovenia	X	X	X	X	X			
Solomon Islands								
Somalia	X	X						X
South Africa	X	X						X
Spain	X	X	X	X	X			
Sri Lanka	X	X						
Sudan	X							X
Suriname	X	X				X	X	
Swaziland	X							X
Sweden	X	X	X	X	X			
Switzerland	X			X	X			
Syrian Arab Republic	X							
Tajikistan	X	X			X			
Thailand	X							

	ICCPR	ICCPR-OP1	EU Charter	European Convention	OSCE	American Declaration	American Convention	African Charter
Timor-Leste	X							
Togo	X	X						X
Tonga								
Trinidad and Tobago	X					X	X	
Tunisia	X							X
Turkey	X			X	X			
Turkmenistan	X	X			X			
Tuvalu								
Uganda	X	X						X
Ukraine	X	X		X	X			
United Arab Emirates								
United Kingdom	X		X	X	X			
United Republic of Tanzania	X							X
United States of America	X				X	X		
Uruguay	X	X				X	X	
Uzbekistan	X	X			X			
Vanuatu								
Venezuela	X	X				X	X	
Viet Nam	X							
Yemen	X							
Zambia	X	X						X
Zimbabwe	X							X

Appendix VII

SUPPORTING DOCUMENTS FOR THE TURKMENISTAN CASE STUDY

 OFFICE OF THE HIGH COMMISSIONER FOR HUMAN RIGHTS

Situation of human rights in Turkmenistan
Commission on Human Rights resolution 2003/11

The Commission on Human Rights,

Reaffirming that all Member States have an obligation to promote and protect human rights and fundamental freedoms as stated in the Charter of the United Nations and the Universal Declaration of Human Rights and the duty to fulfil the obligations they have undertaken under the International Covenants on Human Rights and other applicable human rights instruments,

Mindful that Turkmenistan is a party to the International Covenant on Economic, Social and Cultural Rights, the International Covenant on Civil and Political Rights, the International Convention on the Elimination of All Forms of Racial Discrimination and the Convention against Torture and Other Cruel, Inhuman or Degrading Treatment or Punishment,

Reaffirming that no one shall be subjected to arbitrary arrest or detention and that everyone is entitled in full equality to a fair and public hearing, by an independent and impartial tribunal, in the determination of their rights and obligations and of any criminal charge against them,

Reaffirming also that everyone has the right to freedom of opinion and expression,

Reaffirming further that the fight against terrorism should be conducted in full respect of human rights and democratic principles,

Deeply concerned about the events of 25 November 2002 and the consequences thereof,

Taking note of the meeting on 22 January 2003 in Vienna between the Minister for Foreign Affairs of Turkmenistan and the permanent representatives of the group of 10 participating States of the Organization for Security and Cooperation in Europe that had invoked the Moscow mechanism of that organization,

1. *Expresses its appreciation* at the recent announcement by the Government of Turkmenistan that it will uphold the decision by the Turkmen Peoples' Council in December 1999 to abolish the death penalty;

2. *Expresses its concern* at the restrictions imposed on the realization of the right of everyone to education by the introduction of measures by the Government of Turkmenistan which have drastically reduced the number of years of compulsory education and the number of university places;

3. *Expresses its grave concern*:

(*a*) At the persistence of a governmental policy based on the repression of all political opposition activities and on the abuse of the legal system through arbitrary detention, imprisonment and surveillance of persons who try to exercise their freedoms of thought, expression, assembly and association, and harassment of their families;

(*b*) At the suppression of independent media and freedom of expression, at attempts to restrict the access of the international media and at restrictions on the freedom to seek, receive and impart information and ideas of all kinds, regardless of frontiers, either orally, in writing or in print, in the form of art, or through any other media of choice;

(*c*) At restrictions on the exercise of the freedom of thought, conscience and religion, despite guarantees contained in the Constitution of Turkmenistan and in the International Covenant on Civil and Political Rights, including by the harassment and persecution of members of independent faith groups and the discriminatory use of the registration procedures for such groups;

(*d*) At the heavy prison sentences given to objectors to compulsory military service on religious grounds, such as Jehovah's Witnesses, and the lack of alternative service compatible with the reasons for conscientious objection, of a non-combatant or civilian character, in the public interest and not of a punitive nature;

(*e*) At the discrimination by the Government of Turkmenistan against ethnic Russian, Uzbek and other minorities in the fields of education and employment, which is contrary to the Constitution of Turkmenistan and the International Covenant on Economic, Social and Cultural Rights;

(*f*) At the creation of almost insurmountable obstacles to marriages of Turkmen with foreigners, inter alia through the imposition of an obligation to pay a large sum of money before such marriages can take place;

(*g*) At the introduction of new exit visa requirements for Turkmen nationals and at the unreasonable registration regulations for foreign nationals introduced on 1 March 2003, which curtail enjoyment of the right to liberty of movement and freedom to leave the country;

(*h*) At the manner in which the elections of 6 April 2003 were organized and conducted, which did not represent a free and fair process;

4. *Deplores*:

(*a*) The treatment of accused individuals in violation of the International Covenant on Civil and Political Rights following the events of 25 November 2002, including arbitrary detentions, arbitrary arrests, convictions in the absence of the observation of minimum rules of due process, including the ability to prepare and execute one's defence with counsel of one's own choosing, imposition of sentences in violation of the principle *nulla poena sine lege*, the harassment of family members of the accused and the arbitrary confiscation of their homes and property and, especially, their announced eviction and reports of forced displacement to remote areas of the country;

(*b*) The conduct of the Turkmen authorities with regard to the lack of fair trials of the accused, the reliance on confessional evidence which may have been extracted by torture or the threat of torture, the closed court proceedings, contrary to article 105 of the Constitution of Turkmenistan, which provides that trials should be open, except in a narrowly defined set of circumstances, and the refusal to allow diplomatic missions or international observers in Ashgabat access to the trials as observers;

(*c*) The reluctance of the Government of Turkmenistan to cooperate with the Moscow mechanism of the Organization for Security and Cooperation in Europe and to allow the Rapporteur of that organization to examine concerns arising from the events of 25 November 2002, as well as to respect its human rights commitments as a participant State of the Organization for Security and Cooperation in Europe and a member of the United Nations;

5. *Calls upon* the Government of Turkmenistan:

(*a*) To ensure full respect for all human rights and fundamental freedoms, in particular the freedoms of expression, religion, association and assembly, the right to a fair trial by an independent and impartial tribunal established by law and the protection of the rights of persons belonging to ethnic and religious minorities, and to take the necessary measures to refrain from subjecting conscientious objectors to imprisonment;

(*b*) To grant urgently access by independent bodies, including the International Committee of the Red Cross, to the persons detained following the events of 25 November 2002;

(*c*) To put an end to forced displacement and guarantee freedom of movement inside the country;

(*d*) To fulfil its responsibility to ensure that those responsible for human rights violations are brought to justice;

(*e*) To remove restrictions on the activities of non-governmental organizations, particularly human rights non-governmental organizations, and other civil society actors;

(*f*) To implement the recommendations outlined in the report of the Rapporteur of the Organization for Security and Cooperation in Europe;

(*g*) To develop a constructive dialogue with the United Nations High Commissioner for Human Rights and his Office;

(*h*) To cooperate fully with all the mechanisms of the Commission on Human Rights, including the Special Rapporteurs on the independence of judges and lawyers, on the question of torture, on extrajudicial, summary and arbitrary executions, on the promotion and protection of the right to freedom of opinion and expression, and on freedom of religion or belief, as well as the Working Group on Arbitrary Detention and the Special Representatives of the Secretary-General on internally displaced persons and on the situation of human rights defenders, including by issuing invitations to visit the country;

(*i*) To submit reports to all relevant United Nations treaty bodies and to ensure full implementation of their recommendations;

6. *Urges* the Government of Turkmenistan immediately and unconditionally to release all prisoners of conscience;

7. *Calls upon* the Special Rapporteurs on the independence of judges and lawyers, on the question of torture, on extrajudicial, summary and arbitrary executions, on freedom of opinion and expression, and on freedom of religion or belief as well as the Working Group on Arbitrary Detention and the Special Representatives of the Secretary-General on internally displaced

persons, and on the situation of human rights defenders to seek invitations from the Government of Turkmenistan to visit the country;

8.   *Requests* the Secretary-General to bring the present resolution to the attention of all relevant parts of the United Nations system;

9.   *Decides* to continue its consideration of this question at its sixtieth session.

51st meeting
16 April 2003
[Adopted by a recorded vote of 23 votes to 16, with 14 abstentions. See chap. IX.]

Congress of the United States
Washington, DC 20515

October 20, 2003

The Honorable Colin L. Powell
Secretary of State
US Department of State
Washington, DC 20520

Dear Secretary Powell:

We write urging the designation of Saudi Arabia, Turkmenistan and Vietnam as "Countries of Particular Concern" (CPC), as provided by the International Religious Freedom Act. Each has a well-documented record of "particularly severe violations of religious freedom" and are three notable and egregious violators of religious freedom that warrant CPC designation. As President Bush stressed in the National Security Strategy, "freedom is the non-negotiable demand of human dignity."

Saudi Arabia represents possibly the worst situation for religious freedom anywhere in the world. In fact, every Country Reports on Human Rights Practices issued by the Department since 1999 and the Annual Report on International Religious Freedom have repeatedly declared "freedom of religion does not exist"in Saudi Arabia. Notably, this extraordinary and accurate assertion is not made for any of the current CPC countries, placing Saudi Arabia in a class of its own.

Islam is the official religion of the kingdom. Non-Muslim groups are not allowed to worship in public and risk being detained, imprisoned, tortured, or deported. Conversion from Islam to another religion is considered apostasy and punishable by death. Other Islamic sects outside the Wahhabi order are forbidden and face significant discrimination and harassment. In legal proceedings, judges may discount or reject the testimony of non-Muslims or persons who do not adhere to the "correct" Islamic doctrine. Islamic religious education is limited to Wahhabi Islam and is reportedly anti-Semitic and anti-Israel.

Non-Muslim clergy are prohibited from meeting with co-religionists who travel to Saudi Arabia. Catholics and Orthodox Christians who require a priest to receive requisite sacraments are affected in particular. Non-Muslims are not allowed the freedom of expression and the distribution of religious materials such as Bibles is illegal. Muslims or non-Muslims wearing in public religious symbols of any kind risk confrontation with the religious police, the Mutawwa'in. The Mutawwa'in also enforce the Saudi law requiring women to wear the "abaya," a black robe that covers the entire body, along with covering the head and face. Women who do not fully comply with these standards are harassed by the authorities.

Freedom of religion does not exist in Turkmenistan, either. Minority religious groups are unable to meet the nearly impossible registration requirements and the National Security Committee breaks up peaceful, unregistered religious meetings in private homes. Groups are denied permission to meet publicly and have no choice but to operate under the threat of harsh reprisals, such as home raids, imprisonment, deportation, internal exile, house eviction and even torture. Even the two registered religious groups, the Russian Orthodox Church and the Sunni Muslim community, are under strict state control with members punished should they dare to speak out.

Over the past year there was a marked increase in police action, systematically crushing non-state sanctioned religious communities. Seventh-day Adventists are reportedly forced to conduct baptisms in caves. In April, police banned Baptists from meeting in Balkanabad. In May, authorities raided and closed a meeting of Hare Krishnas in Ashgabad, and law enforcement officers broke up a Baptist Sunday morning service in Turkmenbashi. In June, authorities temporarily detained and heavily fined leaders of a Baptist church ministering to deaf meeting "illegally" in Turkmenabad, and five members of a non-denominational Protestant church in the town of Abadan were fined after a police raid.

In Vietnam, Buddhists, Protestants, Catholics and minority groups suffer intense persecution at the hand of brutal communist rulers. In January 2003, the Communist Party's Central Committee issued a resolution calling for the establishment of Party cells within each of Vietnam's six approved religions in order to foil "hostile forces." While all religious groups in Vietnam face great restrictions and suffer some form of persecution, the Montagnard ethnic group has been singled out for persecution largely due to their support of the United States during the Vietnam War.

Reportedly, between September 2001 and December 2002, the Government of Vietnam forcibly closed 354 of the 412 churches in Dak Lak province and 56 pastors from the Central Highlands "disappeared." The Unified

Buddhist Church of Vietnam (UCBV), the largest religious denomination in the country, has also been declared illegal by the government with its clergy, like Thich Tri Luc, often imprisoned and harassed. Independent Protestants are subjected to particularly harsh treatment by authorities, reportedly including raids on homes and house churches, detention, imprisonment, confiscation of religious and personal property, physical and psychological abuse. Serious restrictions of the Catholic Church's activities have caused a severe shortage of priests; Father Nguyen Van Ly and three relatives have been sentenced for lengthy jail terms.

The "systematic, ongoing, and egregious violations" and government policies leading to imprisonment, internal deportations and torture in Saudi Arabia, Turkmenistan and Vietnam certainly meet the criteria outlined in the legislation as "particularly severe violations of religious freedom." Mr. Secretary, in the interest of advancing the cause of freedom, including the right to freedom of thought, conscience, religion or belief, we strongly urge you to uphold human dignity by exercising your authority and designating Saudi Arabia, Turkmenistan, and Vietnam as countries of particular concern.

Sincerely,

Benjamin L. Cardin, M.C.

Christopher H. Smith, M.C.

Russell D. Feingold, U.S.S.

Ben Nighthorse Campbell, U.S.S.

Saxby Chambliss, U.S.S.

Sam Brownback, U.S.S.

Frank R. Lautenberg, U.S.S.

Frank R. Wolf, M.C.

Ileana Ros-Lehtinen, M.C.

Elton Gallegly, M.C.

Robert B. Aderholt, M.C.

Edward J. Markey, M.C.

Don Nickles, U.S.S.

Eliot L. Engel, M.C.

Dana Rohrabacher, M.C.

Jerrold Nadler, M.C.

Zoe Lofgren, M.C.

Jo Ann Davis, M.C.

Trent Franks, M.C.

Carolyn B. Maloney, M.C.

Betty McCollum, M.C.

Jim Davis, M.C.

Nick Lampson, M.C.

Joseph Crowley, M.C.

Richard H. Baker, M.C.

Max Sandlin, M.C.

James P. McGovern, M.C.

Shelley Berkley, M.C.

Eleanor Holmes Norton, Delegate

Loretta Sanchez, M.C.

Karen McCarthy, M.C.

Lincoln Davis, M.C.

Elijah E. Cummings, M.C.

W. Todd Akin, M.C.

OFFICE OF THE HIGH COMMISSIONER FOR HUMAN RIGHTS

Situation of human rights in Turkmenistan
Commission on Human Rights resolution 2004/12

The Commission on Human Rights,

Reaffirming that all Member States have an obligation to promote and protect human rights and fundamental freedoms and the duty to fulfil the obligations they have undertaken under the international human rights instruments to which they are parties,

Mindful that Turkmenistan is a party to the International Covenant on Economic, Social and Cultural Rights, the International Covenant on Civil and Political Rights, the International Convention on the Elimination of All Forms of Racial Discrimination and the Convention against Torture and Other Cruel, Inhuman or Degrading Treatment or Punishment,

Recalling its previous resolution on the subject, 2003/11 of 16 April 2003, and taking note of General Assembly resolution 58/194 of 22 December 2003,

Noting the conclusion of the first needs-assessment mission of the Office of the United Nations High Commissioner for Human Rights to Turkmenistan in March 2004,

Noting with appreciation that the Government of Turkmenistan has received the Personal Envoy of the Chairman-in-Office of the Organization for Security and Cooperation in Europe for Participating States in Central Asia and the High Commissioner for National Minorities of the Organization,

Reaffirming that improving security and the fight against terrorism should be conducted in full respect of human rights and democratic principles,

Welcoming the decree on freedom of movement of 11 March 2004 and hoping that it will apply to the large number of people who, regrettably, were unable to leave the country following the earlier repeal of exit visas, and that it will be followed by further positive measures,

Noting with appreciation the decision on 11 March 2004 by the President of Turkmenistan to issue a decree on religious freedom, with the hope that its provisions will be implemented to allow unfettered registration by all religious minority groups,

Welcoming the demonstrated readiness of the Government of Turkmenistan to discuss human rights matters with interested third parties on an ad hoc basis and to agree on the desirability of continuing dialogue and practical cooperation,

1. *Expresses its grave concern* at:

(*a*) The persistence of a governmental policy based on the repression of all political opposition activities;

(*b*) The abuse of the legal system through arbitrary detention, imprisonment and surveillance of persons who try to exercise their freedoms of thought, expression, assembly and association, and harassment of their families;

(*c*) Restrictions on the freedoms of information and expression, including through the suppression of independent media;

(*d*) Restrictions on the exercise of the freedoms of thought, conscience, religion and belief, including by the harassment and persecution of members of independent faith groups and the discriminatory use of registration procedures for such groups;

(e) Discrimination by the Government of Turkmenistan against ethnic Russian, Uzbek and other minorities in the fields of education and employment;

(*f*) The poor conditions in prisons in Turkmenistan;

2. *Also expresses its grave concern* at the continuing failure of the Government of Turkmenistan to respond to the criticisms identified in the report of the Rapporteur of the Moscow Mechanism of the Organization for Security and Cooperation in Europe as regards the investigation, trial and detention procedures following the reported assassination attempt against President Niyazov in November 2002, as well as the failure of the Turkmen authorities to allow appropriate independent bodies, family members and lawyers access to those convicted, or to provide any kind of evidence to dispel rumours that some of the latter have now died in detention;

3. *Calls upon* the Government of Turkmenistan:

(*a*) To ensure full respect for all human rights and fundamental freedoms, in particular the freedoms of expression, religion, association and assembly, the right to a fair trial by an independent and impartial tribunal established by law and the protection of the rights of persons belonging to ethnic and religious minorities, and to stop imprisoning conscientious objectors;

(*b*) To grant immediate access by appropriate independent bodies, including the International Committee of the Red Cross, as well as lawyers and relatives, to detained persons, especially to persons detained following the events of 25 November 2002;

(*c*) To put an end to forced displacement and guarantee freedom of movement inside the country;

(*d*) To fulfil its responsibility to ensure that those responsible for human rights violations are brought to justice;

(*e*) To remove the new restrictions on the activities of public associations, including non-governmental organizations, stipulated in the new Law on Public Associations adopted on 21 October 2003 and paralleled in the new rules of registration of religious organizations released in January 2004, and to enable non-governmental organizations, particularly human rights organizations, and other civil society actors to carry out their activities without hindrance;

(*f*) To implement fully the recommendations outlined in the report of the Rapporteur of the Moscow Mechanism of the Organization for Security and Cooperation in Europe, to work constructively with the various institutions of the Organization and to facilitate further visits of the Personal Envoy of the Organization's Chairman-in-Office for Participating States in Central Asia and of the Organization's High Commissioner on National Minorities;

(*g*) To develop further a constructive dialogue with the United Nations High Commissioner for Human Rights and her Office and to cooperate fully with all the mechanisms of the Office;

(*h*) To submit reports to all relevant United Nations treaty bodies and to ensure full implementation of their recommendations;

4. *Urges* the Government of Turkmenistan to release immediately and unconditionally all prisoners of conscience;

5. *Requests* the Special Rapporteur on the independence of judges and lawyers, the Special Rapporteur on torture and other cruel, inhuman or degrading treatment or punishment, the Special Rapporteur on extrajudicial, summary or arbitrary executions, the Special Rapporteur on the right to free-

dom of opinion and expression and the Special Rapporteur on freedom of religion or belief, as well as the Working Group on Arbitrary Detention and the Representative of the Secretary-General on internally displaced persons and the Special Representative of the Secretary-General on the situation of human rights defenders to consider visiting Turkmenistan as part of their programme of visits in 2004–2005, and calls upon the Government of Turkmenistan to facilitate such visits;

6.   *Decides* to continue its consideration of this question at its sixty-first session.

50th meeting
15 April 2004
[Adopted by a recorded vote of 25 votes to 11,
with 17 abstentions. See chap. IX - E/2004/23 – E/CN.4/2004/127]

**COMMISSION ON
SECURITY AND COOPERATION
IN EUROPE**
234 FORD HOUSE OFFICE BUILDING
WASHINGTON, DC 20515-6460
(202) 225-1901
Fax: (202) 226-4199
www.csce.gov

June 3, 2004

His Excellency Saparmurat Niyazov
President
Republic of Turkmenistan
Ashgabat, Turkmenistan

Dear President Niyazov:

We write urging you to institute genuine reforms concerning the freedom of thought conscience, religion and belief for the people of Turkmenistan. As a participating State in the Organization for Security and Cooperation in Europe (OSCE), Turkmenistan promised to ensure and facilitate the freedom of the individual to profess and practice a religion or belief, alone or in community with others. We are particularly mindful of the fact that you personally signed the original Helsinki Final Act document on behalf of your country, unreservedly accepting all OSCE commitments and obligations.

The lack of religious freedom in Turkmenistan, despite several recent decrees supposedly intended to improve the legal protection for religious groups, is particularly disturbing. Over the past year, the Helsinki Commission has followed the multiplicity of new laws and presidential decrees governing religious freedom. Concrete action must follow that allows religious communities of all faiths, regardless of registration, to operate freely and openly without harassment or intimidation. OSCE commitments make clear that the full enjoyment of religious freedom by individuals, either alone or in community with others, to freely profess and practice their faith.

To date, only two applicant religious communities have been registered under the latest decrees purporting to relax the registration process. We are also troubled by your March 29 statement on state television that Muslim communities could "not build any more mosques" and that the mosques "should not choose the mullahs themselves" but that would be a government responsibility. These limitations all contravene OSCE commitments and international norms you have personally agreed to implement in Turkmenistan.

Of particular note, we are quite concerned about the imprisonment of a number of individuals. On March 2, a court convicted the former Islamic leader of Turkmenistan Nasrullah ibn Ibadullah, sentencing him to 22 years in jail. In addition, the situation for Kurban Bagdatovich Zakirov is most troubling, as he has been repeatedly jailed for conscientiously objecting to military service. As an example of your desire to facilitate religious freedom for all, we urge you to unconditionally release Mr. Ibadullah and Mr. Zakirov, as well as the five other Jehovah's Witnesses currently in jail (Rinat Babadzhanov, Shohrat Mitogorov, Ruslan Nasyrov, Rozymamed Satlykov, and Aleksandr Matveyev).

The need for Turkmenistan to immediately improve its appalling record on religious freedom is clear, so as to avoid State Department designation as a "Country of Particular Concern" for particularly severe violations of religious freedom. We urge you take the initial steps to increase religious freedom by registering without delay all applicant religious groups allowing them to operate freely and openly, and releasing the aforementioned prisoners.

Sincerely,

Ben Nighthorse Campbell, U.S.S.
Co-Chairman

Christopher H. Smith, M.C.
Chairman

Saxby Chambliss, U.S.S.
Commissioner

Benjamin L. Cardin, M.C.
Ranking Member

Joseph R. Pitts
Commissioner

Frank R. Wolf, M.C.
Commissioner

cc: The Honorable Tracy Jacobson, U.S. Ambassador to Turkmenistan

United Nations   A/RES/59/206

General Assembly

Distr.: General
11 March 2005

Fifty-ninth session
Agenda item 105 (c)

Resolution adopted by the General Assembly

[on the report of the Third Committee (A/59/503/Add.3)]

59/206. Situation of human rights in Turkmenistan

The General Assembly,

Reaffirming that all States Members of the United Nations have the obligation to promote and protect human rights and fundamental freedoms and
the duty to fulfil the obligations that they have undertaken under the various
international instruments in this field,

Recalling its resolution 58/194 of 22 December 2003,

1. *Welcomes*:

(*a*) The limited increase in the ability of members of certain religious
minority groups, including members of the Bahá'í faith, the Baptist church,
the Hare Krishna movement and the Seventh Day Adventist church, to prac-
tise their religion;

(*b*) The release in June 2004 of a number of Jehovah's Witnesses who had
made conscientious objections to undertaking military service, but notes with
concern that other Jehovah's Witnesses continue to be jailed on the same charge;

(*c*) The comments of the Government of Turkmenistan in May 2004 that
interested representatives of the international community were welcome to
visit Turkmen prisons, and notes with satisfaction that the Government has
begun preliminary discussions with representatives of the International Committee of the Red Cross regarding prison access;

(*d*) The fact that the Personal Envoy of the Chairman-in-Office of the Organization for Security and Cooperation in Europe for Participating States in Central Asia, has been given the opportunity for further dialogue with the Government of Turkmenistan, and expresses the hope that a constructive dialogue on human rights issues is to be continued soon;

(*e*) The submission of the national report under the International Convention on the Elimination of All Forms of Racial Discrimination[1] to the Office of the United Nations High Commissioner for Human Rights and the recent submission of the report under the Convention on the Elimination of All Forms of Discrimination against Women[2] to the Division for the Advancement of Women of the Department of Economic and Social Affairs of the Secretariat and the announcement by the Government of Turkmenistan that it intends to submit the reports due under the Convention on the Rights of the Child[3] by the end of 2004;

(*f*) The amendment of 2 November 2004 to the Criminal Code of Turkmenistan rescinding article 223/1, which stipulated criminal penalties for unregistered activities of public associations, including non-governmental organizations;

(*g*) The invitation by the Government of Turkmenistan to the High Commissioner on National Minorities of the Organization for Security and Cooperation in Europe, which was extended on 16 November 2004, to visit the country by the end of 2004;

2. *Expresses its grave concern* at the continuing and serious human rights violations occurring in Turkmenistan, in particular:

(*a*) The persistence of a governmental policy based on the repression of all political opposition activities;

(*b*) The continuing abuse of the legal system through arbitrary detentions, imprisonment and surveillance of persons who try to exercise their freedom of expression, assembly and association, and by harassment of their families;

(*c*) Further restrictions on the freedom of expression and opinion, including the loss of local retransmissions of Russian language programmes on

---

[1] Resolution 2106 A (XX), annex.
[2] United Nations, *Treaty Series*, vol. 1249, No. 20378.
[3] Ibid., vol. 1577, No. 27531.

Radio Mayak, and serious harassment endured by local correspondents and collaborators of Radio Liberty;

(*d*) Continued restrictions on the exercise of the freedom of thought, conscience, religion and belief;

(*e*) Continued discrimination by the Government of Turkmenistan against ethnic minorities in the fields of education and employment and by forced displacements, despite assurances by the Government that it will stop this discrimination;

(*f*) Constraints faced by civil society organizations, including the slow progress in the registration of non-governmental organizations;

3. *Regrets* the decision of the Government of Turkmenistan not to renew the accreditation for the Head of the Centre of the Organization for Security and Cooperation in Europe at Ashgabat, but hopes that the Turkmen authorities will cooperate fully with her successor;

4. *Calls upon* the Government of Turkmenistan:

(*a*) To ensure full respect for all human rights and fundamental freedoms and, in this regard, to implement fully the measures set out in Commission on Human Rights resolutions 2003/11 of 16 April 2003[4] and 2004/12 of 15 April 2004;[5]

(*b*) To work closely with the Office of the High Commissioner for Human Rights with regard to the areas of concern and to cooperate fully with all the mechanisms of the Commission on Human Rights and all the relevant United Nations treaty bodies;

(*c*) To implement fully the recommendations outlined in the report of the Rapporteur of the Moscow Mechanism of the Organization for Security and Cooperation in Europe and to work constructively with the various institutions of the Organization, in particular following the visit of the Personal Envoy of the Chairman-in-Office of the Organization for Participating States in Central Asia, to work towards implementation of those recommendations and to make the necessary arrangements to facilitate fully a visit by the High Commissioner on National Minorities of the Organization by the end of 2004;

---

[4] See *Official Records of the Economic and Social Council, 2003, Supplement No. 3* (E/2003/23), chap. II, sect. A.

[5] Ibid., *2004, Supplement No. 3* (E/2004/23), chap. II, sect. A.

(*d*) To release immediately and unconditionally all prisoners of conscience;

(*e*) To give real substance to the May 2004 offer of the Government of Turkmenistan for interested representatives of the international community to visit Turkmen prisons by providing appropriate independent bodies, including the International Committee of the Red Cross, with full access to all places of detention in accordance with the usual modalities for those organizations and ensuring that lawyers and relatives have full and repeated access to all those in detention, including those convicted of involvement in the attempted coup d'état of 25 November 2002;

(*f*) To ensure that the forthcoming parliamentary elections will be held consistent with the commitments of the Organization for Security and Cooperation in Europe and other international standards for democratic elections;

(*g*) To remove the remaining restrictions on the activities of public associations, including non-governmental organizations, and to enable those organizations, in particular human rights organizations, and other civil society actors to carry out their activities without hindrance, building upon the amendment of 2 November 2004 to the Criminal Code of Turkmenistan abolishing criminal penalties for unregistered activities of public associations;

5. *Requests* the Secretary-General to submit a report to the General Assembly at its sixtieth session on the implementation of the present resolution.

74th plenary meeting
20 December 2004

September 28, 2005

Secretary of State Condoleezza Rice
U.S. Department of State
Washington D.C. 20520

Dear Secretary of State Rice,

As a coalition of non-governmental organizations, we are writing to express our concern over the dire and worsening situation of religious freedom in Turkmenistan, and to urge you to secure meaningful, measurable, and sustainable short-term improvements. If no such improvements are achieved, we call on you to designate Turkmenistan as a "country of particular concern" this year under the terms of the International Religious Freedom Act of 1998 (IRFA).

The widespread repression of free religious expression in Turkmenistan has been comprehensively and amply documented by the U.S. Department of State in its annual International Religious Freedom Reports and Country Reports on Human Rights Practices, by the U.S. Commission on International Religious Freedom, and by the independent watchdog group Forum 18 News Service and other rights monitors. These excellent reports obviate the need for detailing the systematic violations in Turkmenistan here.

We note only that there is no freedom of religion in Turkmenistan, that the situation is worsening, and there have been severe violations of religious freedom as defined in the statute. Evidence that the situation has worsened recently includes:

- Followers of minority religions – both registered and unregistered – are repeatedly harassed by police and security in the form of house raids, confiscation of religious materials, threats, and beatings. In some cases, these include followers of groups that were registered since the president introduced simplified registration procedures at the U.S. government's request;
- Several mosques have been unjustifiably demolished;
- President Niyazov publicly expressed the wish that no more mosques

be built in Turkmenistan, coinciding with the completion of the building of the country's largest mosque, whose construction adheres to state dictums;

- Islamic religious training has been effectively eliminated in Turkmenistan through drastic cut-backs in faculty and students at the country's last remaining Muslim theological department; and

- President Niyazov announced that he is preparing to introduce a forthcoming list of accepted Islamic rituals which Muslims must observe.

Indeed, we would argue that state control of religious expression in Turkmenistan has reached a new height. The state no longer simply controls religion; it is actively trying to eliminate even state-controlled religions in order to establish a new religion based on the personality of the president. For example:

- State propaganda refers to the president as a prophet, and glorification of the president is required as the preface to all prayers;

- Citizens are required to refer to the president's historical and political book as the "Holy" Ruhnama and to study, discuss in specially convened groups, memorize, and integrate it into their daily lives, much as religious groups do with their holy texts;

- The president has built the region's largest mosque, but the mosque has aroused concern among Muslims that it features quotations from the secular president's "holy" book, Ruhnama (Book of the Soul);

- Places of worship in Turkmenistan are required to have a "president's corner," featuring images of the president and a copy of his "holy" book, much as icons, crosses, holy remains, and holy books are present in places of worship; and

- In February of this year Muslim leaders from across the country were told by the state Council for Religious Affairs that it was "a priority task for clergymen to disseminate the lofty ideas in our great leader's sacred books on the duties of parents and children." (Forum 18)

Failure to comply with these and other requirements of the presidential personality cult has resulted in denial of employment and education; harassment; firings of relatives; threats of rape; severe beatings; and the arrest, imprisonment, and internal exile of several imams and the arrest of the former chief Mufti of Turkmenistan. Presidential restrictions on schools, places of worship, and the workplace insure that all citizens are affected to some degree, regardless of their religious beliefs.

Among the statutorily "severe" violations that have been committed recently are:

- Arbitrary detention and arrest: Former Mufti Nasrulla ibn Ibadulla was arbitrarily arrested in 2003 and is now being held on a 22-year prison sentence on charges that were not publicly disclosed, but were believed to have been motivated by his non-compliance with the practice of Islam as allowed by President Niyazov. This year, the government continues to bar disclosure of the charges against him and to deny him the right to even humanitarian visits.

- Torture: According to an October 2004 Forum 18 report, Jehovah's Witness Kurban Zakirov was reportedly subjected to injections of psychotropic substances during his three-year detention. The report cites the Jehovah's Witnesses as reporting that "His arms are covered all over by injection marks and his behaviour has become odd." They added that "his mental and emotional wellbeing has been ruined and his personality distorted." Baptist Shagildy Atakov was also reportedly subjected to this form of torture during his three-year arbitrary incarceration.

The fact that these violations were initiated in the previous designation cycles indicates only that CPC designation should have been authorized earlier and that it is now overdue. We also wish to underscore that a country that prohibits all free exercise of religious rights, as Turkmenistan does, must surely be considered a severe violator.

Bad Faith on the Part of the Government of Turkmenistan

That religious freedom violations persist and worsen is clear proof of the central government's continuing tolerance, at minimum, of such violations, and of its lack of commitment to ending them.

The registration issue may be the best example of the government's bad-faith implementation of reforms urged by the U.S. government. Unregistered religious activities – for example by unregistered Baptists and Jehovah's Witnesses – remain illegal under the Administrative Code, in defiance of the country's international human rights obligations. Following registration, the Hare Krishna community in Ashgabat was nonetheless barred from celebrating one of their major festivals, Rama Navami. Registered Baptist, Hare Krishna and Adventist communities have all encountered problems in finding places to rent for worship. The ban on using private homes for religious meetings is a major barrier to the functioning of these religious communities. The services of registered Baptists in the towns of Dashoguz and Mary have been attacked by police, reportedly on the pretext that Baptists are registered only in the capital, not throughout Turkmenistan. Baptists strongly dispute this claim, but even registered Baptists in the capital have yet to receive permission to meet for worship. The bitter experience of newly registered communities, such as the Hare Krishna, has undoubtedly deterred unregistered communities from registering and casts doubt on the benefit that registration can bring in an overwhelmingly hostile political environment.

Proposed Benchmarks for Improvement

In light of the effective use of IRFA leverage in the past with respect to the government of Turkmenistan, we urge you to test the government's resolve by asking it to meet the following suggested benchmarks:

1. The government of Turkmenistan must cease all forms of harassment and undue interference in the activities of religious groups or individuals for their religious beliefs immediately.

2. The government of Turkmenistan must amend the law "On Religion and Religious Organizations" of November 2003 and all relevant legislative acts and administrative orders in order to remove all undue restrictions on religious activity, including the ban on religious gatherings, unregistered groups, independent religious education, and others. Punishments and penalties for affiliation with unregistered religious groups must also be removed from the Civil-Administrative Code of the Republic of Turkmenistan (Article 205).

3. The former Mufti Nasrulla ibn Ibadulla must be released from prison immediately and unconditionally.

Failure to give Turkmenistan CPC status this year without achievement of these and other meaningful and sustainable improvements risks exposing last year's threats of designation as meaningless. This, in turn, would jeopardize the credibility of IRFA's unique, proven leverage with respect to Turkmenistan and other countries in the future. It would also cast doubt among the citizens of an overwhelmingly Muslim country on the U.S. government's credibility as a champion of religious freedom. Like many concerned with religious freedom in Turkmenistan, we welcomed the government of Turkmenistan's release from prison of ten conscientious objectors (six in June 2004, and four more in April 2005) and hailed its decision in March 2004 to lower the number of signatures required for the registration process. We were likewise encouraged when several small groups that had previously been denied registration soon thereafter became registered. It is clear that these achievements were secured thanks to the U.S. government's fair, forceful, and effective use of IRFA leverage.

But the government of Turkmenistan's defiance of its legal obligations and self-proclaimed commitment to its own democratic path must not just be modified; it must end. The U.S. government can once again demonstrate its resolve in fighting religious persecution worldwide by calling things by their proper names with regard to Turkmenistan. The government of Turkmenistan falls both squarely and egregiously into IRFA's focus on governments that have "engaged in or tolerated systematic and egregious violations of religious freedom." Apart from securing meaningful, measurable and sustainable improvements in its record on protecting religious rights within a pre-determined timeline, there can be no legitimate justification for a CPC waiver on Turkmenistan this year. Barring such improvements, we strongly endorse the U.S. Commission for International Religious Freedom's August 8 appeal and respectfully urge you to accord Turkmenistan long overdue CPC designation this year.

Thank you for your attention to these concerns.
   Sincerely,

   Environmental Justice Foundation
   Human Rights Watch
   Institute for War and Peace Reporting
   International Crisis Group
   International Helsinki Federation for Human Rights
   International League for Human Rights
   Memorial Human Rights Center
   Turkmenistan Helsinki Foundation
   Turkmenistan Initiative for Human Rights
   Lawrence Uzzell

cc: Ambassador-at-Large John V. Hanford III
Office of International Religious Freedom
U.S. Department of State

Ambassador Michael Kozak
Senior Director for Democracy, Human Rights and International
Organizations
National Security Council

Paula Dobriansky
Under-Secretary of State for Democracy and Global Affairs
U.S. Department of State

Ambassador Glyn T. Davies
Acting Assistant Secretary for Democracy, Human Rights and Labor
U.S. Department of State

Ambassador Tracey A. Jacobson
U.S. Embassy, Ashgabat

Senator Sam Brownback

Senator Tom Lantos

Senator Ben Nighthorse Campbell

Representative Joseph Pitts

Representative Christopher Smith

Ambassador Meret B. Orazov
Embassy of Turkmenistan to the U.S.

Mr. Michael Cromartie
Chairman, U.S. Commission on International Religious Freedom

United Nations   A/RES/60/172

 General Assembly

Distr.: General
9 March 2006

Sixtieth session
Agenda item 71 (*c*)

Resolution adopted by the General Assembly

[*on the report of the Third Committee (A/60/509/Add.3 and Corr.1)*]

60/172. Situation of human rights in Turkmenistan

The General Assembly,

Reaffirming that all States Members of the United Nations have the obligation to promote and protect human rights and fundamental freedoms and the duty to fulfil the obligations that they have undertaken under the various international instruments in this field,

Recalling its resolutions 58/194 of 22 December 2003 and 59/206 of 20 December 2004, and Commission on Human Rights resolutions 2003/11 of 16 April 2003[1] and 2004/12 of 15 April 2004,[2]

Noting the conclusion of the first needs-assessment mission of the Office of the United Nations High Commissioner for Human Rights to Turkmenistan in March 2004 and the ongoing consultations to finalize a possible technical cooperation project,

Noting with appreciation that the Government of Turkmenistan has received the Chairman-in-Office and the High Commissioner on National Minorities of the Organization for Security and Cooperation in Europe,

Welcoming the report of the Secretary-General of 20 September 2005,[3] which concludes that, while the Government of Turkmenistan has made some progress in addressing human rights issues and has shown readiness

---

[1] See *Official Records of the Economic and Social Council, 2003, Supplement No. 3* (E/2003/23), chap. II, sect. A.
[2] Ibid., *2004, Supplement No. 3* (E/2004/23), chap. II, sect. A.
[3] A/60/367.

to cooperate with the international community, there was a lack of overall improvement in addressing serious human rights violations,

Reaffirming that improving security and the fight against terrorism should be conducted in accordance with international law, in particular international human rights, humanitarian and refugee law, and democratic principles,

1. *Welcomes:*

(*a*) The fact that additional minority religious groups have been allowed to worship for the first time as a result of the removal of a legal impediment to the full realization of the right to freedom of thought, conscience, religion or belief, but notes that serious violations of these freedoms continue;

(*b*) The release in April 2005 of four Jehovah's Witnesses who had made conscientious objections to undertaking military service;

(*c*) The lifting of criminal penalties for the activities of non-registered nongovernmental organizations in November 2004, while nevertheless noting that difficulties in the registration process for non-governmental organizations and private organizations continue and that other significant restrictions continue to hinder their activities;

(*d*) The submission, within the past year, of the national report under the International Convention on the Elimination of All Forms of Racial Discrimination[4] to the Committee on the Elimination of Racial Discrimination, as well as the reports due under the Convention on the Rights of the Child[5] and the Convention on the Elimination of All Forms of Discrimination against Women,[6] while encouraging the Government of Turkmenistan to comply with its outstanding reporting obligations to the Human Rights Committee, the Committee on Economic, Social and Cultural Rights and the Committee against Torture;

(*e*) The demonstrated readiness of the Government of Turkmenistan to discuss human rights matters with interested third parties on an ad hoc basis and to agree on the desirability of continuing dialogue and practical cooperation;

(*f*) The statements made by the President of Turkmenistan in April 2005 on democratic reforms, and urges that those reforms be truly democratic, in line with established international norms;

[4] 4 Resolution 2106 A (XX), annex.
[5] United Nations, *Treaty Series*, vol. 1577, No. 27531.
[6] Ibid., vol. 1249, No. 20378.

(*g*) The accession by Turkmenistan to the following United Nations protocols and conventions, and urges the Government of Turkmenistan to implement its obligations under these instruments:

(i) The Optional Protocol to the Convention on the Rights of the Child on the involvement of children in armed conflict;[7]

(ii) The Optional Protocol to the Convention on the Rights of the Child on the sale of children, child prostitution and child pornography;[8]

(iii) The United Nations Convention against Transnational Organized Crime, its Protocol to Prevent, Suppress and Punish Trafficking in Persons, Especially Women and Children and its Protocol against the Smuggling of Migrants by Land, Sea and Air;[9]

(*h*) The public statements of the President of Turkmenistan recommending the abolition of the practice of removing children from school for the cotton harvest and reprimanding a local governor for the use of child labour in the fields, as well as a law passed on 1 February 2005 prohibiting the employment of minors under the age of 15 and stipulating that no form of child labour should interfere with a child's education, and calls upon the Government of Turkmenistan to ensure that the law is fully implemented;

(*i*) The decision of the Government of Turkmenistan to grant citizenship or permanent resident status to more than sixteen thousand refugees, including a significant number of Tajik refugees, who had fled Tajikistan between 1992 and 1999 and whose naturalization under the Turkmen Nationality Law had been advocated for many years by the United Nations High Commissioner for Refugees;

(*j*) The abolition of exit visas as a requirement for leaving the country;

2. *Expresses its grave concern* at the continuing and serious human rights violations occurring in Turkmenistan, in particular:

(*a*) The persistence of a governmental policy based on the repression of all political opposition activities;

(*b*) The continuing abuse of the legal system through arbitrary detentions, imprisonment and surveillance of persons who try to exercise their freedom of expression, assembly and association, and harassment of their families;

---

[7] Ibid., vol. 2173, No. 27531.
[8] Ibid., vol. 2171, No. 27531.
[9] Resolution 55/25, annexes I–III.

(*c*) The poor conditions in prisons in Turkmenistan and credible reports of ongoing torture and mistreatment of detainees;

(*d*) The failure of the Government of Turkmenistan to grant access to detainees to the International Committee of the Red Cross, according to the usual terms of the Committee, as well as to international monitors;

(*e*) The complete control of the media by the Government of Turkmenistan, its censorship of all newspapers and access to the Internet and intolerance of independent criticism of government policy, as well as further restrictions on the freedom of expression and opinion, including shutting down of the last remaining Russian-language radio station, Radio Mayak, even if satellite television is permitted and widely used, harassing of local correspondents and collaborators of Radio Liberty and prohibition of all contact between local journalists and foreigners without the express consent of the Government;

(*f*) Continuing restrictions on the exercise of the freedom of thought, conscience, religion or belief, including the use of registration procedures as a means to limit the right to freedom of thought, conscience and religion of members of certain religious communities;

(*g*) Continuing discrimination by the Government of Turkmenistan against ethnic Russian, Uzbek and other minorities, inter alia, in the fields of education and employment and access to media, despite assurances by the Government that it will stop this discrimination, taking note in this regard of the concluding observations of the Committee on the Elimination of Racial Discrimination of August 2005;[10]

(*h*) Forced displacement of its citizens, including a disproportionate displacement of ethnic minorities;

(*i*) Continuing restrictions on the exercise of the right of peaceful assembly, including increased constraints faced by civil society organizations, such as the slow progress in the registration of non-governmental organizations under the procedures set out in the law of 2003 on public associations;

(*j*) The continuing failure of the Government of Turkmenistan to respond to the criticisms identified in the report of the Rapporteur of the Moscow Mechanism of the Organization for Security and Cooperation in Europe with regard to the investigation, trial and detention procedures following the reported assassination attempt against the President of Turkmenistan in

---

[10] See *Official Records of the General Assembly, Sixtieth Session, Supplement No. 18* (A/60/18), chap. III.

November 2002, as well as the failure of the Turkmen authorities to allow appropriate independent bodies, family members and lawyers access to those convicted, or to provide any kind of evidence to dispel rumours that some of those convicted have died in detention;

(*k*) Arbitrary or unlawful interference with individuals' privacy, family, home or correspondence and violations of the freedom to leave one's country;

(*l*) Reported instances of hate speech against national and ethnic minorities, including statements attributed to high-ranking government officials and public figures supporting an approach to Turkmen ethnic purity, as noted in the concluding observations of the Committee on the Elimination of Racial Discrimination of August 2005;

3. *Urges* the Government of Turkmenistan:

(*a*) To ensure full respect for all human rights and fundamental freedoms and, in this regard, to implement fully the measures set out in General Assembly resolutions 58/194 and 59/206 and Commission on Human Rights resolutions 2003/11 and 2004/12;

(*b*) To work closely with the Office of the United Nations High Commissioner for Human Rights with regard to the areas of concern and to cooperate fully with all the mechanisms of the Commission on Human Rights, in particular to consider favourably requests made by a number of special rapporteurs of the Commission to visit the country, as recalled in the report of the Secretary-General,[3] and with all the relevant United Nations treaty bodies;

(*c*) To implement fully the recommendations outlined in the report of the Rapporteur of the Moscow Mechanism of the Organization for Security and Cooperation in Europe and to work constructively with the various institutions of the Organization, and to facilitate further visits of the Organization's Chairman-in-Office as well as his Personal Envoy for participating States in Central Asia, and of the Organization's High Commissioner on National Minorities;

(*d*) To follow through on the presentation of the Government of Turkmenistan to the Commission on Human Rights in April 2004 and the meetings of the Government of Turkmenistan with the International Committee of the Red Cross in 2005 by finalizing an agreement allowing the Committee to visit Turkmen prisons with full and repeated access to all places of detention in accordance with the usual modalities for that organization, and by providing international monitors, lawyers and relatives with full and repeated access to all those in detention, including those convicted of involvement in the coup attempt of 25 November 2002;

(*e*) To respect the right of everyone to freedom of thought, conscience, religion or belief, whether a member of a religious group or not, and to cease the harassment, detention and persecution of members of religious minorities, whether registered or unregistered;

(*f*) To bring laws and practices governing registration of public associations, including non-governmental organizations, into line with the standards of the Organization for Security and Cooperation in Europe and to enable nongovernmental organizations, particularly human rights organizations, and other civil society actors, including independent media, to carry out their activities without hindrance;

(*g*) To submit reports to the United Nations treaty bodies to which it has assumed a reporting obligation and to give due regard to the recommendations and concluding observations of those treaty bodies, the most recent being the recommendations and concluding observations of the Committee on the Elimination of Racial Discrimination;

(*h*) To fulfil its responsibility to ensure that those responsible for human rights violations are brought to justice;

4. *Requests* the Secretary-General to submit a report to the General Assembly at its sixty-first session on the implementation of the present resolution.

64th plenary meeting
16 December 2005

Appendix VIII

Supporting Documents for the Vietnam Case Study

INSTITUTE *for* GLOBAL ENGAGEMENT

promoting sustainable environments for religious freedom

Chris Seiple
President
Institute for Global Engagement

Testimony before the
Congressional Human Rights Caucus (CHRC)
CHRC Taskforce on International Religious Freedom (TIRF)
Congressional Caucus on Vietnam (CCV)

On

**Religious Freedom in Vietnam:
An Update**

6 December 2007
1030—1200
2255 Rayburn HOB

Introduction

Congresswoman Sanchez, distinguished members of the Congressional Human Rights Caucus (CHRC), the CHRC Task Force on International Religious Freedom, and the Congressional Caucus on Vietnam: Thank you for the opportunity to share my observations about religious freedom in Vietnam, and how we can continue to move forward.

Last month at this time I was in Vietnam's Northwest region, visiting with government officials and religious communities to get a first-hand account of the religious freedom situation there; it was my second trip to the Northwest in the past seventeen months. I also spent some time in Hanoi, meeting national leaders and attending a conference on religion and rule of law that my organization, the Institute for Global Engagement, cosponsored with the Vietnamese Academy for Social Sciences, Vietnam's pre-eminent think-tank, and the Vietnam-USA Society.

This was my fifth trip to Vietnam in the past three years. During these trips I have had the great privilege to meet regularly with government officials and religious leaders in the Central Highlands, the Northwest, and in Hanoi. We have never been refused an interview and we have never been refused access to a region (while focusing on the evangelical church in Vietnam, which has suffered the most).

Vietnam is a country amidst serious transition and strategic transformation. Intelligent and industrious, the Vietnamese people—both the government and citizens—have made the collective decision to not only participate in the world economy, but to join the global civil society as well. In time, I am convinced that Vietnam will be a leader in each.

Vietnam's economy, for example, grew at 8+% the last two years. This is a remarkable statistic considering that Vietnam's biggest trading partners are also former enemies (the Japanese, the French, the Americans, and the Chinese). As a result, the poverty rate has decreased from 58% in 1993, to 20% in 2004, while per capita has increased from $170 to $620 in the same timeframe. As the World Bank states, "Vietnam is one of the best-performing developing economies in the world...It has the potential to be one of the great success stories in development" ("Vietnam: Laying the Foundation for Steady Growth," The International Development Fund, The World Bank, February 2007; available from: http://www.worldbank.org/ida).

These trends and statistics indicate something beyond economic benchmarks. Most of all, they indicate a desire to not let the past—from previous military enemies to failed economic policies—influence the future. They also indicate a comprehensive and systematic desire to quickly provide the most basic of human rights—the right not to live in poverty—as the basis for strong civil society.

In other words, it is difficult to be concerned about religious freedom when there is no bread on the table. This unprecedented progress in poverty reduction therefore enables time to consider and implement equally foundational elements to a strong civil society that participates in a rapidly deepening and expanding global civil society; namely, a religious freedom that is sensitive to culture and consistent with the rule of law.

Toward this end, there have been significant and positive developments, at least for Protestant believers. These improvements—as delineated in the October 2007 report by the Evangelical Fellowship of Canada, "A Slowdown and New Complications: The Protestant Experience with Religious Freedom in Vietnam"—are as follows:

- Large-scale, government sponsored programs to force renunciation of Christianity, especially among Vietnam's ethnic minority Christians, have ceased.

- The registration of congregations, though sometimes with limited benefits, is underway. In February it was estimated that some 800 of the estimated 4,500 Protestant congregations (18 per cent) in Vietnam had some kind of registration...The number of registered churches is slowly increasing.

- Permission has been granted to print many Christian books, in addition to the Bible, and the New Testament in the languages of Vietnam's minority groups.

- Protestant religious prisoners of conscience identified by the US have been released...

- A "legislative framework" for more enlightened treatment of religion, religious communities, and believers was developed in 2004 and 2005. The potential benefits, however, have not been fully realized because of slow implementation and the unchanged mindset of many local officials.

- Some groups have been emboldened by Vietnam's claims to greater religious tolerance and have been more aggressive in their struggle with the government to realize those advances. Earlier they would not have dared to assert their rights (page 4).

I should also note the obvious: The U.S. Ambassador-at-Large for Religious Freedom, John Hanford, has played an instrumental role in persistently and patiently working with the Vietnamese government to help effect these changes.

The Current State of Religious Freedom: Step-by-Step

In understanding religious freedom—the cornerstone of civil society because of its inherent respect for the other—it is critical to keep in mind that values do not take place in a vacuum. They are lived out everyday amidst the messiness of life.

And as we think about other countries, we would do well to remember our own evolution toward our present state of imperfection. For example, religion was not disestablished in the U.S. until the 1830s, and African-Americans did not have the right to vote nationwide until 1870, with women gaining that same right less than one-hundred years ago. So a strong dose of practicality, not to mention humility, is required when we consider other countries… especially as we reflect on how long it takes for a law to be put in place that mirrors a change in mindset.

There is no unified and transparent framework for governing religion in Vietnam today. The government, however, has put in place a series of ordinances, decrees, and guidelines that begin to create a new framework for how religion and the state work together for society's sake. At the same time, the government has been recognizing various Protestant denominations, even as it has created and implemented training courses to explain and discuss this new framework at the local level. Far from complete, this framework has emerged in just three years. It is unprecedented in Vietnamese history, and it was unimaginable just three years ago.

To be sure, as Vietnamese officials will confirm, significant issues remain. There is much more training to do for local government officials and religious leaders. The registration and recognition process is still unclear to many local religious leaders. Church applications are ignored and/or intentionally delayed. Prayer groups and Christian leaders are, depending on the province, routinely harassed. There are many land issues regarding church property. Ethnic minority children who are Christian are sometimes denied access to public schools. New converts are too often pressured to return to their traditional religion.

But these actions do not meet the definition of "systematic, ongoing, egregious" violations of religious freedom, per the International Religious

Freedom Act if 1998's definition. Rather, depending on the local leader, there is the intentional and sometimes violent harassment of believers.

Even cases of seeming bureaucratic inertia are not as they seem. For example, last year I visited an unregistered Hmong house church in the Ta Phin Commune of Sa Pa district in Lao Cai province. This church met freely in the pastor's home (it was not allowed to build a church building), had 40 members and a loving pastor (with a 5th grade education). It was not clear if the church members had a basic understanding of Christian theology. There was also great confusion about the application process to become a registered church of the Evangelical Church of Vietnam—North (ECVN-N, a denomination registered and recognized by the government).

A month ago today, I visited that same church. Everything was still the same, except now the church had 80 members. I asked about the application process and I was told that it had not yet been properly completed! Apparently, although these Hmong families had lived in Ta Phin for generations, there were translation problems (from Hmong to Vietnamese) with the application. To boot, the government wanted to make sure that this church was "comfortable with" and "understood" its faith and denominational identity because its members had only been Christian for a couple of years.

Our response to this official answer could have been immediate and American—after all, it had been over a year and the application hadn't been processed, and who was the government to check theology? Here was a confession we could write about in the *Washington Post*!

Instead, we were able to move beyond the official answer and have a non-threatening conversation with productive results. Why? Because we had a pre-existing relationship with these officials, and because we had allowed significant time in our schedule to take as long as needed to understand just this situation.

The theology, it turned out, was a real issue, not as a function of a repressive government, but as a function of a government made up of local people who cared about the culture and stability of their commune.

This church, we discovered, had been visited by representatives of another denomination (recently registered). This particular denomination, from the south (another issue in and of itself in the north), has been alleged to make converts by passing out money. Whatever the case, the competing denomination had created confusion within a young church that was led by theologically-untrained pastors.

In a group-based society in an underdeveloped region with little education, this kind of issue can become divisive, and quickly. The local government is continuing to assess the situation, still more comfortable with one registered denomination than another. Meanwhile, the church continues to meet freely in the pastor's home, appreciative of the fact that its size has essentially doubled in the past year.

I recognize that this story is but one, and that it is anecdotal. And I do not tell the story to discount the intentional stalling of church registrations that does take place.

I share this story to encourage patience. This story should remind all of us that it is always much easier to point fingers, and then find the proof necessary to fit into our own preconceptions, than to work for solutions that endure.

Life is messy. And it requires innovative persistence and programs to promote religious freedom at the intersection of culture and the rule of law.

Moving Ahead: Top-Down & Bottom-Up

In the International Religious Freedom Act of 1998, there are specific expectations that the U.S. government will work actively to promote religious freedom. For example, in Title V, "Promotion of Religious Freedom," Section 501 (a) (2), it says that the "United States should make a priority of promoting and developing legal protections and cultural respect for religious freedom." Earlier in the IRFA, the law states that the U.S. Commission on Religious Freedom "in evaluating the United States Government policies with respect to countries found to be taking deliberate steps and making significant improvement in respect for the rights of religious freedom, shall consider and recommend policy options…"

It would be interesting to have a hearing that discussed practical policies and programs that the United States could use to promote religious freedom in countries that are clearly taking systematic steps to change their religious freedom environment. It would also be interesting to talk about how America—through government and non-government organizations—might come alongside the steps a particular country was taking.

It has been our direct experience at IGE that promoting religious freedom is indeed possible, but only through a relational diplomacy that simultaneously works from the top-down and the bottom-up.

From the top-down, we have partnered through a written agreement with the Vietnam-USA Society to co-sponsor annual conferences with the Vietnamese Academy of Social Sciences (the Institute for Research on Religion). We have now had two such conferences in Hanoi, working together to create a habitual space through which a practical discussion of religion and rule of law is routinized.

We should not underestimate the importance of this space and dialogue! It did not exist three years ago. Through this space Vietnam is in discussion with international and regional experts about the various and interrelated dimensions of religion, culture, rule of law, and national security. Without such a discussion, it is impossible for Vietnam to assess for itself what lessons apply to Vietnam in the near-term; let alone which lessons help Vietnam evolve toward a rule of law that allows religion and state to peacefully coexist such that both serve society.

Also from the top-down, we engaged the Vietnamese Embassy last year regarding a "training" document that officials were using in the Northwest. This document acknowledged the reality of religion in the Northwest (itself a step forward), but was very negative in its words and tone toward Christians. We asked the embassy to take up the issue and push for the manual's text and tone to be edited.

Last month, a new version was released. While we are now conducting a comprehensive assessment of the two versions, two excerpts illustrate the step-by-step process of progress. For example, in the 2006 version, page twenty-one records: "In recent times, the Protestant faith has been influenced by progressive tendencies in the world *and many denominations have separated themselves from the bad forces.*"

In this year's version, however, page eighteen states: "In recent times, the Protestant faith has been influenced by progressive tendencies in the world *so many denominations have made important contributions to peace, stability and development of mankind.*"

In the first excerpt, religion is a neutral at best. Obviously it had a bad past, and now it is merely separated from that past. The second excerpt, however, demonstrates that religion can actually be positive, contributing to the solution.

Words make a difference. And while I'm sure this second version needs many more revisions, as most documents do, this simple edit is a critical step toward a better understanding; something that is absolutely imperative when considering that it usually takes a generation of training and education to change a mindset.

From the bottom-up, IGE and our Vietnamese partners have worked hard to include Glocal Ventures Inc.—a church-based development NGO from Dallas, Texas—in the promotion of religious freedom. Glocal Ventures has been working in Vietnam's northwest for several years, serving the ethnic minorities. Through a long series of discussions, all parties have developed a framework through which the Glocal Ventures "model" can be expanded to other provinces. Why is this so important?

First and foremost, Glocal Ventures provides development assistance to people who need it. But because Glocal Ventures is not only faith-based, but church-based, its efforts demonstrate that faith and church are positive factors. Vietnamese officials appreciate the positive impact that communities of faith have made toward the socio-economic development of Vietnam's rural areas. They also appreciate the opportunity to let more Americans see for themselves what Vietnam is like as Glocal Ventures facilitates the expertise of church members from across America to serve the Vietnamese.

Also from the bottom-up, we are in discussion with our Vietnamese friends about how we might assist religious freedom training for government officials and religious leaders, as well as theological training for pastors. If government officials and religious leaders are trained together, not only will both know more about religious freedom, both will be more comfortable with the other as stereotypes are ameliorated, even eliminated.

In addition, theological training for aspiring pastors not only helps faith communities to better understand their religion and its requirements to serve society, theologically trained pastors also prevent local congregations from being politically manipulated by those seeking their own, non-religious, purposes (e.g., separatism). At the end of our visit to Ta Phin commune, for example, the provincial deputy minister for religion and ethnicity suggested that we work with them to explore these very possibilities.

These ideas were confirmed in subsequent meetings in Hanoi with the National Committee on Religious Affairs (CRA), the Ministry for Public Security, and President Triet. As one CRA official said in response to my trip report and suggestions for how we might move ahead: "You strike the right notes in your summary. The reality is that we have good policies but the implementation is not perfect. The education level is low at the local level, but local officials have to face the reality of something new."

Conclusion

Vietnam is a country in serious transition amidst strategic transformation. It is tackling several challenges head-on. It is working to develop its economy and reduce poverty—a fundamental human right. It is also working to develop a religious freedom framework and therefore enable an even stronger civil society.

Despite continuing issues of harassment at the local level, the government has affirmed and demonstrated that religious freedom is not just an abstract value that it indirectly assents to, but that religious freedom is important to its national security and governance (not just its foreign policy). Otherwise, religion and rule-of-law conference would not take place, access to sensitive regions would not be granted, security documents would not be revised, and Protestant Christianity—still a minority religion—would not have been addressed.

The above developments don't negate the still-existent challenges. Clearly, however, significant internal political forces are at work, forces that seek to affirm rule of law in the context of religion and religious freedom.

In the context of this internal evolution and our bilateral relationship, the U.S. government and its citizens should continue to exercise vigilance in supporting openness to reform. We need to enhance our communications in order to correct misperceptions and investigate and address the abuses that do take place. We need to work toward a national law regarding religion; for increased registrations; and for greater opportunity for churches to construct buildings. But, we need to promote religious freedom *together*—with the Vietnamese government and people—in a way that honors the genuine paradigm shift that is now taking place.

This kind of progress does not come easy. In fact, it is the direct result of the difficult and long-term work of building relationships of trust and respect. Through a relational diplomacy that operates simultaneously from the top-down and the bottom-up, it is indeed possible to understand one another and, as a result, develop solutions that are sustainable, if only because we've developed them together.

Thank you again Congresswoman Sanchez for inviting me to participate in this vital discussion.

About the Institute for Global Engagement

The Institute for Global Engagement (IGE) promotes sustainable environments for religious freedom worldwide. As a faith-based organization, IGE believes firmly in universal human dignity and is committed to the protection of all faiths through the rule of law. IGE pursues this mission with a balanced approach, encouraging governments to protect religious freedom (*top-down* engagement) and equipping citizens to exercise that freedom responsibly (*bottom-up* engagement).

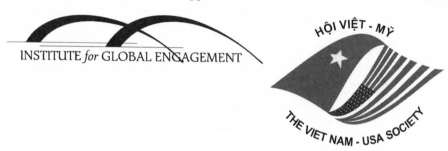

Memorandum of Understanding
Between
The Vietnam-USA Society and the Institute for Global Engagement
Article 4 Protocol
Community-to-Community Relationships

In accordance with Article 7 of the 9 September 2006 Memorandum of Understanding (MOU) between the Vietnam-USA Society (VUS) and the Institute for Global Engagement (IGE), this protocol establishes the practical parameters for implementing Article 4 of the MOU: Promote community-to-community relations between America and Vietnam focusing on Vietnam's socio-economic development by carefully expanding the model of humanitarian and development assistance projects implemented by the "Glocal Ventures, Inc. (GVI) in Lao Cai province to other provinces upon the approval of the local authorities in compliance with the Regulations on the Operation of Foreign Non-Governmental Organizations in Vietnam promulgated in accordance with Decision No. 340/TTg dated 24 May, 1996 of the Prime Minister of the Socialist Republic of Vietnam (hereinafter referred to as the Regulations).

Foremost, this protocol re-affirms our purpose of strengthening and sustaining Vietnam-U.S. relations by building on the significant progress made by Vietnam in religious freedom. In particular, this protocol recalls our principles of cooperation as stated in the 1 July 2005 Letter of Intent, and reflected again in our September MOU. We commit again to working together through consensus, mutually respecting:

- One another's national cultural and historical context;
- The rule of law and each country's legal system; and,
- The need for timely consultation.

Fundamental principles for the implementation of the Article 4:

Community-to-Community Relations

1.   All Article 4 projects shall take place in accordance with the goals and principles of the 9 September 2006 MOU between VUS and IGE.

2.   All projects will be designed and implemented in support of Vietnam's five-year development plan (see Appendix A).

3.   All projects shall be approved by authorized bodies in Vietnam according to the relevant legal regulations in Vietnam. Under the approved projects, agreements with Vietnamese partners can be signed with necessary consultation with the Committee for International Non-governmental Organization (COMINGO) to assure the legality of such agreements.

4.   All projects will take reference to the basic model of humanitarian and development assistance projects implemented by GVI (see Appendix B). Specific development projects are to be determined after assessment of the communities' needs.

5.   GVI will design projects/programs and sign MOU with the authorities in each province where it works, including the relevant community leaders. This MOU will include the following elements:

   a.   An MOU steering committee that reflects relevant community sectors such that implementation decisions are made in a timely and effective fashion. The steering committee may establish an "executive committee" of one local government official, one project beneficiary representative and one representative of GVI.

   b.   A mutual and ongoing assessment mechanism that:

      i.   Identifies the community's needs;

      ii.   Develops a plan with objectives and metrics to meet those needs;

      iii. Ensures that this plan supports Vietnam's five-year development plan; and,

      iv.   Compares and measures, on a regular basis, the plan's objectives against the results, adjusting as necessary.

   c.   A mechanism through which the visiting expertise of American communities is appropriately implemented in a consistent manner.

6.   IGE and GVI will screen all non-Vietnamese experts for participation in projects.

7.   GVI will train all non-Vietnamese experts before they work in Vietnam, ensuring they will operate in a manner that is culturally respectful, follows best practices, and honors the principles of the MOU, and this protocol.

8. GVI will conduct project assessments/evaluation with PACCOM or other related agencies at least once per year, and send IGE and VUS the evaluation reports. These reports will also include upcoming objectives and planned projects.

Together, the articles of this protocol help promote socio-economic development for the people of Vietnam, strengthen and sustain U.S.-Vietnam relations.

Signed 4 November 2007 in Hanoi, Vietnam

Hoang Cong Thuy
Secretary General
Vietnam-USA Society

Chris Seiple
President
Institute for Global Engagement

Memorandum of Understanding
between
the Vietnam-USA Society and the Institute for Global Engagement

The Vietnam-USA Society (VUS) and the Institute for Global Engagement (IGE) agree to continue working together to strengthen U.S.–Vietnam understanding and cooperation, building and expanding upon the work begun through the 1 July 2005 Letter of Intent. To this end, VUS and IGE will work to encourage and sustain progress already being made in ensuring religious freedom and the rule of law in Vietnam through the next steps, detailed below.

Principles of Cooperation
VUS and IGE re-affirm the principles of cooperation stated in the 2005 Letter of Intent, agreeing to work together through consensus, mutually respecting:

- One another's national cultural and historical context
- The rule of law and each country's legal system
- The need for timely consultation

Next Steps
IGE and VUS will work together to:

1. Maintain frequent communication to foster better mutual understanding about the actual religious situation in Vietnam and America.

2. Continue facilitating annual reciprocal visits of U.S. and Vietnamese religious, government, academic, NGO, and business leaders such that the relationship between Vietnam and the United States is strengthened through mutual understanding.

3. Institutionalize, on a regular basis, a conference series on "Religion and Rule of Law in Southeast Asia" to deepen regional understanding

of effective religion legislation and implementation through comparative discussion, beginning in the fall of 2007.

4.   Promote community-to-community relations between America and Vietnam focusing on Vietnam's socio-economic development by carefully expanding the "Glocal Ventures" model established in Lao Cai province to other provinces.

5.   Facilitate, as appropriate, intra-faith discussions between Vietnam and the U.S about religious freedom and its responsible exercise.

6.   Facilitate, as appropriate, provincial level training seminars for local Vietnamese officials and religious leaders on Vietnam's religion regulation and the need for its compliance, building trust as a result.

7.   Develop and implement a pilot program for articles 4, 5, and 6 in 2007. Protocols for these pilot programs will be worked out jointly by VUS and IGE in close consultation with relevant Vietnamese authorities.

Together, these steps are designed to further respect and guarantee of religious freedom in Vietnam consistent with Vietnamese culture and the rule of law, building on the significant progress already made, thereby strengthening and sustaining U.S.-Vietnam relations.

Signed 9 September 2006 in Hanoi, Vietnam

Hoang Cong Thuy
Secretary General
Vietnam-USA Society

Chris Seiple
President
Institute for Global Engagement

INSTITUTE *for* GLOBAL ENGAGEMENT

promoting sustainable environments for religious freedom worldwide

VIETNAM, RELIGIOUS FREEDOM & PNTR

Chris Seiple

President, Institute for Global Engagement

testimony before the
United States Senate
Committee on Finance

On

"S.3945—A bill to authorize the extension of nondiscriminatory treatment
(normal trade relations treatment) to the products of Vietnam"

12 July 2006

Chairman Grassley, Senator Baucus, Members of the Committee,

Thank you for the privilege of speaking with you about Vietnam, religious freedom, and whether or not to establish permanent normal trade relations with Vietnam.

My family is familiar with this country, its blood literally a part of Vietnamese soil. Two of my uncles served as Marine infantry officers in Vietnam, earning three purple hearts among three tours. I was born in the great state of Iowa because my Hawkeye mother, Margaret Ann, went home to have me while my father, Bob, a Marine aviator, flew 300 combat missions out of Da Nang. As a result, our family has a clear-eyed instinct for engaging the world as it is; an instinct confirmed by my own nine years of experience as a Marine infantry officer.

Yet we are also a family of faith. We believe in things like forgiveness and reconciliation. My father, for example, has long worked to build bridges to Vietnam. In 1988, he brought World Vision, the world's largest faith-based relief and development NGO, back to Vietnam in order to serve its people. Similarly, the Institute for Global Engagement—the organization he founded after serving as the first U.S. Ambassador-at-Large for International Religious Freedom—has worked to serve the Vietnamese people since 2001.

The Institute for Global Engagement (IGE) is a "think tank with legs" that promotes sustainable environments for religious freedom worldwide. We take a comprehensive approach that first seeks to understand the nexus of faith, culture, security, development and the rule of law within a given society. We then use relational diplomacy to simultaneously engage both the government (top-down) and the grassroots (bottom-up). The result, we pray, is respectful dialogue and practical agreements that help transition countries toward sustainable religious freedom.

As a faith-based organization, we are well-positioned to engage complex places where religion is a core issue. By way of brief example, two months ago, IGE took an American delegation of Muslims and Christians to Pakistan's Northwest Frontier Province (NWFP) and Tribal Areas. Working in support of a Memorandum of Understanding that we signed last year with the NWFP government, we established a scholarship program for Muslim students and minorities from the Afghanistan-Pakistan border regions at the University of Science and Technology in Bannu. At the program's core is education on religious freedom and respect—perhaps the best long-term tool we have for fighting terrorism.

Our work in Vietnam reflects the same principles. This September marks my fourth trip to Vietnam since the U.S. designated Vietnam a "country of particular concern" (CPC) in September 2004. Over the course of these visits, to include several meetings with Vietnamese officials visiting the U.S., I have had the opportunity to meet and observe many government and religious leaders in Hanoi, as well as at the provincial level (particularly in the Central and Northwest Highlands).

(I should note that the focus of our work is with the Christian ethnic minorities of the Central and Northwest Highlands because these faith-based groups are the largest and have suffered the most.)

While there are many technical and tactical issues to debate regarding PNTR with Vietnam, religious freedom in Vietnam, and the relationship between the two, I believe that we can distill these discussions to two strategic questions:

1. Has Vietnam begun to move toward a rule-of-law system that will preserve, protect and promote religious freedom in Vietnam, as well as enhance the trade between our two countries?

2. And, if so, how should the United States practically encourage Vietnam to continue moving in the right direction?

Vietnam has made the strategic decision to seek a strong bilateral relationship with the United States, which requires the removal of CPC designation. One cabinet level official remarked to me last year: "Whether we like it or not, we recognize religious freedom as a permanent U.S. national interest." As a result, I believe, the decision has been made at the highest levels—and confirmed at the 10th Party Congress this past April—to do whatever it takes to remove CPC designation, and prevent further U.S. sanctions.

In other words, in the last two years, a strategic shift has taken place in the Vietnamese mindset. This shift, irrespective of origin, has begun to provide for the religious freedom of all Vietnamese citizens. This change is confirmed in the conversations I've had with senior Vietnamese officials and demonstrated in the talking points advanced by provincial authorities at the beginning of each meeting.

Evidence of this shift began with the promulgation of nationwide ordinances (November 2004), instructions (February 2005), and guidelines (March 2005) on religious freedom. Although significant discrepancies among these documents must be clarified—for example, the registration process for faith-based groups is unclear when the three documents are laid side-by-side—the government has begun the unprecedented process of training officials at all levels about these decrees and how religious freedom should be addressed. This shift has also created the space in which religious freedom organizations like IGE can contribute to an opening civil society by providing third party accountability regarding religious freedom. Finally there is increasing awareness among government officials that faith-based groups contribute to social stability by: 1) providing for the poor and needy, 2) alleviating the financial responsibility of the state to provide the same services; and 3) by serving as a moral bulwark against the increased corruption that inevitably accompanies an economy in transition.

This evolution of word and deed among government officials at the national and provincial level mark the beginning of a new pattern in the history of Vietnam's human rights.

To be sure, the implementation of these changes is uneven and there are too many examples of people of faith, to include Buddhists, being harassed because of their belief system (in some places much more than others). Yet these positive changes continue to take place, deepening and broadening the opportunity for a rule-of-law system to take root and permanently provide for religious freedom as well as normal trade relations.

In this overall context, I believe that the United States should honor Vietnam's good faith effort in religious freedom, lift CPC, and then establish PNTR.

These two particular actions send the strong signal that we both *respect* the efforts made thus far by the Vietnamese government to establish the rule of law (especially the protection of religious freedom), and that we *expect* the government of Vietnam to continue creating the rule-of-law structure necessary to promote religious freedom and free trade in a sustainable manner. If such efforts do not continue at a reasonable pace, the U.S. should be ready to quickly reinstate CPC designation, possibly with sanctions.

Perhaps most importantly, removing CPC, then establishing PNTR, encourages the progressive elements among Vietnam's leadership. Vietnam possesses many true patriots amidst its government's bureaucracy. I have met many of these national servants who want what is truly best for their country and their citizens. If we do not tangibly support them, hardliners gain the advantage and impede the progress we all seek.

To maintain the current momentum, both governments should agree to a rule-of-law roadmap that, in particular, ensures steady progress in religious freedom. A critical component of that roadmap, I believe, is the continuation of the practical, confidence-building steps that have been taken thus far by the Vietnamese through the partnership between IGE and the Vietnam-USA Society (VUS).

On 1 July 2005, IGE and VUS signed an agreement to take three tangible steps together to build religious freedom in Vietnam whereby: 1) IGE would host a Vietnamese delegation of government and religious officials in Washington, D.C. (February 2006); 2) IGE would take a delegation of scholars and pastors to Vietnam (June 2006); and 3) IGE would co-sponsor a conference on religion and rule of law in Hanoi (September 2006).

The first step called for a delegation of Vietnamese government and religious leaders to come to America (which took place this past February). For the first time in Vietnamese diplomatic history, the government did not choose its country's religious representatives for a delegation; instead, these authentic voices from the Christian community were selected by IGE. Importantly, during the course of our meetings with U.S. officials, these pastors were not afraid to sometimes disagree with the government officials—demonstrating an emerging public square for honest discussion of religious freedom issues among Vietnamese.

These discussions took more formal form on 28 February, when the delegation participated in an off-the-record conference of experts that IGE co-sponsored with Georgetown University and The George Washington University. This forum—the first of its kind—provided an opportunity for American and Vietnamese officials and practitioners to meet and discuss the many issues related to religious freedom, including the current U.S. CPC designation.

The second step of our agreement called for IGE to bring a delegation of scholars and pastors to Vietnam to understand the progress and challenges of implementing religious freedom in the Central and Northwest Highlands (which we did last month). While our conversations in Hanoi with the Communist Party, Ministry of Foreign Affairs, the National Committee for Religious Affairs, and Buddhist and Christian leaders confirmed Vietnam's strategic commitment to promoting religious freedom, our experiences at the provincial levels also confirmed the uneven progress made in implementing these religious freedom reforms.

In Vietnam's Northwest, Protestant evangelicalism is growing rapidly with 1200 "house Churches" (which are comprised almost entirely of the Hmong ethnic minority, with a few ethnic Dzao) seeking recognition and registration from the government under the auspices of the Evangelical Church of Vietnam (North). Although Hanoi has officially encouraged the recognition and registration of these churches, provincial authorities still practice bureaucratic discrimination against the Hmong Christians. Certain local authorities regularly tell Christians that they cannot state their religion on their identification cards while returning unopened church registration applications to the congregations. If someone is not officially Protestant, and if no church application has been received, then the government can maintain the appearance that there are no problems. This clumsy approach serves no one except those who prefer CPC designation to continue.

Still, unregistered house churches are increasingly allowed to meet. The first full-time Catholic priest since 1950 has been installed in the town of Sa

Pa (Lao Cai). And our trip itself was an indication of continuing movement in the right direction. According to officials in Hanoi and the Northwest, IGE is the only international NGO to have been allowed into the Northwest. It is also important to note that we were not refused access to areas or people by local officials. Indeed, local officials and pastors spoke openly about how Christians and government officials have contributed to recent problems.

Meanwhile several complicating factors make it difficult to discern whether or not religious freedom violations have taken place. The Hmong tribes tend to practice a "slash and burn" form of agriculture as they migrate among provinces (and international borders). These habits create tension with local residents, as well as government officials who are trying to establish development programs for a region where roughly 50% of the people live on less than 50 cents/day. The extreme geography of the region only accentuates development efforts as many remote villages do not have access to the outside world during rainy season when landslides, impassable trails and roads, and swollen rivers prevent travel.

When Hmong convert to Christianity, there is often tension within the family as the non-Christian members of the family feel that the Christians have betrayed the family, its ancestors and the culture (a feel shared by neighbors and the local shaman). There are often issues of land inheritance associated with the conversion, depending on the age of the convert, as younger members of the family feel left out.

Making the situation more complex is the Hmong word "Vang Chu." In a spiritual context, it can be translated as "God" or "Christian." In a political context, however, "Vang Chu" can mean "king" or "lord," reminding local officials of Hmong separatism as well as Hmong support for the U.S. during the Vietnam War.

The final complicating factor is the Christians themselves. First, the Evangelical Church of Vietnam (North)—which must recognize and take responsibility for the 1200 Hmong churches before the government will register them—does not have a presence in any of the Northwest provinces. Each of the 1200 Hmong churches must go to the Hanoi headquarters of the Evangelical Church of Vietnam (North) to coordinate its actions with the provincial government where the church wants to register.

Second, a seminary does not exist to serve the Northwest's 120,000 Christians (some estimate as many as 250,000). Without certified pastors, the government will not recognize these 1200 churches. Untrained pastors also limit the spiritual maturity of these believers. Third, for example, an unregistered and aggressive house church from the south—Lien Huu Co Doc (roughly, "Christian Alliance Church")—is growing quickly in the Northwest. Unfortunately, most reports suggest that this church is buying converts, even churches, in order to demonstrate its "success" worldwide. Without a proper understanding of Christianity, and extremely poor to begin with, Hmong Christians are susceptible to these financial advances.

On the other hand, we also visited the Central Highlands provinces of Dak Lak and Gia Lai during this second step of our religious freedom agreement with the Vietnam-USA Society. Previously known for the severe persecution of Christians, these provinces are now moving forward to provide for the spiritual needs of its 200,000 Christians. In Dak Lak, the province has made land, and building permits, available to the nine officially registered churches (which now only lack money to build). Churches with thousands of members are now worshipping freely. The future is even brighter in Gia Lai. Twenty-nine churches have been registered in the last two years and 235 designated places of worship are being organized into churches. Plagued with a shortage of certified pastors (there are only nine), the local Evangelical Church of Vietnam (South) council has worked directly with the provincial authorities to establish three different seminary tracks.

The difference between the Central and Northwest Highlands is threefold. First, the local government leadership is making a comprehensive effort to implement Hanoi's decrees, and educate its officials. Second, the Evangelical Church of Vietnam (South) is organized at the provincial level, working directly with the People's Provincial Committees. Third, the government and the church recognize that more seminary graduates serves both of them.

More pastors equates to better churches which live out the faith by taking care of the poor (while also alleviating some of the state's financial burden to otherwise provide these services). More pastors also means more Christians who better understand the tenets of their faith and are thus less susceptible to personality cults or separatist movements.

The third component of IGE's religious freedom agreement with the Vietnam-USA Society is to co-convene Southeast Asia's first-ever conference on religion and rule of law in Hanoi this September. Working with the Vietnamese Academy of Social Sciences' Institute for Religious Studies, Brigham Young University Law's International Center for Law and Religion Studies, and Emory University Law's Center for the Study of Law and Religion, this conference will give regional policymakers, scholars, and government officials an opportunity to learn from their comparative countries' examples.

Together, these three steps are tangible indicators of where and how Vietnam is moving toward a more transparent, rule of law system that will one day protect and promote the religious freedom of its citizens. Progress is uneven to be sure, especially in the Northwest. But it is also quite clear that national and provincial authorities are headed in the right direction.

In summary, as one observer put it, "Vietnam wants to change, it's just not sure how to." So how should we continue to work with Vietnam?

First, we need to establish a rule-of-law roadmap for moving ahead on religious freedom. The immediate step is to end the bureaucratic discrimination taking place in Vietnam's Northwest by eliminating all issues related to identification cards and by registering at least half of the 1200 Hmong churches in that region.

Second, Vietnam must clarify the discrepancies among the ordinances, instructions and guidelines on religious freedom if government officials are to be comprehensively educated and trained about them. That said, joint classes at the district and commune levels—where government and religious officials are taught together—would help immensely. As information is distributed and people are taught how to observe the rule of law, stereotypes between potential antagonists are reduced by sharing a common classroom.

Third, we need to send a strong and unambiguous message to Vietnam's leaders that we are willing to work with them. Establishing PNTR and lifting CPC sends that signal. And we should communicate that if Vietnam falters or backslides, we will not hesitate to re-impose CPC designation and impose sanctions.

Fourth, we need to encourage a more clearly defined structural process through which the Evangelical Church of Vietnam—North and South— coordinates with provincial authorities and provides seminary training to more pastors.

Fifth, and finally, we need to broaden and deepen the kind of people-to-people diplomacy that has been taking place between IGE and the Vietnam-USA Society. For example, at the end of our September 2006 conference on religion and rule of law in Southeast Asia, IGE will renew our commitment to the Vietnam-USA Society by signing a Memorandum of Understanding (MOU). The MOU will institutionalize this historic regional dialogue, establishing an annual conference series on religion and rule of law.

The MOU will also deepen mutual understanding and foster new initiatives through ongoing reciprocal visits of U.S. and Vietnam faith, business, academia, and government leaders. New initiatives achieved through the MOU might include local economic development projects; business investment; training for local government officials and religious leaders; seminary scholarships for pastors; and establishing a mechanism for regular contact between religious leaders and government officials.

This kind of progress does not come easy. In fact, it is the direct result of the difficult and long-term work of building relationships of trust and respect. Through relational diplomacy—between states and between peoples—it is indeed possible to understand one another and, as a result, develop solutions that are sustainable, if only because we have developed them together.

Thank you again, Mr. Chairman, for inviting me to participate in this vital discussion.

About Chris Seiple:

Chris Seiple is the President of the Institute for Global Engagement (www.globalengage.org). Next month he defends his Ph.D. dissertation on "U.S.-Uzbekistan Relations, 1991-2005" at the Fletcher School of Law & Diplomacy at Tufts University. He also holds an M.A. in National Security Affairs (Special Operations/Low Intensity Conflict) from the Naval Postgraduate School in Monterey, California, and a B.A. in International Relations (East European/Soviet Studies) from Stanford University. He is a Senior Fellow at the Foreign Policy Research Institute and a member of the International Institute for Strategic Studies and the Council on Foreign Relations. He is the founder of the Council on Faith & International Affairs.

About the Institute for Global Engagement:

The Institute for Global Engagement (IGE) promotes sustainable environments for religious freedom worldwide. As a faith-based organization, IGE believes firmly in universal human dignity and is committed to the protection of all faiths through the rule of law. IGE encourages governments to respect their citizens' right to religious freedom and educates people of faith to exercise that right responsibly. Operating at the nexus of faith, culture, security, development, and the rule of law, IGE's relational diplomacy—currently focused on East and Central Asia—enables respectful dialogue and practical agreements that help transition countries toward sustainable religious freedom.

Letter of Intent
between
The Vietnam-USA Society & The Institute for Global Engagement

Purpose

With this letter, the Vietnam-USA Society (VUS) and the Institute for Global Engagement (IGE) express their willingness to work together for a strengthened and deepened mutual understanding between the peoples of Viet Nam and the United States, thus promoting bilateral cooperation and friendly relations between the two countries in all dimensions.

VUS and IGE agree to cooperate in facilitating people-to-people diplomacy, through promoting experts' dialogues and exchange in all fields—e.g., social, economic, political, cultural, etc., including religious freedom and human rights.

Principles of Cooperation

We will work together through consensus, mutually respecting:

- One another's cultural and historical context
- The rule of law and each country's legal system
- The need for timely consultation

First Steps

We will coordinate joint efforts towards realization of the following initiatives:

- Co-sponsor an expert dialogue on human rights and religious affairs in Washington, D.C. (Fall 2005)

- Support the organization of a conference on the rule of law and religion in Hanoi, hosted by the Institute for Research on Religions (Fall 2006)

- Facilitating IGE field visits for further understanding of the implementation of the ordinance on faith and religions at local level (ongoing)

It is our intent to formalize this relationship as a Memorandum of Understanding by September 2005, after further consultation with our respective partners in each country.

Done in Hanoi on July 1, 2005

Thuy Hoang
Secretary General, VUS

Chris Seiple
President, IGE

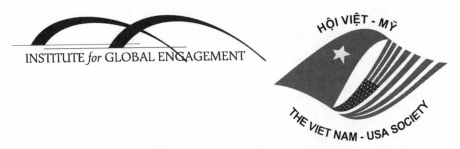

IGE-VUS Memorandum of Understanding
Between
The Vietnam-USA Society and the Institute for Global Engagement
Article 6 Protocol
Provincial Level Training Seminars on Vietnam's Religion Regulation

In accordance with Article 7 of the 9 September 2006 Memorandum of Understanding (MOU) between the Vietnam-USA Society (VUS) and the Institute for Global Engagement (IGE), this protocol establishes the practical parameters for implementing Article 6 of the MOU: Facilitate provincial level training seminars for local Vietnamese officials and religious leaders on Vietnam's religion regulation and the need for its compliance.

Foremost, this protocol re-affirms our purpose of strengthening and sustaining Vietnam-U.S. understanding and cooperation by building on the significant progress made by Vietnam in religious freedom. In particular, this protocol recalls our principles of cooperation as stated in the 1 July 2005 Letter of Intent, and reflected again in our 9 September 2006 MOU. We commit again to working together through consensus, mutually respecting:

- One another's national, cultural, and historical context;
- The rule of law and each country's legal system; and,
- The need for timely consultation.

Fundamental principles for the implementation of the Article 6:

1. The coordination to implement Article 6 shall take place in accordance with the goals and principles of the 9 September 2006 MOU between VUS and IGE.

2. GCRA and IGE will be working together to establish and maintain a routine communication and coordination process of pilot provincial training seminars in accordance with the following guidelines:

a. GCRA will consult and coordinate with Vietnamese local authorities to determine the format (contents, participants, timing and place) and the pilot training seminars.

b. The pilot training seminars will be conducted in accordance with the following Vietnamese government's documents:

   i. Resolution #25 NQ/TW on 12 March 2003 of the 9th Plenum of the Central Committee of the Communist Party concerning the religion task;

   ii. The Ordinance on Belief and Religion passed by the Standing Committee of the National Assembly (the 6th Plenum) of 18 June 2004;

   iii. Instruction #01/2005/CT-TTg of 4 February 2005 of the Prime Ministers concerning some tasks involving Protestant Christianity; and,

   iv. Decree #22/2005/ND-CP of 1 March 2005 of the National Government regarding guidance to carry out some provisions of the Ordinance concerning religion and belief.

c. GCRA's coordination with local authorities and religious communities will take place throughout the training process to ensure that the pilot training seminars encourage and build mutual understanding and cooperation between government officials and religious leaders.

d. Training assessments/evaluations of the pilot seminars with trainers and trainees will be conducted by GCRA. These reports will conclude with a section discussing future seminars and objectives. IGE and COMINGO (Government Committee for Foreign NGO Affairs) will be properly informed of these assessments/evaluations and reports.

3. IGE will provide financial assistance to GCRA's budget for the pilot seminars. GCRA and IGE will prepare anticipated cost and expenses report prior and after each seminar. These financial reports shall be included in the evaluation reports. IGE will be fully informed with these reports.

4. This protocol has been made in three identical copies. One for each undersigned party and one for GCRA.

Together, the articles of this protocol help facilitate provincial level training seminars for local Vietnamese officials and religious leaders on Vietnam's religion regulation and the need for its compliance, building trust and harmonious relationship between the two groups.

Signed 13 October 2008 in Hanoi, Vietnam

Hoang Cong Thuy
Secretary General
Vietnam-USA Society

Chris Seiple
President
Institute for Global Engagement

Notes

Chapter 1

1 A/HRC/2/3, para. 35. Report of the Special Rapporteur on Freedom of Religion or Belief and the Special Rapporteur on Contemporary Forms of Racism on the incitement to racial and religious hatred and the promotion of tolerance.

2 1998 International Religious Freedom Act, section 3(13)(A).

3 ICCPR art. 18(3).

Chapter 2

1 E/CN.4/1998/6, para. 115.

2 General Assembly resolution 60/251 of 15 March 2006.

3 Human Rights Council resolution 5/1, para. 85.

4 ECOSOC resolution 2000/3, art. 3.

5 ECOSOC resolution 1996/31, para. 22.

6 ECOSOC resolution 1996/31, para. 23.

7 ECOSOC resolution 1996/31, para. 24.

Chapter 5

1 http://www.osce.org/hcnm/.

Chapter 6

1 Article 25 of the Rules of Procedure of the IACHR.

2 Article 63.2 of the American Convention.

Chapter 7

1 Article 58, African Charter on Human and Peoples' Rights.

2   Article 3, Protocol to the African Charter on Human and Peoples' Rights on the Establishment of an African Court on Human and Peoples' Rights.

3   Article 27, Protocol.

4   http://www.pan-african-parliament.org/.

CHAPTER 8

1   This chapter will not discuss U.S. mechanisms to combat domestic religious freedom violations, since this guidebook does not examine the domestic structures of any country. Chapter 8 focuses on the United States because of the numerous bodies that exist to promote religious freedom abroad.

2   Section 502B(a) of the Foreign Assistance.

3   Sec. 302(a)(3) of HR 4444.

CHAPTER 10

1   For more about religious freedom conditions in Turkmenistan during this period, review articles from Forum 18 (www.forum18.org) from 2002–2005 and the U.S. religious freedom reports on Turkmenistan from the same period (www.state.gov/g/drl/rls/irf/).

2   "Situation of human rights in Turkmenistan," Commission on Human Rights resolution 2003/11, 59th session (2003)—March 17 to April 25, art. 2(c & d). http://www2.ohchr.org/english/bodies/chr/regular-sessions.htm (last viewed April 30, 2008).

3   "Situation of human rights in Turkmenistan," Commission on Human Rights resolution 2004/12, 60th session (2004)—March 15 to April 23, art. 1(d), 3(a). http://www2.ohchr.org/english/bodies/chr/regular-sessions.htm (last viewed April 30, 2008).

4   "Situation of human rights in Turkmenistan," Resolution adopted by the General Assembly, A/RES/59/206, December 20, 2004, art. 1(a & b), 2(d). http://www.unhcr.org/refworld/type,RESOLUTION,,TKM,43f312330,0.html (last viewed September 22, 2008).

5   "Situation of human rights in Turkmenistan," Resolution adopted by the General Assembly, A/RES/60/172, December 16, 2005, art. 1(a-c), 2(f), and 3(e). http://daccessdds.un.org/doc/UNDOC/GEN/N05/497/92/PDF/N0549792.pdf?OpenElement (last viewed April 30, 2008).

6   "International Religious Freedom Report—Turkmenistan," U.S. Department of State, 2003. "Ambassador also raised specific reports and urged ending numerically-based registration for religious minority groups in multiple meetings with the Foreign Minister in 2003." http://www.state.gov/g/drl/rls/irf/2003/24440.htm (last viewed April 30, 2008). "U.S. Deputy Assistant Secretary of State Laura E. Kennedy Visits Turkmenistan," *United States Mission in Turkmenistan*

Quarterly Journal (Winter, February 2005), p. 2. Following her talks with President Niyazov, Ambassador Kennedy said, "I also appreciated the opportunity to discuss some areas of particular concern to the U.S. government, including religious freedom, the development of civil society, access to prisoners, resumption of Radio Mayak broadcasts and some other issues." http://turkmenistan.usembassy.gov/uploads/Ww/zn/WwznAbHkwyAqU9deHkHtug/newsletter_winter05.pdf (last viewed April 30, 2008).

7   "U.S. Ambassador to OSCE Discusses Human Rights in Ashgabat," *United States Mission in Turkmenistan Monthly Newsletter* (August–September 2003), page 2. http://turkmenistan.usembassy.gov/uploads/HF/Rf/HFRfRtN_Feq5tz2ieaJNhQ/Newsletter0306.pdf (last viewed April 30, 2008). "Statement of U.S. Delegation on the Freedom of Thought, Conscience, Religion or Belief," October 7, 2003. http://osce.usmission.gov/archive/2003/10/FREEDOM_OF_THOUGHT.pdf (last viewed April 30, 2008).

8   "Consolidated Summary of the Human Dimension Implementation Meeting," The Organization for Security and Cooperation in Europe, Warsaw, October 6–17, 2003. http://www.osce.org/documents/odihr/2003/11/1033_en.pdf (last viewed April 30, 2008).

9   "Commission Releases Report, Recommendations on Turkmenistan," March 14, 2002. http://www.uscirf.gov/index.php?option=com_content&task=view&id=184&Itemid=53 (last viewed April 30, 2008).

10   "Turkmenistan: Stop Religious Persecution—NGO Coalition Call on US Secretary of State Condoleezza Rice to Designate Turkmenistan as a 'Country of Particular Concern,'" Human Rights Watch, September 28, 2005. http://hrw.org/english/docs/2005/09/28/turkme11796.htm (last viewed April 30, 2008).

11   "Helsinki Commission Members: Turkmenistan Has Place on Powell's List of Religious Freedom Violators," United States Helsinki Commission, October 21, 2003. http://csce.gov/index.cfm?FuseAction=ContentRecords.ViewDetail&ContentRecord_id=330&Region_id=104&Issue_id=0&ContentType=P&ContentRecordType=P&CFID=7964132&CFTOKEN=69930094 (last viewed April 30, 2008).

12   "Helsinki Commission Briefing Reviews Religious Freedom in Turkmenistan," United States Helsinki Commission, May 7, 2004. http://csce.gov/index.cfm?FuseAction=ContentRecords.ViewDetail&ContentRecord_id=363&Region_id=104&Issue_id=0&ContentType=P&ContentRecordType=P&CFID=7964132&CFTOKEN=69930094 (last viewed April 30, 2008).

13   "Letter to President Niyazov," United States Helsinki Commission, June 3, 2004. http://www.csce.gov/index.cfm?Fuseaction=UserGroups.Home&ContentRecord_id=242&ContentType=R&ContentRecordType=R&UserGroup_id=104&Subaction=ByDate&CFID=6909454&CFTOKEN=18936789 (last viewed April 30, 2008).

CHAPTER II

1   For further reading on Vietnam, see the following texts: Robert Templer, *Shadows and Wind* (New York: Penguin Books, 1999); Bao Ninh, *The Sorrow of War* (New York: Pantheon Books, 1995); Van H. Nguyen, *Vietnam: Journeys of Body, Mind, and Spirit* (Berkeley: University of California Press, 2003); Shawn F. McHale, *Print and Power: Buddhism, Confucianism, and Communism in the Making of Modern Vietnam* (Honolulu: University of Hawaii Press, 2003); Niel L. Jamieson, *Understanding Vietnam* (Berkeley: University of California Press, 1993); Bernard B. Fall, *Hell in a Very Small Place: The Siege of Dien Bien Phu* (Cambridge, Mass.: Da Capo Press, 1966); Duong V. M. Elliott, *The Sacred Willow: Four Generations in the Life of a Vietnamese Family* (New York: Oxford University Press, 1999); and Thu H. Duong, *Paradise of the Blind* (U.S. edition; New York: William Morrow, 1993).

2   As Protestant evangelicals were the most persecuted group in Vietnam, IGE focused its efforts on this particular group.

3   "Vietnam: Laying the Foundation for Steady Growth," The International Development Fund, The World Bank, February 2007. http://www.worldbank.org/ida (last viewed April 30, 2008).

4   These documents have been published in English by the Government Committee for Religious Affairs as "Vietnamese Legal Documents on Belief and Religion" (Hanoi: Religion Publishing House, 2007).

5   After Seiple spoke on Capitol Hill in the fall of 2007 to a group of congressional staffers and shared this story, a staffer told him, "That's all we ever do."

6   The LOI and subsequent agreements between IGE and VUS can be found in the appendix.

7   The hearing focused on S.3495—"A bill to authorize the extension of nondiscriminatory treatment (normal trade relations treatment) to the products of Vietnam." http://finance.senate.gov/sitepages/hearing071206.htm (last visited April 30, 2008).

8   Emphasis in original. For a transcript and links to articles about IGE's work in Vietnam, visit http://www.globalengage.org/media/release.aspx?id=9082 (last visited April 30, 2008).

9   GVI is the legal mechanism through which Northwood Church (Dallas, Texas) serves the marginalized minorities of Vietnam's Northwest Highlands. Per IGE's September 2006 agreement with the Vietnamese, the GVI "model" in the Northwest is to be expanded to the Central Highlands. Toward that end, GVI was officially recognized last year and IGE has worked to enable GVI to partner with local provinces and even Vietnamese churches in the Central Highlands. While this partnership of American and Vietnamese churches will serve the poorest of the poor, the example also demonstrates to the government that people of faith can be a part of the solution while building a common community.

Index

Middle East, 54, 73

Midrand (South Africa), 111

Ministerial Council, OSCE, 79

Moldova, 54, 57

Mongella, Gertrude I., 112

monitoring bodies: AU, 106–7; CoE, 68, 70, 71; EU, 58–59; ICCPR, 19; OAS, 94, 96, 99–100; OSCE, 80–85; UN, 26–27, 29, 34, 37, 136; United States, 114–21

Montenegro, 57

Morocco, 57

Muslims, discrimination against, 34, 59, 72, 85, 138, 148–49

Nairobi (Kenya), 15

National Focal Points, RAXEN, EU, 59–60

National Security Council, U.S., 144–45

national security justification, 14, 62

Netherlands, 10, 46, 83

New York City (United States), 15, 25

NGOs (nongovernmental organizations): as early warning system, 39; overview, 125–27; policy of AU toward, 102–3, 105, 106; policy of CECC toward, 121; policy of CoE toward, 62; policy of EU toward, 44; policy of OAS toward, 89–90; policy of OSCE toward, 76, 87; policy of UN toward, 40; Turkmenistan case study, 135–38; types of activities of, 127–33; Vietnam case study, 139–46; see also accreditation

Nigeria, 35

Ninth International Conference, OAS, 89

Niyazov, Saparmurat, 135–37

nongovernmental organizations; see NGOs

non-state actors, 11–12, 110

North Korea; see Korea, Democratic People's Republic of

North West Frontier Province (NWFP; Pakistan), 148–49

Northwest Highlands (Vietnam), 140–46

Northwood Church, 145

Norway, 10

Nuremberg trials, 7

OAS; see Organization of American States

Office for Democratic Institutions and Human Rights (ODIHR), OSCE, 80–83, 119–20

Office for International Religious Freedom (IRF Office), U.S., 114–16

Office of High Commissioner for Human Rights (OHCHR), UN, 21, 37

Order of Business, Committee of Ministers, CoE, 67

Organization for Security and Cooperation in Europe, (OSCE): field operations, 85–86; HCNM, 83–84; HDIM, 79, 86–87, 137; ODIHR, 80–83, 119–20; overview, 75–79; Parliamentary Assembly, 88; Permanent Council and Chairman-in-Office, 79–80, 84–85; SHDM, 79, 87; Turkmenistan case study, 136–37; Vienna Concluding Document, 75, 77–79

Organization of African Unity (OAU), 101–2, 109

Organization of American States (OAS): General Assembly, 93, 94; IACHR, 94–97; Inter-American Court of Human Rights, 97–99; Inter-American Institute of Human Rights, 99–100; overview, 89–92; Permanent Council, 93

Organization of the Islamic Conference (OIC), 28

overregulation, 12–13